THE
BOOK
OF
BOOKS

THE RADICAL
IMPACT OF THE
KING JAMES BIBLE
1611–2011

MELVYN BRAGG

THE BOOK OF BOOKS

THE RADICAL IMPACT OF THE KING JAMES BIBLE 1611–2011

HODDER & STOUGHTON

First published in Great Britain in 2011 by Hodder & Stoughton
An Hachette UK company

1

Copyright © Melvyn Bragg 2011

The right of Melvyn Bragg to be identified as the Author of the Work has been
asserted by him in accordance with the Copyright, Designs and Patents Act 1988.

A CIP catalogue record for this title is available from the British Library

Hardback ISBN 978 1 444 70515 7
Trade Paperback ISBN 978 1 444 70517 1

Typeset in Garamond Three by Hewer Text UK Ltd, Edinburgh

Printed and bound in the UK by CPI Mackays, Chatham ME5 8TD

Hodder & Stoughton policy is to use papers that are natural, renewable and recyclable
products and made from wood grown in sustainable forests. The logging and manufacturing
processes are expected to conform to the environmental regulations of the country of origin.

Hodder & Stoughton Ltd
338 Euston Road
London NW1 3BH

www.hodder.co.uk

To the Reverend Marie-Elsa Bragg
With love

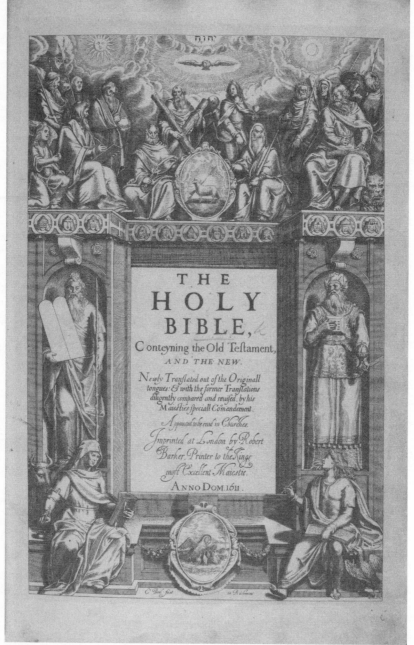

CONTENTS

Prologue   1

PART ONE
FROM HAMPTON COURT TO NEW ENGLAND

Chapter One	The Scope of It	5
Chapter Two	The Road to 1611	12
Chapter Three	The Foundation is Laid	21
Chapter Four	The King James Version is Commissioned	32
Chapter Five	The Four Companies	41
Chapter Six	The *Mayflower* and the Covenant	53
Chapter Seven	The Bible in the Civil Wars (1642-51)	68
Chapter Eight	The New Map	81
Chapter Nine	The Great Awakening	93

PART TWO
THE IMPACT ON CULTURE

Chapter Ten	The Royal Society (1660): Early Modern Science and the Bible	109
Chapter Eleven	Language	119
Chapter Twelve	The Bible Itself as Literature	130

Chapter Thirteen   From Shakespeare –
The Bible and Literature (1)   140

Chapter Fourteen   American Literature and the
Twentieth Century –
The Bible and Literature (2)   164

Chapter Fifteen   The Eighteenth-Century
Enlightenment   182

Chapter Sixteen   The Matter of Richard Dawkins:
The New Enlightenment   194

Chapter Seventeen   Mary Wollstonecraft and William
Wilberforce   210

PART THREE
THE IMPACT ON SOCIETY

Chapter Eighteen   Slavery and the Civil War
in America (1)   229

Chapter Nineteen   Slavery and the Civil War
in America (2)   243

Chapter Twenty   The Bible and Education   259

Chapter Twenty-One   On a Mission Around the World   271

Chapter Twenty-Two   The Bible and Sex   287

Chapter Twenty-Three   The Bible and Women   310

Chapter Twenty-Four   Christian Socialism and the
Social Gospel   324

Chapter Twenty-Five   The Bible and Democracy   335

Afterword   345

Acknowledgements   349

Select Bibliography   351

Index   355

PROLOGUE

In 1953, Queen Elizabeth II was crowned in Westminster Abbey. She swore her oath on the King James Bible. This version of the Bible was printed in English in 1611. It was inspired by James I, who was also crowned in Westminster Abbey, 350 years before Elizabeth II. His cousin, Elizabeth I, had, on the last day of her life, indicated that he was to be her successor.

The Bible was a book which changed and moulded the English-speaking peoples. In America, Abraham Lincoln was sworn in as President on the King James Version as were other Presidents including George Washington, Ronald Reagan and Barack Obama.

This is no mere ceremonial token either in the United Kingdom or in the United States, Australia, Canada, New Zealand and elsewhere. This binding ritual signifies and honours a bond of faith and an acknowledgement of the unique reach and power of this book.

You may be a Christian. You may be anti-Christian, or of another religion, or none. You may be an atheist fundamentalist and think the Bible is monstrous, a book to be dismissed or derided.

But whoever you are in the English-speaking world, I hope to persuade you to consider that the King James Version of the Bible has driven the making of that world over the last 400 years, often in most unexpected ways.

PART ONE
FROM HAMPTON COURT
TO NEW ENGLAND

CHAPTER ONE
THE SCOPE OF IT

The King James Bible has been called the Book of Books. It has a good claim to this title. It consists of sixty-six different 'books'. It has sold more than any other single book since its publication in 1611. It has carried the Protestant faith around the globe. And, by the law of unexpected consequences, its impact, alongside and often outside its vital role in spreading the Word, has been radical and amazingly wide-ranging. This Bible is one of the fundamental makers of the modern world. It has set free not only its readers and its preachers but those who have used it as a springboard to achieve gains and enrichment in our world never before enjoyed by so many. This book walks with us in our life today.

Its impact on the English-speaking world is unparalleled. It can touch on mysteries which seem beyond our reach yet at times we sense them to be there. It can teach us day-to-day morality. It gave us myths and stories which are as familiar to us as the histories of our own families and communities. It stands still as a book of great language and beauty.

There has never been a book to match it. It has a fair claim to be the most pivotal book ever written, a claim made by poets and statesmen and supported by tens of millions of readers and congregations. It declared itself to be the Word of God. Many people have believed and cleaved to that and some still do. But everyone, even atheists, has benefited from many of its unexpected consequences.

The King James Bible was the steel of will and belief that forged America and other British colonies. It has inspired missionaries around the globe and consoled the hopeless in their desperation. It was used by the enforcers of slavery and later by the liberators of slaves, and transformed into liberation theology by the slaves themselves. It became the bedding of gospel music and the spirituals which set in motion soul, blues, jazz and rock, the unique cultural gift of America to the world. It has defined and re-defined sexual attitudes. It has fortified and provoked philosophy.

Followers of the King James Version – as it is known in America – provided the vocabulary, the seedbed and construction model for the early development of democracy. It was the consolidating voice of two world empires. It unleashed and motivated philanthropic movements of a size and effectiveness which bettered the lives of ordinary people throughout the English-speaking world. Its ferocious sense of mission transformed and sometimes destroyed native cultures.

For centuries the King James Bible fed some of the finest thinkers and artists and men of science and politics; others it persecuted. This English version came out of persistent demands for a voice in their own tongue, a demand which, despite persecution, could not be extinguished in medieval England. It had grown into an irresistible force by the time of Henry VIII in the 1530s. The lasting version was finally secured by King James in 1611.

'It was wonderful to see with what joy the Book of God was received,' wrote a commentator at the time of its publication '. . . not only among the learneder sort . . . but generally all England

6

over among all the vulgar and common people; with what greediness God's word was read . . . Some got others to read it to them if they could not themselves . . . even little boys flocked among the rest to hear portions of the Holy Scriptures read.' In their own tongue: that was the first and still the most radical part of its impact.

Since 1611 it has flooded over the world. 'It is the best book that God has given to man,' said Abraham Lincoln. Charles Dickens wrote: 'The New Testament is the very best book that ever was or ever will be known in the world.' 'It is impossible rightly to govern the world without God and the Bible,' said George Washington, the founding President of the United States.

This is a story of the present every bit as much as it is of the past. When American soldiers in Iraq and Afghanistan looked through the sights on their guns, they may not have seen it, but inscribed minutely there are words justifying war taken from the King James Bible. John viii, 12 for example: 'he that followeth me shall not walk in darkness, but shall have the light of life,' and 2 Corinthians iv, 6: 'For God, who commanded the light to shine out of darkness, hath shined in our hearts, to give the light of the knowledge of the glory of God in the face of Jesus Christ.'

When the Nobel-prize-winning novelist Toni Morrison wrote *Beloved*, she called on that Bible again and again, bringing to bear its spirit and its words, her inspiration and her material. Behind the gallant, desperate and often flawed attempts to feed the poor of the world and release them from their oppression stands the most magnificent morality in print – the Sermon on the Mount from the King James Bible. In verses called the Beatitudes:

Blessed are the poor in spirit: for theirs is the kingdom of heaven . . .
Blessed are the peacemakers: for they shall be called the children of God.

7

When biologists seek the origin of life or physicists look for the formation of the universe in the particle accelerator at CERN, how far is that from the Christian belief in a prime mover? And how much does the modern scientific idea of a First Cause, a Big Bang, owe to the Christian Newton and his conviction that there was indeed a First Cause: God? After all, the Big Bang could just as well be the *end* of something. There is, it seems to me, something biblical in claiming it was the beginning. Atheists, like Richard Dawkins, seek to define themselves by the destruction of what they see as the corrupt temple of the Bible. Their zeal can appear rather like religious fundamentalism and share its inflexibility.

Artists have plundered its stories for 400 years and time before then. Along the path that led to the publication in 1611 are atrocities, tortures and burnings at the stake. But the men who wanted the Word of God in English would not be deterred. Men were destroyed for trying to get the Bible published in English: others took their place. It is a heroic story. And because of them we speak out of that book still, every day of our lives.

When we 'put words into someone's mouth' and 'see the writing on the wall' or 'cast the first stone', when we say 'you are the salt of the earth', or 'a thorn in the flesh', when we 'fight the good fight' or 'go from strength to strength' or 'when the blind lead the blind', or are 'sick unto death' or 'broken-hearted', or 'clear-eyed', or talk of 'the powers that be' – in these and literally thousands more ways we talk the language of the 400-year-old King James Bible. And 'beautiful', that too makes its first appearance in the translation which became the keystone of the Bible. 'It is,' wrote American journalist and satirist H.L. Mencken 'the most beautiful piece of writing in any language.'

Its words comprise 8,674 from Hebrew, 5,624 from Greek, 12,143 from Old English. From those many roots grew a bounteous tree, a tangle of faith and work, thought and debate, violence, prejudice, terror, poetry, song and hope.

It has gone through these last 400 years responding to different times, meeting and seeking out new demands, changing its powers. It has been and still is the book for peacemakers and the book for warmongers, the book that ignites rejoicing and the book that incites fury, the book worshipped and the book scorned, but above all the book that affected minds, hearts and destinies profoundly over centuries. 'It is no mere book,' wrote Napoleon, 'but a living creature with a power that conquers all that oppose it.'

Just after the Easter of this year, 2010, I went to Westminster Abbey where King James I was crowned in 1603. Significantly, it was the first coronation to take place in an entirely English liturgy. At last the English language, in that Shakespearean age, needed no assistance from ancient or foreign tongues. In 1066, William the Conqueror's coronation had been in Latin and French.

I went there on the afternoon of that Sunday to hear the Anglican Church's jewel of a service, Choral Evensong. I was raised an Anglican in the Church of England.

In this abbey, which has witnessed thirty-eight coronations, the blessing of power was God-given from the tyranny of Henry VIII to the constitutional democracy of Elizabeth II. Here too lie the tombs and commemorative plaques of the famous dead. Out of those you can pick examples from many whose work and life had been shaped by the King James Bible: William Blake, Sir Winston Churchill, Isaac Newton, Charles Dickens, T.S. Eliot, Martin Luther King, Florence Nightingale, Handel, William Shakespeare, William Wilberforce . . .

In that service I heard one of the dozens of cathedral and college choirs which up and down the land on most days of the week sing a religious service as their predecessors did for more than a thousand years. The arches meeting in the high Gothic stone ceiling rang with the affirmation of a religion triumphant still in some parts of the world, beleaguered, disdained or ignored in others, but here in the singing, its resonance still evident. What began with a flourish of trumpets in 1611 calling together our island tribes became a global orchestra of sounds and themes, now rising, now fading, but for many the soul goes marching on.

Ten years after the King James Bible was published, the Pilgrim Fathers set sail for America. They found and they founded a New World. It became a great democracy. It was a world based on the book, the Word of God. And America propagates its faith like no other people has ever done. The Gideon Society alone places 60 million new Bibles a year in over 181 countries and many Americans pray their way into the theatres of war and peace and the work and play of their daily lives.

Even in England, now seen to be at an ebb tide of formal Christianity, this book can still arouse passionate eloquence. It is accepted that the two greatest speeches in the House of Commons, a stone's throw from Westminster Abbey, were by Christians and rifted with the King James Bible. Those were by Winston Churchill in 1940, just after the outbreak of the Second World War, and by William Wilberforce when he made his first speech for the ending of the slave trade in 1789. The parliamentary tradition is not dead. On 9 December 2009, David Simpson, the Member of Parliament for the Northern Ireland constituency of Upper Bann, demanded a debate, calling on the government to commemorate the four hundredth anniversary of the King James Bible.

'The great Winston Churchill,' he said, 'noted that the scholars who produced it had forged an enduring link, literary and religious, between the English-speaking people of the world.' David Simpson went on:

It is not only our literature and language that has been influenced by the King James Bible. It has had an extraordinary beneficial influence upon political and constitutional affairs. It was the Bible of Milton and the Protectorate, later it was the Bible of the Glorious Revolution, which gave us constitutional monarchy and parliamentary democracy. It was the Bible of Whitefield and the Wesleys, that saved the realm from the brutality and blood of the French Revolution. It was the Bible carried by the founding fathers of the United States that helped to force that land and give the world that great democratic powerhouse . . .

Hospitals were built and charities created as a result of its influence. The hungry were fed, the sick nursed, the poor given shelter . . . lives that lay in ruins were made whole and souls that were held in bondage were set at liberty.

The anthem was taken up by other speakers, most notably Dr William McCrea, MP for South Antrim, who quoted from John Wesley: 'Oh, give me that Book! At any price give me the Book of God. Let me be a man of one Book.' Dr McCrea continued: 'It has been burned but there is not the smell of fire about it. It has been buried but no man has ever kept it in the grave . . . This book sets men free . . .'

How and why did such a book come to be written? With what was that core so fire-filled that it became the sun to a solar system of human life? How did what was asserted to be the Word of God become the key which unlocked so many doors of history, Christian, non-Christian, even anti-Christian?

The writing of this book is a story that begins in blood, fear, murder and acts of high courage by dedicated scribes who lived and died to see the Scriptures in English. And the finest of those scribes and martyrs to the Word was William Tyndale.

CHAPTER TWO
THE ROAD TO 1611

William Tyndale, born in 1494, martyred in 1536, has a good claim to be both the founder of the King James Bible and the father of the English language. As a man he provoked awe and protective affection from those who knew him; fear and hatred from those who hunted him down to silence him.

His life's work was to translate the Bible into English. It was an obsession which, like many of the tunnel-visioned and unsleeping obsessions of the very great, was seeded when he was young. When he was ten, and already knew Latin, we are told, as well as English, he read that King Athelstane, Alfred the Great's grandson, had some of the Scriptures translated into English. From whatever mysterious force, this fact seized on him. From then on, this became the life purpose of this brilliant boy, who went to Oxford University when he was twelve. He *had* to translate the Scriptures into English, it was his vocation, and from this sole purpose he never faltered.

He made himself master of the languages necessary to fulfil his mission: Latin, Greek, Hebrew, French, Spanish, Italian. He was acknowledged by his peers to be outstandingly accomplished in all of them. As for his English, it reads like a rare, perhaps transcendent gift. Even those who dismiss Christianity concede that

Tyndale's words and sentences form much of the basic structure, grandeur and memorability of the English tongue.

His translation of the New Testament came out in 1525. It was the first printed Bible in English. Technology, as so often, energised and restructured society's view of its possibilities. Fortune, timing, favoured his cause. So much else did not. In his short life he was mostly penurious, often hungry, isolated, hounded, vilified and cruelly, deliberately, misrepresented. Tyndale lived a life which would have done credit to an Apostle. He laid down his life to put what he thought of as soul-saving words on to the English tongue for the benefit of the common people.

He was a Roman Catholic whose work would become a beacon for Protestants of all denominations all over the world. He was a defender of the divinity of the King who persecuted him, planned his assassination and tried by whatever means to wipe his work off the face of the earth.

He was a quiet, fervent scholar whose voice shook the almighty Holy Roman Empire, rattled the gilded cage of Henry VIII and goaded the corrupted papacy into a panic of revenge. Tyndale is the keystone of the King James Version of the Bible which was published seventy-five years after he was burned at the stake.

But he was not the first. The way had been paved before him.

In 1382, another Oxford scholar, John Wycliffe, had organised the first version of the Bible in English. He was not a translator but a brilliant intellectual general whose battle plan was to wrest the Bible from the Latinists and make it available in English. We tend to think of medieval Oxford as the elite and exclusive battery farm for tame clerics and lawyers who would go on to do the bidding of the authoritarian Church and state. It was in Oxford that they were plumped up for the privileged slots waiting for them after university. But there were among them independent and courageous young men who had minds willing to be tested. And within that smaller cluster of questioning young men there were those who rebelled against the authority of a Church which decreed that the Bible must be in Latin.

Wycliffe, a major philosopher and theologian, was critical of what he saw as the materialism, impiety and dictatorial management of the Roman Catholic Church of which he was a member. Wycliffe, too, had his precursors, notably John Ball whose plain fundamentalist Christianity had helped drive on the Peasants' Revolt in 1381 which had all but toppled the Church and the aristocracy. And before John Ball there had been other attempts to put at least some small part of the Scriptures into the language of the people who made up the overwhelming majority of the congregation but whose voice was not heard. In the eighth century the Venerable Bede translated St John's Gospel into English, but alas it is lost. King Alfred the Great in the ninth century had the Gospels translated and may himself have worked on them. Certain Psalms and favoured passages had been rendered into English a little later but they were sporadic and modest efforts.

John Wycliffe's project was on a different scale. He invited the finest Latin scholars in Oxford to translate St Jerome's Latin masterwork into English. This was completed and published in 1382, precisely 1,000 years after Pope Damasus had invited Eusebius Hieronymus (St Jerome) to pull together a hotchpotch of Latin variants and old Greek translations. This was the Vulgate and it stayed unchanged and unchallenged for a millennium. St Jerome's version became known as the Vulgate because of its common use in Roman Catholic churches.

Latin was the language of the Roman Empire which under the Emperor Constantine embraced Christianity as its official religion. Latin became the language of the Pope whose empire was also centred in Rome. When military Rome was conquered and its empire overrun, its language lived on in the Roman Church. Length of time and usage and Catholic politics made this Latin seem sacred, invincible and untouchable. Wycliffe and his Oxford scholars challenged that and their English manuscripts were distributed all over the kingdom by the scholars themselves. Oxford bred a revolutionary cell right inside an ostensibly safe breeding ground of the Catholic Church.

We are talking about a degree of centralised regulation in medieval Christian Europe which had a great deal in common with Stalin's Russia, Mao's China and with much of Hitler's Germany.

The Roman Church, rich, its tentacles in every niche of society, could be a vital ally in war, a diplomatic master force whose nuncios infiltrated all the courts of Europe. It was often crucial in the web of strategic alliances. Above all, it had a monopoly on eternal life. Eternal life was the deep and guiding passion of the time. The Vatican said you could only gain everlasting life – the majestic promise of the Christian Church – if you did what the Church told you to do. That obedience included forced attendance at church and the payment of taxes to support battalions of clergy. And accepting that the Bible had to be in Latin and not in your own tongue.

Daily life was subject to scrutiny in every town and village; your sex life was monitored. All rebellious thoughts were to be confessed and were punished, any opinions not in line with the Church's teaching were censored. Torture and murder were the enforcers. Those suspected of even doubting the workings of this monumental monotheistic machine were forced into humiliating public trials and told to 'abjure or burn' – to offer a grovelling and public apology or be eaten by fire.

Wycliffe wanted to burst out of what he saw as these man-made bonds for which he saw no justification in the Bible. He saw the

Catholic Church structure as an offence against true faith. Its teaching had become a corruption of the true message of Jesus Christ. It was no more than a degenerate institution. Behind the screen of its astounding cathedrals, its magnificent pageants, its music, its luring of artists and even the unique benefits of its hospitals and schools, Wycliffe, the severe Oxford scholar, saw the false gods of greed and oppression. He also realised that much of its power came from its control over religious language. He spoke out and demanded that everyone ought to have the right to read or hear the Bible in their own tongue.

His translators were writing in the age of the mystery plays – one of the few ways in which ordinary people could receive the Bible stories in English, though they had to be performed outside the churches and cathedrals. It was the time of Chaucer, who brought in the dawn of English literature, and of *Piers Plowman*, the epic English poem written by William Langland, a Wycliffe sympathiser.

From the start there was heavy criticism of the very idea of a translation into English. One chronicler complained that 'the pearl of the Gospel is scattered abroad and trodden underfoot by swine'. But the swine wanted to be fed and immediately and for a century afterwards these Oxford manuscripts were in high demand.

This translation from the Latin could be literal and lumpen: 'Lord go from me for I am a man sinner' and 'I forsooth am the Lord thy God full jealous'. And Latinate words weave through the text: 'mandement', 'descrive', 'cratch', but also 'professions', 'multitude' and 'glory'. But this was the first proper English oasis in a thousand years. It began:

In the beginning God made of nougt heune and erthe. Forsooth the erthe was idel and voide, and derknessis weren on the face of the depth; and the spirit of the Lord was boren on the wateris And God seid, Light be maad, and Ligt was maad.

[In the beginning God made of naught heaven and earth. Forsooth, the earth was idle and void, and darkness was on the face of the depth, and the spirit of God was borne on the waters. And God said 'Light be made!' And light was made.]

Although the fortress of Latin had not been taken and would be secure for about 150 years, a breach had been made and the Bible in English had begun its long campaign.

The medieval Oxford scholars, long-woollen-gowned, staff in hand, took to the mud tracks of medieval England with their concealed manuscript Bibles in English. They travelled secretly through unculled forests and barely inhabited wildlands, hiding in safe houses, forever fugitive. They were a guerrilla movement and they were called Lollards. Their mission was to give people access to the Word of God in English.

The authorities would not endure it. They summoned Wycliffe to London to meet a synod of bishops and other churchmen in 1382, the year the translation was completed. It was a show trial. Wycliffe was condemned for heresy. His Bibles were outlawed. Anyone caught with a copy was to be tortured and killed. Yet the Lollards persisted; for more than a century they roved the land and passed on the Word.

Revenge could not be severe enough. More than forty years later, Wycliffe's bones were dug up and burned. This, it was believed, would deprive him of eternal life for at the Last Judgement the body had to rise from the grave and reunite with the soul.

His remains were burned on a little bridge that spanned the River Swift, a tributary of the Avon. His ashes were thrown into the stream. Soon afterwards, a Lollard prophecy appeared:

The Avon to the Severn runs
The Severn to the sea.
And Wycliffe's dust shall spread abroad
Wide as the waters be.

In English.

What was it that the Church was so afraid of?

The elders of the Church knew as well as Wycliffe and certainly Tyndale that the Bible had in its history moved through several languages and versions. Moses had brought down the tablets chiselled in Hebrew. Christ had preached to assemblies in their own languages – Aramaic and Syriac. The Greek version arrived to meet the needs of a Greek-speaking empire as did Roman versions. This culminated with Latin in the fourth-century Vulgate of St Jerome. But after that the Word of God was frozen. Despite the many languages the Church had dominion over, only the increasingly ancient Latin was permitted to speak for Christianity. To dispute that was a sin, seen as an attempt to undermine the foundations of the Church.

Language can be a means of control. It has always been used and abused by those claiming omnipotence. The medieval Roman Church's mission was to impose recognition of its omnipotence the world over.

The Church attracted men of wisdom, scholarship and compassion. It also attracted ambition, corruption and brutal politicians. To save their souls, to celebrate their faith, to give thanks or express sorrow and repentance, the faithful were encouraged to offer gifts, often vast gifts, of land and money. This made the Church rich and ripe for plucking. The enterprise of some church-going men – in the profitable wool trade in England for example – turned them into princely landowners and successful merchants in England's biggest manufacturing and trading business, and they paid into the treasure of the monasteries to express their thanks and seek favour with the Almighty. The treasure was there to be plundered.

The ancient credentials of Jerome's Vulgate helped make the Bible an oracle. Its antiquity made it hard to challenge. To have lasted so long was surely in itself proof of truth. Its spiritual supremacy was absolute. This was good for commerce. Selling safe passages to heaven, dealing in relics and monetising miracles were profitable and the Church grew more and more fat on dealing with these practices. And Latin padlocked the faith which under-pinned the whole edifice.

The longer it lasted the more inviolable the Latin became. Very few could read or speak it. Even the clergy were not necessarily familiar with it. In the sixteenth century the Bishop of Gloucester did a survey of 311 deacons, archdeacons and priests of his diocese. He found that 168 could not remember the Ten Commandments and 40 could not say the Lord's Prayer.

It is doubtful whether this mattered to the more cynical and worldly prelates who tended to take the choicest pickings. Perhaps they thought the less general understanding the better. Good that the Word of the Lord was owned by the few. In effect the Catholic Church had long ago become just another arm of the ruling caste. From the beginning of the institutionalised Church, the rich families had sent in their younger sons (after the court and the army) and sometimes their daughters to take command of these plump Godly landholdings. They saw the new wealth, the thousands of acres, the magnificent monasteries and abbeys, the treasures piled up on earth, and they wanted to own it.

From the seventh century, in England, the Church's leaders had largely been a cadet branch of the old aristocracy. By the Middle Ages, the Church was seen by the ruling classes as just another route to increase their grip on the top. With their mistresses and robes of silk, their booty and their immunity from the laws of the land, these churchly princes and prelates were not accountable to other mortals. And they guarded the Word as their ultimate weapon.

The Latin Vulgate had become an icon, as revered as a saint. Verses from it were whispered at the altar so that the common herd could hear nothing. They were separated from the crucial rituals by screens which blocked out the officiating cadre. Mystery plays and simple stories had to serve for them. The language of God was sacred and the sacred became secret and the secrecy spawned ignorance, spun fear. The traditional mechanisms of tyrannical suppression evolved over the centuries.

To throw off the language – to let in fresh air, and new words – was unthinkable. Save for a few brave and evangelical scholars. But when they tried, in all good faith and with no intention but to improve and to purify a Church to which they were devoted, they were set upon. When it feared its supremacy challenged, as it did at the beginning of the sixteenth century, the Church reacted swiftly.

William Tyndale walked into the perfect storm.

CHAPTER THREE
THE FOUNDATION IS LAID

At the centre of the storm was Martin Luther. The scriptural work and political actions of this German priest had an eruptive effect. The fallout is still with us. For not only in 1517 did he attack with learning and virulence the many failings and corruptions of the Church, in 1522 he translated the New Testament into German. The Church was destabilised. The violence of his preaching was believed to have stirred up a peasants' revolt against the princes and the states in 1524–5 in which more than 50,000 people were slaughtered. Out of this turbulence came the Protestant Reformation which ripped apart the Catholic monolith for ever and set a new course in European and American history and beyond which was to reconfigure the world.

He put the fear of revolution into the kings and prelates. They looked at what we might for convenience call 'Germany' and cowered. They feared for their titles, their booty and their lives. Few more than Henry VIII, who, in his full pomp as king, said that he hated Luther more than any man on earth. Henry's defence of the Pope and the Catholic Church against Luther's 1517 eruption had earned him a most coveted title, a gift from Rome, 'Defender of the Faith'.

Henry became a militant and a fanatical Roman Catholic. With the help of Wolsey, a cardinal and Lord Chancellor of England, his spies raked the land for dissidents. Wolsey, dressed in gowns suppurating in silk and satin, his fingers glittering with precious stones, his entourage pharaonic in its splendour, relished the hunting down of those godly men. He loved to toy with them in mock and mocking trials, to have them tortured but he did not condemn people to burning at the stake. Others, including Sir Thomas More, applauded and supported Henry's anti-Protestant zeal.

Into this London stepped William Tyndale, unblemished in his Catholic devotion and a monarchist who had argued that the King was outside the law and subject only to God's law. Outwardly he was a gentle scholar but one who proved to have within him a will which would not be broken. He never once gave in or gave up his vow to make the Bible accessible even to 'a plough-boy'.

At Oxford in the early sixteenth century he had been drawn to the ideas of the Lollards, who were still at large. The hand-copied manuscript translations of the Bible were still passed on, more than a century after the death of John Wycliffe, despite persecution, torture and executions. The English hunger for a Bible of their own was not to be thwarted. Tyndale was ordained priest in 1521. Despite his academic distinction, which had been developed at Oxford and was then burnished at Cambridge where he inherited the example of the recently resident Dutch humanist scholar Erasmus, he turned away from further formal study.

It is a speculation but I think that he was already preparing himself for what he knew would be an unorthodox vocation. He became a chaplain and tutor to the family of Sir John Walsh in the village of Little Sodbury in the Cotswolds, a lush and hilly area of the rich wool trade in the west of England.

He was twenty-six, a wonderfully accomplished linguist, with a gift for poetry. He was in a sympathetic community which included Christian Brethren, another name for the Lollards. Soon he was preaching in the open air outside the church on College Green and his ideas were nettling some of the local bigwigs. At one stage he was accused of heresy, and brought before the vicar-general, who 'threatened me and rated me as if I had been a dog'. It was a taste of what was to come. Most importantly, he had begun to take up his vocation as a translator. He was on his way and so was the King James Bible.

The much praised Greek translation of Erasmus, then thought the greatest scholar in Europe, was his ideal. And his purpose was clear: to put the Scripture plainly before the lay people in their mother tongue, that they might see and hear for themselves the words and the meaning of the Scriptures. A few years later, near his death, when he was racked by persecution, abuse, poverty and exile, he still held to his resolution, to continue his work 'out of pity and compassion which I had and yet have, on the darkness of my brethren, and to bring them to the knowledge of Christ'.

Unsurprisingly, having flagged up his position in a country which was alarmed at all that he stood for, he found no position in London. Partly, he himself thought, because he was unimpressive and awkward in any interview about his future. Perhaps his character was too transparent for comfort, his meek demeanour thought to be camouflage. For whatever reason, aged thirty, he sailed for Hamburg in 1524. He would never again set foot in England.

It is thought that he went to Wittenberg where he met and very possibly worked with Luther – the new Satan. He certainly admired Luther. That sealed his fate. The English court turned on him and set out to silence him and to hunt him down.

He went to Cologne and worked on his first translation of the New Testament, for which he went back to the original Greek. It was finished and printed a year later. Six thousand copies were about to be shipped to London when a self-appointed spy, Johan Dobneck, alerted the authorities in Cologne and in England. He informed the Bishop of London, and, via Wolsey, Henry VIII. The English saw a dangerous association with Luther and with the brutal Peasants' Revolt and went into a frenzy of counter-measures. Tyndale, no less determined, when tipped off about Dobneck, seized as many printed Bibles as he could and took to a boat on the Rhine. For a time, it was touch and go whether his translation would survive. It was here that Tyndale again proved his tenacity. He was determined not to have his translation banned from its destination.

Henry VIII put the English ports on alert. It has been said that he sent out the navy to search all ships coming from the Netherlands. Certainly warehouses on the Thames were raided and ransacked in the pursuit of the New Testament in the English language. Diplomatic letters and ambassadors urged the authorities in the Low Countries (Tyndale's current location in a life on the run), to crack down on the production of this subversive and inflammatory book. The Lord Chancellor was commanded to prevent their import, clergy to prevent their circulation.

But in England there was a willing underground, stemming from the Lollards. Most of all there were Christians who wanted to read the Gospels and the Epistles in their own language. Between 1525 and 1528 it is estimated that about 18,000 copies of Tyndale's New Testament were printed and, despite seizures, most of them got into the hands of those who wanted them. Printing made huge numbers available. Far too many to net anything but a fraction.

The energy of Tyndale's New Testament came partly from the invention of print. Francis Bacon in the reign of Elizabeth I asserted that print, gunpowder and the navigational compass had changed the world. Without print, Tyndale's work would most likely have followed that of Wycliffe along untrodden ways to remote safe houses, the contraband of faith smuggled through the lines for a minority. Print meant mass. Battalions replaced the single spies.

People fell in love with Tyndale's translation because of its beauty, the sense of certainty, the way in which it seemed to be at the heart of this newly emerging, exotic, vivacious and proud language, his own language. Perhaps above all else it was loved because it was written to be spoken. Tyndale knew the limitations of literacy in the country which had now exiled him and it was on those people that his mind was fixed as his scholarship and great artistry unrolled the scrolls of ancient time.

> In the beginning was the Word, and the Word was with God and the Word was God. The same was in the beginning with God. All things were made by Him; And without Him was not anything made that was made. In Him was life and the life was the light of men.

New words and phrases were planted in the English language, words that have flourished ever since. 'Let there be light', 'fell flat on his face', 'filthy lucre', 'let my people go', 'the apple of his eye', 'a man after his own heart', 'signs of the times', 'ye of little faith', 'the meek shall inherit the earth', 'fisherman', 'under the sun', 'to rise and shine', 'the land of the living', 'sour grapes', 'landlady', 'sea-shore', 'two-edged', 'it came to pass', 'from time to time' and hundreds more. He is bitten into our tongue.

And he gave us, in English, the Beatitudes, the most radical and compelling affirmation of morality, and one of the most sublime poems in the language, which begins:

Blessed are the poor in spirit: for theirs is the Kingdom of Heaven.

Blessed are they that mourn, for they shall be comforted.

Blessed are the meek, for they shall inherit the earth.

Which Tyndale's words have done.

The movement for a Bible in English, which had gathered for so long, now had its champion. Tyndale's version of the New Testament was the fuse. God's English could no longer be silenced. The English ruling classes panicked.

The Bishop of London, Tunstall, had a plan. He would arrange to buy up all the books at source, ship them to London and burn them on the steps of St Paul's Cathedral.

'Well, I am the gladder,' said Tyndale, 'for these two benefits will come thereof: I shall get money of him for those books to bring myself out of debt and the whole world shall cry out upon the burning of God's word.' Which is what happened and Tyndale continued rewriting and refining his work. Yet it hurt. Especially when he was accused of deliberate deceit and profanation of the Scriptures. He knew that his only aim was to educate. There was no heresy in him. He was damned out of fear and politics and not for anything he wrote or said.

The campaign to stop Tyndale intensified. In the 1520s, Sir Thomas More was called up for service. Thomas More, a renowned scholar, was an admired friend of other liberal humanist scholars across Europe, especially of Erasmus, who wrote of him in the highest terms. He said that being in More's company 'you would say that Plato's Academy was renewed again'. He wrote of More's 'gentleness and amiable manners'. There was More's *Utopia*, a classic. And he had at one stage, like Erasmus, approved of vernacular translations of the Bible and attempted a few passages himself. He seemed, given the hardness of the age, a kindly man.

Yet once licensed by Bishop Tunstall in 1528 to read all heretical works and refute them, he bared his fangs in swiftly written dialogues. Tyndale became his chief prey. Tyndale wanted a ploughboy to be able to read the Bible? More, who abhorred free speech, was alarmed that the Bible might be available 'for every lewd lad'.

In this he differed from his friend Erasmus, who found himself twice snared in these disputes. Luther claimed him for a master although Erasmus opposed Luther's violent expression of their joint position and disassociated himself from the bloody consequences of the German wars. Now Thomas More saw Erasmus as an ally. Yet Erasmus wanted the Bible to be translated into every language and read as widely as possible. More's frenzy against Tyndale was nourished by his concern for the future of the ancient position of the Church and monarchy. He saw it threatened and his liberal humanism was thrown overboard.

More savaged Tyndale's translation. He even claimed it was not the New Testament but a forgery. He brought no proof and nor could he substantiate in any but the most minor way 'its faults . . . wherein there were noted wrong above a thousand texts'.

Tyndale's reply, *Answer Unto Sir Thomas More's Dialogue*, carefully refuted the false claims of Henry VIII's bulldog. More's counter-response, *Confutation of Tyndale's answer*, included descriptions of Tyndale as 'a beast' discharging 'a filthy foam of blasphemies out of his brutish beastly mouth', a 'hellhound' fit for 'the dogs of hell to feed on'. He called him the son of the devil himself.

Whenever Tyndale challenged him on detail, More's method was to bluster. And he descended into a sort of madness. In his defence of Roman Catholicism, he claimed, for instance, that, as some miracles had it, the heads of saints could be buried in two places.

More was fighting for the rights of the Roman Catholic position to be infallible and to be whatever it decided it wanted to be.

He saw it as sanctified by time and service. Any change, he thought, would inevitably destroy the sacrament of Holy Truth, the papacy and the monarchy. Everything must be accepted as it had been. To dislodge one pebble would be to set off the avalanche.

The vitriol against Tyndale's translation and the burning and murdering of anyone offering the slightest disagreement to the Old Church's view show what was at stake. Power was to be taken from those who had held it for so long that they believed that it belonged to them by right. Their authority had been exercised for so many centuries that the prospect of its being diminished in any way was felt to be fatal. They wanted the populace to be subservient, silent and grateful. Anything else was unacceptable. Tyndale's print-popular New Testament had breached the fortifications of a privilege so deeply founded in the past that it seemed God-given and unchallengeable. It was not to be tolerated.

While this battle of the pamphlets was going on and Tyndale was being harried from town to town in Europe, evading both the King's spies and the agents of the Holy Roman Emperor, he began to translate the Old Testament. To do this he found a way to learn Hebrew, a language in which he rejoiced. 'Where did Tyndale learn Hebrew?' asks David Daniell in his biography. 'The straightforward answer is that we do not know. Because so little Hebrew was known in England in the 1520s, he must have learnt it somewhere on the Continent, where Hebrew studies were gathering pace.'

He would have had access to a Hebrew grammar and a dictionary and 'a printed Hebrew text of scripture would not have been too hard to come by from a German bookseller.' And we know he was 'unusually skilled with languages'. Tyndale saw a close affinity between Hebrew and the English form. 'The manner of speaking in both is one,' he wrote, 'so that in a thousand places there needs not but to translate it into the English, word for word.'

He found similarities with Anglo-Saxon and used Hebraic contractions and words so boldly they are now embedded in English.

To the first five books of the Old Testament, Genesis, Exodus, Leviticus, Numbers and Deuteronomy, known as the Pentateuch or the Torah, he gave provocative marginal notes when he shipped them to England. Many of them directly criticised the Pope. Despite a shipwreck on the way from Antwerp to Hamburg in which he lost his whole manuscript and his reference books, he reconstructed the work in a few months, assisted by Miles Coverdale, a biblical scholar. His work rate was as prodigious as his erudition. References are made again and again to his working day and night. The project was always urgent, time always pressing him on.

In 1533, Henry VIII married Anne Boleyn, who was six months' pregnant. Thomas Cranmer, who arranged the marriage, became Archbishop of Canterbury and soon afterwards Thomas Cromwell became Chancellor. Wolsey, having failed to secure the divorce, was discarded. The King, now Supreme Ruler, wanted an English Bible for his new non-papist Church. All finally ought to have been ripe for Tyndale. But Miles Coverdale's version of 1539 was chosen. Tyndale was still the enemy.

We are told that Thomas Cromwell put out one or two feelers to Antwerp to help Tyndale. We know there were attempts to persuade him to return to England but, wisely, he suspected it to be an invitation to his trial and execution. He refused. But in these encounters we have a glimpse of the man, worn away, indigent, devoted to good works when not at his books. John Foxe, in his *Book of Martyrs*, wrote of him: 'He was a man without any spot or blemish of rancour or violence, full of mercy and compassion, so that no man living was able to reprove him of any sin or crime.'

Tyndale found what he thought of as safe lodgings in Antwerp and it was there, in 1535, that the assassins finally caught him.

One of them, the leader, Henry Phillips, was an Oxford man, which might have helped him into an acquaintanceship in which Tyndale trusted. Phillips led him to ambush, and fingered Tyndale, who was seized by the officers of the Holy Roman Emperor. There was no fight. They 'pitied to see his simplicity'.

They took him to Vilvoorde Castle and he was put in a dungeon for seventeen months. English residents in the city tried but failed to secure his release.

In the first winter, he wrote a letter to the prison governor. He asked that some things could be fetched from his belongings in his lodgings.

A warmer cap, for I suffer greatly from the cold and have a cough . . . a warmer coat also for what I have is very thin; a piece of cloth too with which to patch my leggings and a woollen shirt . . . for my clothes are all worn out . . . And I ask to be allowed to have a lamp in the evening for it is wearisome to sit alone in the dark. But most of all I beg and beseech your clemency that the commissary will kindly permit me to have my Hebrew bible, grammar and dictionary, that I may continue with my work.

It seems the books at least were brought to Vilvoorde and he continued to work on the Old Testament. He was condemned officially for his belief in justification by faith. He had written that 'the New Testament is an everlasting covenant made unto the children of God through faith in Christ and upon the deservings of Christ . . . there is an inward justification of a man before God which is by faith alone.'

He was found guilty of heresy and on 6 October 1536 tied to the stake and strangled by the hangman. His last words were: 'Lord, open the King of England's eyes!' and then he was 'with fire consumed'.

There will be space further to discuss his language and its influence. Here enough to say that from his New Testament and his core work on the Old came the building blocks, the character and the beauty of the King James Bible. Out of his dedication and genius came words which still line our speech and writing and thoughts today. In the history of the King James Bible there were others before and after him. But many are like myself and view William Tyndale's life and work as the founding and empowering sacrifice.

CHAPTER FOUR
THE KING JAMES VERSION
IS COMMISSIONED

When Elizabeth I lay on her deathbed in March 1603, she was surrounded by some very apprehensive men. Who was to succeed her? She had been the Pope's prime official target for assassination; there had been rebellions within her own country; a great fleet, the Spanish Armada, had set out from a Catholic country, Spain, immeasurably more powerful than her own. Its aim was to invade her England and destroy her rule. But it failed. Over the years she had managed to navigate her way through the poisonous domestic conspiracies of Catholics and the resentments of Presbyterians.

Elizabeth I was probably the best educated person to sit on the throne of England. She had seen the greatest flowering of artistic, entrepreneurial and intellectual genius in her country's history. And her island realm had begun to call itself an empire.

She had been a monarch for more than forty years. Now, clearly at the end of her days, she had still not announced her successor. It was a time of murderous politics, when killing was often the preferred option for succession to a crown and paid assassins slunk around Europe like plague rats. These her last days, 22 March and 23 March in 1603, were a dangerous time for her courtiers as they watched the dying of a monarch, married to her country as she had said. But even now it seemed that she would not declare her successor.

We are told that 'her face became haggard and her frame shrank almost to a skeleton. At last her taste for finery disappeared, and she refused to change her dresses for a week. A strange melancholy settled down upon her. Gradually her mind gave way . . . food and rest became alike distasteful. She sat day and night propped up with pillows on a stool, her finger on her lips, her eyes fixed on the floor without a word.' The Privy Council was summoned on 22 March.

She had lost the power of speech. But when yet again they asked her who should succeed her and brought up the name of the King of Scotland, she did the final service for her country. At the sound of his name she raised her wasted arms above her head and brought the fingers together to form a crown. It was done. The next morning she died 'mildly like a lamb, easily like a ripe apple from the tree'.

The messengers on horses saddled and bridled in anticipation immediately raced the 400 miles north to Edinburgh up what became the Great North Road, along dark tracks, through rivers and forests, buying fresh mounts along the way, riding, bloodied and bruised, day and night to the Scottish capital to tell King James VI of Scotland that he had been proclaimed James I of Scotland and England, Ireland, Wales and France.

As they rode north, Sir Robert Cecil, first Earl of Salisbury, went with trumpeters and heralds to the gates of Whitehall and Cheapside to proclaim that the Queen was dead, long live the King. There were bonfires to celebrate the peaceful transition and to prepare the way for the imperial funeral of Elizabeth I and the majestic journey south of the new King. New to London, he had been King of Scotland for more than thirty years. It was a crown he had inherited when he was a one-year-old child. And he had children of his own! There would be heirs. The throne was doubly assured. This was the man who would commission the Bible known by his name.

His childhood would have been called traumatic had the word been invented. His mother was Mary Queen of Scots. She was an ardent Catholic and a magnet for conspirators against her cousin, Elizabeth I. Mary's lover had been slaughtered in front of her; rival groups had kidnapped the child and held him prisoner in grim, cold, isolated Caledonian castles. The country was racked by the clashing and tormented arguments of fanatically stern Presbyterians who demanded the King's attention and were wholly unafraid to tick him off. He declared himself a lover of Presbyterianism.

There was then the death and execution of his exiled Roman Catholic mother and a life spent in sifting the signs coming from Elizabeth in London. Out of this, remarkably, he emerged as a man very sure of himself. Perhaps his scholarship grounded him.

His learning, especially his biblical learning, was on a par with that of the best biblical scholars of the day when such learning dominated the intellectual agenda. Biblical scholarship was then seen as the greatest discipline of the intellect as well as being the golden key to the word of God Himself as delivered in the Scriptures. The child James was taught Latin before he knew Scots.

At the age of eight, his learning was such that he could call on anyone to open the Bible and whatever the chapter or verses, he would instantly be able to translate it from Latin into French and from French into English. As an adolescent he became obsessed with making metrical translations of the Psalms; he boasted that he had read the Bible in most languages and could argue the case as well as any man. His love of books extended to poetry and philosophy; he wrote poetry and a book about the evils of tobacco. But the Bible was the hub of his learning.

He walked awkwardly because of a childhood bout of rickets; he wore heavily padded clothes to ward off a dagger thrust; he was unprepossessing in an age when the dandyism of the male was peacocked abroad, particularly in London. This was a man who wrote a book on demonology and – on biblical authority, 'thou shalt not suffer a witch to live' (Exodus) – had 'witches' burned to death after questioning them himself at a trial in Edinburgh. This was also a man who wrote the defining book on the Divine Right of Kings and believed that the King was God's representative on earth, that the King was outside the law and that kings alone could and did speak directly to God, who ruled Above as the King ruled Below.

His journey south from Edinburgh, which took months, was, for James and his family, a triumphal entry into a form of paradise, unforeseen. He was greeted with crowds wherever he went. Merchants of towns and cities gave him heavy purses of gold. Great landowners entertained him in houses luxurious beyond any dwelling he had ever seen. His passion for deer hunting was indulged in the richest forests he had known. Entertainments were provided for himself and his family. No flattery was too thick to lay on. He was seduced, ravished and, on that dalliance of a journey south, wholly converted to the opulence and flattering of England. He came in from a small cold country and, still vigorous in his early middle years, found treasures. His debts became a scandal.

Along the way south he was petitioned by Presbyterians. They were well organised. They were alight at the prospect of a King who had praised the Presbyterian Church in Scotland and declared himself to be happy with it and proud to be part of it. The beleaguered Presbyterians of England, strong in determination and educational influence but a minority in numbers and with no supporters at court, saw their chance and seized it. All the way along the road the man who would be crowned king in Westminster received closely argued documents, signed, it was claimed, by 1,000 Presbyterian clergy sympathetic to the cause. His past was not easily to be cast off.

There was yet another visitation of the plague in London in 1603 and James's coronation was celebrated only briefly in the capital. He was then hurried away eight miles up the River Thames to Hampton Court. This was to be where his Bible was to be born.

Hampton Court, a palace of a thousand rooms, princely halls, and gardens and ornaments fit for kings and queens, was just one of the stupendous buildings ordered and paid for by Thomas Wolsey. He was the son of a butcher in the town of Ipswich in the east of England. He had won a scholarship to Magdalen College, Oxford, and at fifteen earned his BA, 'a rare thing and seldom seen'. He scaled the ladder of the medieval academic world, was ordained, became Dean of Lincoln Cathedral and then chaplain to Henry VIII.

With the King's admiration and favour filling his sails, this precocious boy turned into a heat-seeking missile aimed at greater and greater power. He became one of the mighty diplomats of Europe, Archbishop of York, Lord Chancellor of England and a cardinal with a firm eye on the papacy as his final earthly posting. In Church and state he carried all before him and pursued a ruthless policy of appropriating rich Church titles and lands. Precious stones ringed his fingers, rarest satins and silks clothed him, mistresses and sycophants constantly plumped up the pillowed comforts of a sovereign's life in his palace beside the Thames.

James took to Hampton Court as to the manner born. He began what became an addiction to extravagance. There were feasts and masques, in one of which his young wife and her friends appeared lightly masked but otherwise gauzed in near nakedness. Shakespeare and his company were bidden up river to preview *Macbeth* in the Great Hall. Shakespeare's three witches were thought to have entertained the new King. This second kingship called up some luxuriating part of James's mind. The sensualities of that frozen kidnapped boy bullied by Presbyterians, used as a pawn by ambitious Scottish noblemen, now demanded to be sated. He found a new world and although he had delivered a lover's farewell to Scotland, saying he would return there often, he went back only once in twenty-two years. He was King of England now and he pillaged this paradise ruthlessly.

Since Tyndale's Bible, the first printed Bible in English, there had been several others. Despite some notes and small amendments, it was the case that again and again Tyndale's version remained the basis for these subsequent translations into Early Modern English. Tyndale was only lightly edited by Miles Coverdale for his 1539 Bible: the Great Bible, 'authorised' by Henry VIII, had Tyndale's work on the New Testament and the early books of the Old Testament as its foundation. The Geneva Bible (1560), which became the most influential of all until the King James Version, took Tyndale's Bible and the Great Bible as its basis, as did the Bishops' Bible of 1568. Even the Douay-Rheims New Testament of 1582, a Roman Catholic version, used Tyndale.

These several Bibles were confusing and an embarrassment. Towards the end of Elizabeth's reign Parliament spoke of the need to reduce 'the diversity of Bibles now extant in the English tongue'. Nothing was done.

It was an ideal opportunity for this new biblically erudite King. In January 1604, a few months after the hurried coronation in Westminster Abbey, and following his spectacular Twelfth Night theatricals, King James opened the Hampton Court Conference.

Religion was the potent political and intellectual currency of the day. It was the only arena of great debate and James used this occasion to show off his paces. The Privy Council was there, as were many bishops. Although it was they who had suggested it, there were only four Puritan clerics and they were not even invited to the opening service. So much, they would have been right to think, for James's recent passionate declaration of loyalty to the Presbyterian Church in Scotland.

On the first day James made a five-hour speech, much of it in Latin. He attacked the Church of England so expertly and relentlessly that some thought he had shipped his Presbyterianism down from Edinburgh intact. Only the canniest listeners, like Launcelot Andrewes, Dean of Westminster, saw him as 'playing' the Puritan. But the speech left no one in any doubt of his learning and his religious zeal. Indeed, some thought his vehemence was rather coarse, even boastful.

Then on the second day, the Puritans, high on expectation, were allowed in to the court. He turned on them. His opening speech, only one hour this time, was on the subject 'Religion is the soul of a Kingdom and Unity the life of Religion'. I think that he had studied the triangular balancing act of Elizabeth I. She enforced, in law, the state's Protestantism; kept many of the Catholic forms and practices; and tolerated at arm's length the radical Puritans. Above all she was seen to be moderate. James knew about lack of moderation from his Scottish experience. This now seemed too raw and too disruptive from the perspective of this more complex and nuanced terrain.

So when the Puritans came forward with their rather modest proposals, minor changes in the rights of the Church – to forbid the making of the sign of the Cross at certain points in the service and the enforced wearing of a wedding ring and the end of absentee clergy, which had enabled Wolsey, for instance, to pile up his wealth – James turned down all of their requests.

'I will have one doctrine and one discipline, one religion in substance and in ceremony,' said James. The more they pressed the angrier he became, until he declared: 'If this be all they have to say, I will make them contain themselves or harry them out of the land.' In the ecstasy of this accomodating and sumptuous Anglicanism, he had sown the seeds of what was to become an exodus of some of the best educated and most serious-minded people in the kingdom. In his excitement at pleasing the English establishment in his newfound land, he had paved the way for the nonconformists to leave England and found their own newfound land – America.

In one other respect the mysterious law of unexpected consequences was already at work at that Hampton Court Conference. For one of the four Puritans, John Reynolds, president of Corpus Christi College, Oxford, petitioned the King to consider a new translation of the Bible. The Anglican establishment objected most strongly, but on this one subject, possibly flattered by the glory that would accrue to him, or perhaps as a consolation prize for the Presbyterians, the King acceded. And the politician in him realised that a single Bible, ultimately authorised and controlled by the King himself, and a King as steeped in Bible scholarship as he was, could play a starring role in bringing and holding his new domain together.

Out of Wolsey's most Catholic Hampton Court on the Thames came one Bible, one authorised version controlled by one King. One King by Divine Right. One Bible that would eliminate those radical suggestions which appeared in the margins of the Geneva Bible. One Bible that would show the world what the King and God and the heavenly and earthly kingdom were really made of. A book to re-order the world.

Which it did.

CHAPTER FIVE
THE FOUR COMPANIES

James began work immediately. He had already said at the conference: 'I profess I could never yet see a Bible translated well into English . . . I wish some special pains were taken for an uniform translation which should be done by the best learned men in both universities, then revised by Bishops, presented to the Privy Council, lastly ratified by Royal Authority, to be read in the whole church, and none other.'

That became his battle plan. And the book that proved that a work of lasting value, unique significance and unparalleled popularity could be assembled by committee got under way. King James put his oar in even before the work had begun. Not only did he outline the schedule – and see that it was followed – he marked the cards of those he chose to make the new translation.

The Geneva Bible, the most popular of all the Bibles published at that time, had irritated James in Edinburgh where he had to bite his tongue. In London it was loosened and he rounded on his tormentor. His chief objection to the Geneva Bible was not the translation of the Scriptures but the marginal notes, which he saw as 'untrue, seditious and savouring too much of dangerous and traitorous conceits'. He pointed out that in Exodus i, 17, in its marginal notes the Geneva Bible had *commended* the example of civil disobedience shown by Hebrew midwives. In 2 Chronicles xv, 16, the notes stated that King Asa's mother should have been executed, not just deposed for her idolatry. This, he thought, could be used to reflect badly on his mother, Mary Queen of Scots, who had indeed been executed. Worse, Exodus challenged the Divine Right of a King to be above the law.

There would be no marginal notes in his new Bible. Nor was the word 'tyrant', which appeared more than 400 times in the Geneva Bible, to be used.

James grasped what many later ideologues and rulers and tyrants grasped – that authority was secured by the enforcement of detail. Just as Marxists, Leninists and Maoists argued for months on apparently hair-splittingly different interpretations of their own sacred books, so here James saw the Bible as his outward and visible authority. It would be *his* Bible. No notes.

But the overall guidance still left a great deal of room for manoeuvre. In King James's Bible, the ambiguities of the language and the multiple possible uses to which the stories could be put were to prove both a book for the establishment and, equally, a book with revolutionary potential. Yet at the time of publication it seemed that the Book of Books had become solely the Book of the King. The Scriptures would serve the state and only through the King of the state would they serve God. He wanted the Bible to sound familiar and it did; he wanted it revised by his own selection of great scholars and it was.

The country, at that intellectually blossoming time in its history, was quite remarkably well served with scholars in Latin, Greek, Hebrew, Arabic, Syriac, Dutch, French, Italian, Spanish and Anglo-Saxon. James had only to cast out his net to haul in a glittering catch of linguists.

The scheme was set up in a few months. The preliminary translation took four years. There were nine months of review and revision in London. Then followed final revisions, including that of the King. From the court it would make its way to the Royal Printer.

Fifty-four scholars were sifted from the mass of bibliophiles who had accreted in Oxford and Cambridge and around Westminster. Deaths and illnesses culled the field a little and probably forty-seven were active. A mighty and intellectually dazzling host from a small country to be funnelled into one book. Almost all of them came from the south-east of England, which both characterised and unified the English, which in that period was a quilt of dialects. About 25 per cent of the translators were Puritans, evidence of an impressive fight-back after their humiliation at Hampton Court.

These men took their work with gravity. To them, the Scriptures were the books of eternal life, the guides to daily life, the story of Jesus Christ, the only Saviour, the history of the world and the Word of God. They were not timid in their learning. One of the reasons the book has lasted and was so resonant is that it was scrupulously tested by superbly learned minds whose life's work had been to fathom ancient religious texts. They took translation seriously and, in his preface to the Bible, Miles Smyth defended this memorably. He wrote: 'Translation it is that openeth the window to let in the light; that breaketh the shell that we may eat the kernel; that putteth aside the curtain that we may look into the most holy place; that removeth the cover of the well that we may come by the water, even as Jacob rolled away the stone from the mouth of the well.'

Smyth also wrote: 'we never sought to make a new translation, nor yet a bad one to make a good one, but to make a good one better; or out of many good ones, one principal good one.'

The scholars worked in six committees, two based in Oxford, two in Cambridge and two in Westminster. The Bible was carved up between them. The majority was firmly Anglican. The committees worked separately until completion when two from each committee met to revise and harmonise the whole. The King did not pay them. Either their colleges supported them or they were steered towards well-paid parishes and dioceses which gave them the time to do the work. They worked in an orderly, even a drilled manner, for years. A contemporary, John Selden, in his *Table Talk*, writes: 'the translation in King James' time took an excellent way. That part of the bible was given to him who was most excellent in such a tongue . . . and then they met together, and one read the translation, the rest holding in their hands some Bible, either of the learned tongues, or French, Spanish, Italian etc. If they found any fault they spoke up, if not he read on.'

'He read on.' That is crucial. From the beginning the Bible in England had been a preaching and a teaching Bible. Wycliffe and Tyndale were aware that they were delivering their translated Scriptures into a largely illiterate society. They wrote as scholars for scholars, but they also wrote as preachers for everyone who needed to be reached. Later it would be read not only in churches and in vast open air rallies, but in schools and homes, in meetings and conferences. It would be quoted by soldiers on the battlefield and nurses in hospitals and its poetry would later be translated into the gospel songs. In this as in much else, they modelled themselves on the practice of Jesus Christ who spoke directly to the people.

The scholars had a substantial library at their disposal. Not only the versions in English, beginning with Wycliffe, but the Complutensian Polyglot (of 1517, in which Hebrew, Latin and Greek were printed side by side), the Antwerp Polyglot of 1572, the Tremellius-Junius Bible of 1579, Sebastian Münster's Latin translation of the Old Testament, Theodore Bega's translation of the New Testament; Latin translations of the whole Bible by

Sanctes Pagninus, Leo Judo and Sebastian Castalio; the Zurich
Bible, Luther's German Bible; the French Bibles of Lefèvre
d'Étaples (1534) and Olivétan (1535); Casiodoro de Reina and
Cypriano de Valera (1569) in Spanish; Diodati in Italian; the
1,600-year-old Latin Vulgate by St Jerome and commentaries by
early Church fathers, rabbis and other contemporary scholars.
And, of course, Tyndale.

Since Tyndale's day, Greek and especially Hebrew scholarship
had advanced rapidly; there were more and better Hebrew gram-
mars and the scanning of existing versions was fine-toothed. All
the more remarkable then that Tyndale's final version still
accounted for about 80 per cent of the King James New Testament
and the same percentage obtained in those books he had translated of the Old Testament. Yet the contribution by these later
scholars was important both for the grand authority their reputa-
tions brought to it and for the work of improvement and finessing
they undertook.

The First Westminster Company was led by Dean Launcelot
Andrewes, of whom it was said he 'might have been interpreter
general at Babel'. He went to Cambridge University at sixteen,
where he met and befriended Edmund Spenser, the poet, author of
The Faerie Queen. It appears that he was studious and 'avoided
games of ordinary recreation'. He climbed rapidly up the Church
ladder until he became Dean of Westminster Abbey and one of
the twelve chaplains to Queen Elizabeth I.

We are told that he mastered fifteen languages and had an
outstandingly tenacious memory. Grotius, the leading Dutch
legal authority and historian, said that meeting Andrewes was
'one of the special attractions of a visit to England'. It is said that
King James sometimes slept with Andrewes's sermons under his
pillow and was in awe of him. T.S. Eliot, almost four centuries
later, praised his gift for 'taking a word and developing the world

from it'. Too Latinate and self-absorbed for some, but to the greatest poet of the twentieth century he was a literary hero.

As merely one example, Eliot takes Tyndale's opening lines of Genesis: 'In the beginning God created heaven and earth. The earth was void and empty, and darkness was upon the deep and the spirit of God moved upon the water.'

He then quotes Andrewes, whose words he claims are much superior: 'In the beginning God created the heaven and the earth. And the earth was without form, and void, and darkness was upon the face of the deep. And the spirit of God moved upon the face of the waters.'

Thirty-nine words compared to Tyndale's twenty-nine. The key words 'void', 'darkness', 'deep' are Tyndale. I prefer Tyndale. Nevertheless, T.S. Eliot is to be respected and many have agreed with his judgement about this and others of Andrewes's rephrasings.

Eliot was much indebted to Andrewes. In his poem 'The Journey of the Magi' he took phrases from him for some of his most admired poetry. From a sermon of Andrewes on the Three Wise Men in 1622, he used and echoed: 'It was no summer progress. A cold coming they had of it . . . the ways deep, the winter sharp, the days short, the sun farthest off in solstitio brumali, the very dead of winter.'

Andrewes and his committee met in the Jerusalem Chamber, still part of the original Abbey House at Westminster.

Other members included Hebrew specialists, Greek scholars and Latinists. One was so fluent in Latin that he found it difficult to talk in English at any length. Another had a permanently faithless wife whose public infatuation with sex saddened him but did not sever his marriage nor, it seems, interfere with his concentration on the translation.

The First Cambridge Company was led by Edward Lively, the

Regius Professor of Hebrew, whose thirteen children disabled him
from living a life without debt. There was the Regius Professor of
Divinity from Cambridge, one of the four Puritans who had
attended the Hampton Court Conference. Another scholar had
lived through the reigns of four Tudors and two Stuarts and died
aged 105, still able to read a copy of the Greek Testament in 'very
small type' 'without spectacles'.

The First Oxford Company was headed by John Hardinge,
Regius Professor of Hebrew. The most powerful man on that
committee, though, was John Reynolds, not only President of
Corpus Christi College, Oxford, but the man who had successfully suggested the idea of a new Bible to James I at Hampton
Court. He was variously described as a 'living library' and 'a
university unto himself'. He was a moderate Puritan, understanding of the Roman Catholic position, a tried and trusted friend and
respecter of Jews, and a man who literally, it was thought, wasted
away in his service to translation. He died in 1607 and looked 'the
very skeleton'. Other Puritans were not as tolerant: one, Thomas
Holland, would say, on parting company, 'I commend you to the
love of God and to the hatred of Popery and superstition.'

These three companies devoted themselves to the Old
Testament. The word 'company' for what might better be
described as a 'committee' indicates the power of fashion of the
day. London was a nest of companies: the Actors' Companies, the
Livery companies, the Muscovy Company, the Levant Company,
the East India Company . . . There was something vaguely martial
and also convivial about a company and that seems to have rubbed
off on these biblical companies.

The Second Oxford Company and the Second Westminster
Company worked on the New Testament, the Second Cambridge
Company on the Apocrypha now sadly omitted from the King
James Version.

James drew up fourteen rules after consultation with Bishop (later Archbishop) Bancroft and Robert Cecil, his principal secretary of state. Their aim was to ensure the translation was a conservative one. Perhaps to emphasise that, they kept words and phrases and sentences that had already drifted out of fashion, even archaic, like 'verily' and 'it came to pass'. By retaining them, they ensured that the new Bible from the beginning had a halo of antiquity, a feeling of immemorial validity.

From January 1609, a General Committee of Revision met in London to examine the new version. According to one of the three translators entrusted with the task, only a few of their changes made it into the final version. The companies had done well. From this committee it went to two other translators. One of them, Miles Smyth, wrote the preface. On to Archbishop Bancroft, who made fourteen of his own changes, rather resented by Miles Smyth. It was then finally presented to the King and from the court sent off to the printers.

The Bible was about to be born again and this, the Authorised Version, would, with some retouching along the way, remain the standard English Bible until well into the twentieth century. In many parts of the world it still is and where it has been superseded its loss is often lamented and there are cries to bring it back.

Just as the Scottish King, thrifty in everything save his indulgences, would not pay the translators, so he left the printers to fend for themselves.

Although called the Authorised Version, the King James Bible was never officially authorised. That would have required an Act of Parliament. But within the title the words 'By his majestie's special commandment' and 'Appointed to be read in churches' and the common knowledge of King James's decisive role allow that 'Authorised' to be used without too much historical embarrassment. America has it more accurately with the 'King James Version'.

The printing proved to be a strain. Bibles had been a trade monopoly since the time of Henry VIII and the custom of a cut of the profits, a royalty going to royalty to acknowledge their royal approval, was well established by James's day. Bibles and theological books were not only good business, they were the biggest proportion of the book business. Under Queen Elizabeth I, in 1577, Thomas Barker secured a monopoly on Bibles. A decade later, by intensive lubrications at court, he had it extended for the whole of his lifetime and that of his son, who became the King's Printer, solely responsible in 1611 for the publication of the Bible.

It would be lavish, splendid and very expensive. Barker had to set aside an eye-watering sum, £3,500 (in Jacobean times, a king's ransom). He had to look for partners. They came and they brought troubles and disputes and debts which put him in prison for the last ten years of his life. But even in his cell he remained the King's Printer and held on to the copyright.

It was printed in 1611 with the title 'The Holy Bible, Conteyning the Old Testament and the New: Newly Translated out of the Originall tongues: & with the former Translations diligently compared and revised, by his Majesties speciall Comandement. Appointed to be read in Churches. Imprinted at London by Robert Barker, Printer to the Kings most Excellent Majestie Anno Domini 1611'. The New Testament bore a title, the same but for the opening line: 'the New Testament of our Lord and Saviour Jesus Christ . . .'

It cost twelve shillings bound, ten shillings loose leaf. The folio edition was handsome, heavy and designed to impress. The smaller and cheaper quarto edition was on the streets a year later. There were no illustrations. It contained a table for the reading of the Psalms at matins and evensong, a Church calendar, an almanac and a table of holy days and observances. Some of this dropped away as later versions appeared, most notably in 1629, 1638 and 1762 at Cambridge and, most successfully, in 1769 at Oxford.

Punctuation, spelling and capitalisation were often erratic. Of the 1,500 misprints in the first years some are memorable. For instance there was the omission of '*not*' from the commandment 'thou shalt not commit adultery'. This became known as 'the wicked Bible'. The printers were fined. Then there was the 'vinegar Bible', where 'vinegar' crept in instead of 'vineyard'. And the 'murderer's Bible', where there was 'let the children first be *killed*' instead of '*filled*'. Hating '*life*' became hating '*wife*'.

There were disputes. For example, the same Greek verb meaning 'rejoice' was translated not only as 'rejoice' but also as 'glory'. 'We rejoice in . . .', 'we glory in . . .' and 'we also joy in . . .'. Variation had suited the poetic and illuminating mind of Tyndale and that was one of the characteristics his successors imitated. The fluidity and the rush of richness in and the bounty of almost-synonyms in the Roman-Germanic-Norse-French-English language at the time was too tempting to resist.

But it has been pointed out that literally a liberty had been taken and the cry of Richard III, 'A horse! A horse! My kingdom for a horse!' might not have been improved with the introduction of 'steed' and 'nag'. And though the Authorised Version was more Latinate than earlier versions, Anglo-Saxon words still predominated and Anglo-Saxon monosyllables, as in Shakespeare, gave the language its dynamism: 'Song of Songs', 'King of Kings', 'And the word was made flesh', 'man of war', 'I am the way, the truth and the light', 'three score and ten', 'And the word was with God. And the word was God.'

The fiercest critic of the day was a Puritan Hebrew scholar, Hugh Broughton, who had not been included on the list of translators – very likely because of his tendency to argue with everyone who dared to disagree with him. King James asked for advice from independent scholars and Broughton weighed in. 'It is so ill done . . . Tell his Majesty I had rather be rent in pieces by wild horses than that any such translation by my comment should be urged upon poor churches. It crosseth me and I require it to be burnt!' He was not alone, though his intemperance was exceptional.

At first people did not take to it. In some matters, and certainly in this case, people prefer old lamps to new. The Bishops' Bible ceased to be printed but its translated bulk still stayed on the lecterns in many of the churches. Its words were familiar and it had its hold. It took time for James to decree that his Bible be the sole Bible in churches. After that it took over the lecterns throughout the kingdom.

Then there was the Geneva Bible, much loved, conveniently priced and sized, the portable sustenance of the faith for generations. That too held on and was not entirely supplanted until the middle of the century.

St Jerome, after the years spent turning the Bible into the Latin current in his day at the end of the fourth century, encountered equally harsh opposition which embittered him. He would have been pleased that Thomas Hobbes, the seventeenth-century English philosopher, in his book *Leviathan* quotes the Bible only in the Latin of St Jerome and disdained the King James Version. Many of the educated preferred what they had studied at university. The beauties of the new Bible's prose were to be discovered, admired and then loved rather later.

It was the will of James I that made the book happen. It was the poetry of it and a civil war in the kingdoms of Britain and a purposeful and valiant push west across the Atlantic to America that embedded it.

'The scholars who produced this masterpiece are mostly un-known and unremembered,' wrote Sir Winston Churchill, not, as it turns out, correctly. 'But they forged an enduring link, literary and religious, between the English-speaking people of the world.'

And a scholar's voice, that of Professor Albert Stanborough Cook, of Yale University in the 1920s: 'No other book has penetrated and permeated the hearts and speech of the English race as has the Bible.'

Finally, from the historian Lord Macaulay: 'If everything else in our language should perish, it would alone suffice to show the whole extent of its beauty and power.'

Now, 1611, it was done and out in the world. It would help create new worlds and be part of the rise and fall of empires. It would be crucial in shaping America, its faith, its democracy and its language. All this potential was compact in dangerously crowded, small ships which set off from ports in the west of England to find and found a New England, which they did, Bibles in hand, God's English their guide.

CHAPTER SIX
THE MAYFLOWER AND
THE COVENANT

There is something of the Ark about the *Mayflower*. On 6 September 1620, 102 people set off from Plymouth in Devon on the south coast of England. This boat, the *Mayflower*, was ninety feet long and twenty-five feet wide. Today you can see a full-scale replica berthed in Plymouth, Massachusetts. It is a thing of beauty, gleaming, perfect: and very small.

In 1620 it leaked, stank, bulged with people and furniture, livestock and stores and forced its way across the storm-stricken North Atlantic for sixty-six days. To imagine that small vessel in the turbulence of a Northern Atlantic late autumn is to be reminded of Noah. When the Flood came to drown the earth, God told Noah to build a wooden ark, and in this he put the birds and the beasts and men and women who would survive the Flood and begin God's work on earth once more.

Thirty-five of those on board the *Mayflower* would have embraced the comparison and sought strength from it. These thirty-five believed that they were God's favoured people, heirs to the Israelites of the Old Testament. They had entered into a covenant with each other and with God who expected greater service from them than from anyone else. Their religion was based on Calvinism: they were Separatists, they were the Elect. It is likely that most of them took the Geneva Bible, and their reading of the Bible told them so.

Like the King James Version, it was largely based on the work of Tyndale. When the King James Version took over, which it did in a few years, there was not much that was new. The disturbing marginal notes had gone. But the Separatists would then ink in their own marginal notes. They were the 'Chosen' and they watched every step they took. Few groups in history can have taken their calling with such fearless seriousness. It was those qualities as much as their faith which put their stamp on the language, the constitution and the morality of America. These people of the book were the crucible in the making of the new nation. They made it as a tribute to the book.

They also made it, as they saw it, through God's providence. The following is one of the only known primary source accounts of the journey of the *Mayflower*, written by William Bradford in his *Of Plymouth Plantation*. The extract begins when the *Mayflower* finally set sail successfully, having been beaten back to Plymouth by violent storms:

September 6. These troubles being blown over, and now all being compact together in one ship, they put to sea again with a prosperous wind, which continued divers days together, which was some encouragement unto them; yet according to the usual manner many were afflicted with sea sickness. And I may not omit here a special work of God's providence.

There was a proud and very profane young man, one of the seamen, of a lusty, able body, which made him the more haughty; he would always be condemning the poor people in their sickness, and cursing them daily with grievous execrations, and did not let to tell them, that he hoped to help to cast half of them overboard before they came to their journey's end, and to make merry with what they had; and if he were by any gently reproved, he would curse and swear most bitterly. But it pleased God before they came half seas over, to smite this young man with a grievous disease, of which he died in a desperate manner, and so was himself the first that was thrown overboard. Thus his curses light on his own head, and it was an astonishment to all his fellows, for they noted it to be the just hand of God upon him.

In this next extract, besides once more showing the hardships of the voyage, a more benevolent God is revealed:

And as for the decks and upper works they would caulk them as well as they could, and though with the working of the ship they would not long keep staunch, yet there would otherwise be no great danger, if they did not overpress her with sails. So they committed themselves to the will of God, and resolved to proceed. In sundry of these storms the winds were so fierce, and the seas so high, as they could not bear a knot of sail, but were forced to hull, for divers days together. And in one of them, as they thus lay at hull, in a mighty storm, a lusty young man (called John Howland) coming upon some occasion above the gratings, was, with a seele of the ship thrown into the sea; but it pleased God that he caught hold of the topsail halyards, which hung overboard, and ran out at length; yet he held his hold (though he was sundry fathoms under water) till he was hauled up by the same rope to the brim of the water, and then with a boat hook and other means got into the ship again, and his life saved; and though he was something ill with it, yet he lived many years after, and became a profitable member both in church and commonwealth.

Finally at their destination, they had no doubt what must be done before all else: 'Being thus arrived in a good harbour and brought safe to land, they fell upon their knees and blessed the God of heaven, who had brought them over the vast and furious ocean, and delivered them from all the perils and miseries thereof, again to set their feet on the firm and stable earth, their proper element.'

After sixty-six days, after one death and one birth, they had landed near what they called Plymouth Rock. On rocky ground they built their church. They faced a winter of which one of their number wrote: 'they that know the winters of that country know them to be sharp and violent, and subject to cruel and fierce storms, dangerous to travel to known places, much more to search an unknown coast. Besides, what could they see but a hideous and desolate place, full of wild beasts and wild men – and what multitudes there might be of them, they knew not.'

By the end of that first winter, half of them had died.

They were woefully unprepared for the task of settlement. The author Bill Bryson has written: 'You couldn't have had a more helpless group of people to start a new society. They brought all the wrong stuff, they didn't really bring people who were expert in agriculture or fishing. They were coming with a lot of faith and not a great deal of preparation.' These people had travelled before – to the Netherlands where they had sought refuge for their godly task. But in that country there was a language and an economy with which they were familiar.

They saw alien peoples and the uncultivated wilderness. Yet it was their destination and they sturdily called it 'New England'. Out of this desert walked their saviour. He was an Indian, Tisquantum, nicknamed Squanto. The settlers would have had every justification for adding his appearance to the calendar of miracles. His knowledge, intelligence and kindness got them through that winter and beyond.

Squanto had been kidnapped by English sailors fifteen years

before and taken to London where he was trained to be a guide and an interpreter for the fishermen who regularly travelled the 3,000 miles across the North Atlantic to bring back rich hauls from the teeming, scarcely harvested seas of the North Atlantic and Cape Cod. Squanto escaped, and trekked back to his tribe. He found it all but wiped out by one of the European diseases that were to bring successive plagues to the Native Americans. He travelled on and you might feel justified in saying, 'God alone knows how,' he ended up next to the same rock as the helpless colonists from Devon. As Bill Bryson notes: 'He taught them not only which things would grow but also how to fertilise corn seed by adding little pieces of fish – the fish would rot and actually fertilise the seed – and he taught them how to eat all kinds of things from the sea.'

He spoke English and helped the settlers to reach a balance of accommodation with the tribes whose lands they had moved in on. Some of the settlers thought it beyond mere good fortune and saw it as providence. This *was* the Promised Land and God had held out His hand to them.

Charles I had succeeded his father, James, in 1625. His increasing encouragement of Catholic practices drove out more and more colonists and Separatists. The King badly underestimated the historical and the visceral fear of Roman Catholics. The Pope was considered to be the literal Antichrist: his Church the Empire of Evil, his mission satanic. By 1640, scores of ships had brought over a community of about 25,000 in and around new Plymouth. They came largely from the east of England – especially Lincolnshire, Essex, Kent and London – and the Midlands, particularly Nottinghamshire. Overwhelmingly, they came to stay and they dug in.

They were proud to be English. The place names alone show that: a small selection includes Cambridge, Ipswich, Norwich,

Boston, Hull, Bedford, Falmouth and Plymouth, of course. This was evidence of homesickness perhaps, but also a determination to keep the connection and hold faith with the faith of those they had left behind. It was a new baptism, but also an assertion of their Englishness. There were many who came for reasons other than a search for a place in which to plant a purer Puritan faith. But for many generations it was the religious self-exiles who dominated. By the time the make-up of the population of the New World had grown and changed and its history been forged in godliness, slaughter, injustice and risk, it was these founding Puritans and Separatists who had put down their mark. Their covenant with each other through their faith in the teaching and in the language of the Bible had made its harsh Protestant charac-ter the first draft of the new America.

There was something else going on, more profound and, I think, difficult to grasp in our age. There grew with increasing force in seventeenth-century England, among the Puritans, the belief, frightening to these faith-filled souls, that 'God was leav-ing England'.

In this, as in so much about the seventeenth century, I am indebted to Christopher Hill. Here is a quotation with which he opens the chapter called 'God Is Leaving England', in his book *The English Bible and the Seventeenth-Century Revolution*. He begins with a reference, one of many, taken from the Old Testament.

'The Lord hath a controversy with the inhabitants of the land, because there is no truth, nor mercy, nor knowledge of God in the land.' The land referred to was now thought to be England. The fear was growing that the threat of Catholicism and the Antichrist was not being countered with sufficient rigour. Charles's court flirted with Catholicism and it was becoming dangerously drawn back into its orbit.

In Europe the Thirty Years War between Protestants and Catholics was swinging perilously and savagely against the Protestants. England refused to get involved. Just as Israel had faced the larger powers of Egypt and Babylon, so England now faced the far greater powers of France and Spain. The Puritans thought that their country was not alive to the danger. Why did King Charles not take up arms against the Catholics? God would not stay with people who did not deserve Him.

In 1622, John Brinsley, in his influential *The Third Part of the True Watch*, wrote: 'The withdrawing of the Lord's precious presence from his church is both an evident sign of his displeasure and a manifest threatening of his departure.' England needed to repent its sins. Preacher after preacher called out, but in vain. A verse of one new hymn ran:

> Preserve this hopeless place
> And our disturbed state
> From those that have more wit than grace
> And present counsels hate.

Less than a decade later, in 1631, Thomas Hooker, in a sermon called 'The Danger of Desertion', left no one in any doubt. 'As sure as God is God, God is going from England . . . Stop him at the town's end and let not thy God depart . . . God makes account that New England still be a refuge . . . a rock and a shelter for his righteous ones to run to.'

Which they did; the hundreds turned into thousands. There were those who remained to continue the fight in the Puritan cause in the Civil War and to see their triumphant victory and the Protestant 'Commonwealth' under Oliver Cromwell. This seemed to promise to reunite New and Old England for ever. But before that, the decisive transatlantic shift, the flight which was to create the character of America, had been made. The dreadful warning, that 'God is leaving England', had been heeded and taken literally. And as a consequence the New World was founded on the rock of a tough, Bible-bound, deep-thinking Protestantism.

There had been expeditions and attempted settlements in America before the Pilgrim Fathers – in Virginia, for instance, under Walter Raleigh in the reign of Queen Elizabeth I. There was Jamestown, established in 1607. This was Anglican, rather middle class and more easy-going than those fanatically driven communities further north. Not that the English gentry avoided going to the north. The immigrants of the 1630s were a wide social mix, but it was the Puritans who were dominant for a sealing length of time. 'From the beginning,' as Diarmaid MacCulloch the distinguished theological historian has written, 'they were a 'Commonwealth', whose government lay in the hands of godly adult males who were the investors and the colonists.' Most of them were Puritans: the Separatists – extreme Puritans – were a minority, but, in the early days, disproportionately influential.

The first Governor of Massachusetts, John Winthrop, like his Puritan contemporary Oliver Cromwell, was an East Anglian gentleman. One of the most striking things these Puritans did was to set up a university college, Harvard, in a town they named Cambridge. It was for the training of new clergy. In 1650 Massachusetts had one minister for every 415 persons. In Virginia it was one for 3,239. And by *law* every householder in Massachusetts had to pay a tax for the church or meeting house and by *law* go there for two hours twice on Sundays and for a two-hour lecture in the week.

This and their devotion to the daily study and reading of the Bible and other religious works made them, MacCulloch again, 'possibly the most literate society then existing in the world'.

Almost every Puritan town had a school. What bound them was the central notion of 'the covenant' they had made with God, with each other and with the future. What lined their minds was the Bible, by now, the 1630s, the King James Version.

Their implacable stance saw life as a battle between God and Satan. This set in motion yet another persisting strain in American life: persecution. If you were not with them you were against them, as Jesus Christ Himself had said. And if you were against them you were to be attacked, defeated and, if necessary, destroyed. They used the Old Testament but also English common law to justify the persecution of what they saw as 'immorality'. This included breaking the Sabbath or blasphemy, which were criminalised. Hysterical insanity could take over. In 1642, the New Haven authorities examined a piglet whose face, they said, bore a resemblance to one George Spenser. He was convicted of bestiality. He confessed and was hanged; and so was the sow.

Non-Puritans were not encouraged to come to New England and one of the leading men of the Chosen spoke of 'the lawlessness of liberty of conscience'. Dissenters were given, as another Puritan said, 'free liberty to keep away from us'. When the intellectually adventurous Quakers came, they were prosecuted and their ears were cropped and they were expelled. When four of them returned between 1659 and 1661, they were hanged.

One unexpected consequence of this was that Roger Williams, a minister in Salem in the 1630s, was moved to say that the Puritans had gone too far. He fled to found what became Rhode Island, unique in the English-speaking world for welcoming exiles and Dissenters, Anglicans, Baptists, Quakers and also those from another religion – one both deeply allied and historically alien – Jews.

These New England Puritans hunted down witches. It was a period when medicine was primitive and when magic and 'signs' would be sought out to fill the gaps in knowledge. The devil was held to be ceaseless in his attempts to deform, damage, disrupt, distort and dismantle the plans and purposes of the best of God's people. It was a time of the dramatically inexplicable and in that fear-fraught and fortressed society, vengeance seemed an essential defence. And though 'vengeance is mine, saith the Lord', the Old Testament furnished many dramatic examples not only of a vengeful God but also of vengeful Israelites and their enemies. It was there in the book and so it could be followed as an example.

Witches were a prime target. Overwhelmingly women and mostly of the poorer class. These were usually women canny in their knowledge of traditional country cures. They were powerless and easy to capture. For those in authority they were useful, perhaps in some primitive way: they were essential victims. For such furious and strained endeavours as the Puritans were undertaking, perhaps sacrifices were needed to satisfy the tribe – blood sacrifices, human sacrifices.

Puritan New England was persistent in the matter of witches. In Virginia, there were nine cases, only one suspect and *he* sentenced to a whipping and banishment. In the north ninety-three were tried, sixteen executed.

Then came Salem in 1692. Accusations by feverish adolescent girls were taken seriously and acted upon. Hundreds, mostly women, were accused by them. Eighteen were hanged. Sense returned only when the accusers turned their venomous hysteria on the ruling elite, including the governor's wife. That went too far. 'Further trials were suppressed,' the historian Alan Taylor writes. 'Regarded as a fiasco, the Salem mania became a spectacular flame-out that halted the prosecution of witches in New England.'

But the stain remained. Salem is dead but not buried. Arthur

Miller's play, *The Crucible*, keeps it alive; Senator McCarthy's search for communists in the 1950s was called a 'witch hunt'.

These English, soon to be joined by Irish, Scots and Welsh, Puritans, and other hard-line Protestants, brought to New England a fanaticism allied with righteousness which would begin to clear the new continent of its natives. It would go on to build a capitalist democracy, global industries, new technologies, weaponry, and it would encourage mass education, equality, and princely philanthropy. The dark side led the settlers into the deceits, injustices and crimes of all dominating empires. The King James Version was there, every step of the way, for better and for worse, often the latter.

In 1789, George Washington took his oath of office and opened the Book of Genesis to passages that included Joseph's dying reminder that God had promised the Israelites a new land. 'So help me God,' he said, as has every President of America since. The core tribe among the 'Israelites' in America were the Puritans and, deeper still, the Separatists. At the heart, what drove them was the binding Word of God in the King James Version.

It was the Bible that founded the English language over the Atlantic. It appears to have occurred to scarcely any of them that they should 'go native' and adopt the language of the tribes whose lands they occupied.

Their approach rested on their attitude to the King James Version. Quite simply, it was their book and its words belonged to them. In the 1630s, it began its centuries of dominance as by far the biggest selling and widest read book in America. The words were holy. They were aware that the Old Testament had been written in Hebrew, the New in Greek, the whole in Latin and that modern European nations had put it in their own languages. But the English translation was the supreme authority on all matters, the Book of Books.

They found poetry in it as well as wisdom and their guidance to the Kingdom of Heaven. They read it aloud every day. They took its names for their names, made its parables as their own, swore by it, lived and died by it. It provided meat for their daily conversation and proofs of their earthly destiny. They were married to it and no one could put them asunder.

Their behaviour to other languages echoed that of the Germanic tribes who had brought what became 'English' to the eastern counties of England in the fifth century. It was partly from these eastern counties that the first tide of pilgrims came to the east coast of America. The fifth-century Germanic tribes were in a vulnerable minority among the Celts, as were the Pilgrim Fathers among the American Indians. Yet they had held on to their own language and taken a very modest number of words from the hoard of British-Celtic words of the natives.

Much the same happened in New England 1,100 years later. In America they found new plants, new animals, new geographical features for which they needed new words. Some – comparatively few – came from local tongues. Others in the main came from inventive combinations of English words.

The settlers came largely from flatlands and so the new, often mountainous landscape called out for new words. They invented 'foothill', 'notch', 'gap', 'bluff', 'divide', 'watershed', 'clearing' and 'underbrush'. When they had to bring in native words they did, but they anglicised them to 'raccoon', 'skunk', 'opossum' and 'terrapin', always simplifying them. For native foods they took in 'squash' for the variety of pumpkins. Sometimes there would be more straightforward borrowings, like 'squaw' or 'wigwam', 'totem', 'papoose', 'moccasin' and 'tomahawk'.

Some of the settlers were not immune to the beauty of the native language. William Penn the eminent Quaker wrote: 'I know not a language spoken in Europe that hath words of more sweetness and greatness in Accent and Emphasis than this.' Many place names came from Indian words and numerous rivers including the Susquehanna, the Potomac and the Miramichi. But all of these were minor additions.

The English and, soon following, the Scots and Irish stuck to the language in the book and were reluctant to stray very far away from it. They would coin English words for natural things rather than take them from the Indian – 'mud hen', 'rattlesnake', 'bull-frog', 'potato-bug', 'groundhog', 'reed bed'. Even when describing Native American life, they preferred their own words as in 'warpath', 'paleface', 'medicine man', 'peace pipe', 'big chief'. Their attitude to language reinforced their religious conviction. They had the Words of God through His prophets and His Son: what more could they possibly need save a few phrases which speeded up commonplace understanding?

English had taken on thousands of words from several other languages since about AD 500. It had been promiscuous. But in its beginnings in America it was very prudent. Perhaps Squanto spoiled them. Perhaps the Indian languages were just too difficult. 'Squash' for instance was 'asquat-asquash', 'raccoon', like many other animals, had several names. In this case they included 'rahaugcum' 'raugroughcum', 'arocoune' and 'aroughcum'.

This was a group of people obsessed by the power of the word. Improper speech, blasphemy, slander, cursing, lying, railing, reviling, scolding, threatening and swearing were crimes. Curse God and you were in the stocks. Deny the Scriptures and you would be whipped and possibly hanged. These colonists set out to honour the language and it started in the schoolrooms. This began with the *New England Primer*, which sold over 3 million copies in the seventeenth and eighteenth centuries. Every English-speaking family in America must have worked their way through this clear and well-constructed teaching aid. It was stocked from the Bible.

A. In Adam's Fall we all sinned
B. Heaven to find, the Bible mind
C. Christ crucify'd for sinners died
D. The Deluge drowned the earth around
E. Elijah hid by ravens fed
F. The judgement made Felix afraid
G. As runs the grass our life doth pass
H. My book and Heart must never part
J. Job feels the rod, yet blesses God

Some commentators would call this propaganda. Some have said its effect on the minds of the young could be called 'child abuse'. It set out to promote literacy and you were being made literate in order to study the Bible. But the law of unexpected consequences was to take that literacy far away from study of the King James Version.

The King James Version became an Anglo-American literary story and, more widely, an English-speaking story – Australia, Canada, South Africa, New Zealand, parts of India and Africa. There would be developments which took America further away from the English of the Pilgrim Fathers and other early settlers. There would be great seams of new words from other European and then Eastern immigrants who poured into the United States.

American English, extended and embellished by all these new Americanised tongues, would go on and soon deliver its own greatness in books and speeches and songs. But the genesis of the country's language lay in the King James Version. The vital early achievement of letting no other language speak for this New World was down to the early Puritan settlers. And it could be credited, through the centuries, with making that enormous, patchwork, multiracial continent into a single and often a cohesive force.

John Adams, who would become the second President of the United States, prophesied in a letter in 1780: 'English is destined to be in the next and succeeding centuries more generally the language of the world than Latin was in the last or French in the present age. The reason for this is obvious, because of the increasing population in America, and their universal connection with all nations, will, aided by the influence of England in the world, whether great or small, force their language into general use.'

While the early colonists were digging English into New England, back in the mother country the King James Version became a crucial factor in civil war and revolution.

CHAPTER SEVEN
THE BIBLE IN THE
CIVIL WARS (1642-51)

The King James Bible crept hesitantly into the light. The expensive and bulky Bishops' Bible was chained to the lecterns in the churches. The cheap and argumentative Geneva Bible remained a general favourite. It needed laws to unchain the one and prohibitions to stamp out the other, and that took some time. About a generation. By the mid-1630s, the new version was being read to most congregations and it was in the hands of hungry readers; hundreds of thousands bought it, more listened to it.

The Bible was out of its Latin straitjacket. It could be interpreted by anyone who read it. This state of affairs disturbed the establishment profoundly. What had been theirs was now everybody's and that, they thought, could only cause trouble and they were right. Once released, it was open to comment and challenge and the 'interpretations' were multitudinous. Most of all, many often self-educated reform men and women found that in the Bible there was no direct authority for infant baptism, fasting, marrying with a ring, nor most of the paraphernalia and hierarchical practices in the Churches. This began what became a dangerous course of questioning.

Next they discovered that the Bible could be used to say the unsayable, to change the law, even to kill a king. From being the weapon of the rulers, the Bible in a few years became the weapon of those who for centuries had been ruled over and overruled.

Its public arrival coincided with the bloody, revolutionary Civil Wars in the middle of the seventeenth century. The words of the biblical prophets, the acts of the Old Testament kings and occasionally one or two phrases of Jesus Christ played an essential role in these wars. The King James Version was instrumental in the execution of King James's son. His Bible was out in the world now, with an energy of its own and it was sucked into the conflict.

Christopher Hill, in his magnificent study *The English Bible and the Seventeenth-Century Revolution*, reminds us of the landscape of the thinking of that time. More than a thousand years of Christian presence in the islands of Britain had instructed most of the people in its ways and caught them in its spells. But the people were silenced. Now it changed: the King James Bible became the book through which the people could speak and act.

Since 1517, the shot of the Reformation had set fire to the Christian world and in the mid-seventeenth century its fury flamed higher than ever before. There was in Europe a virulent war, Catholics against Protestants, which was to last for thirty years. The Antichrist (the Pope) had to be slaughtered. The godless Protesters had to be slaughtered. God was claimed by both sides. Paranoia and hatred on both sides were pitched to what we might now call hysterical fanaticism. Religion was all in all. It blotted up all their thought systems and blotted out what did not fit.

It is difficult for many of us now to imagine how binding the Christian faith was in that Civil War conflict. It was in your daily bread, your daily work, it guided your laws, your actions, your words. As if you had been dipped in hot wax and emerged for ever as a candle whose purpose was to be alight for God, the Trinity, Jesus Christ, the Church and hope of eternal life. You could privately, secretly, disagree; you could be disobedient or argumentative or indolent. But in the mid-seventeenth century, in the drama into which the King James Bible was enrolled as a major force, it trapped you as surely as the earth was recently proved to be trapped around the sun.

The Bible was not a programme. It was not any single lesson. It was a well of adaptable wisdom and a pit of fertile contradictions. In the tormented argument which provoked and helped shape the course of action in Britain between 1625 and 1649 it spoke in conflicting tongues and all of them sought and found authority in the words of God or His prophets. It made the war respectable: it justified slaughter: it aided liberation. It was both a source of truth and a serpents' nest.

Henry VIII had appointed himself head of the Church as well as of the state and put religion and politics together in the same box and there they stayed. James I believed that he ruled by Divine Right and was finally answerable only to God. There were grumbles but the strength of English law, Parliament and behind them both Magna Carta, was felt as an effective brake should it be needed. Also James's shrewd intelligence, overlaid though it was with his unceasing over-excitement and over-indulgence in the lush and louche excesses of those rich and promiscuous Englishmen who swarmed about him, just about saw him through.

His son, Charles I, who came to the throne in 1625, was not so intelligent, a hardliner on Divine Right, wholly convinced that he was outside and above the law and did not need Parliament. His promiscuity was not with sensuality but with Catholicism and that was not to be tolerated. His wife was Roman Catholic. He wanted their son to make a good Catholic marriage. He refused to support the Protestant cause in the Thirty Years War.

It is proof of how deeply divinity was thought to hedge a king and how tightly the traditional obligations held, that for seventeen years Charles I seemed to get away with playing the tyrant. But during that time the voraciously read and often radically interpreted Bible undermined his position. By the end of the 1630s the King was under attack from a revolutionary force. The Bible was its battering ram. Having been for centuries the book of authority, it became, now that it was available in English, the book of rebellion. It pervaded the nation.

That greatest of English lawyers, Sir Edward Coke, sought help for his judgements in the Bible and, Christopher Hill tells us, writers on farming and gardening looked into the Bible. People wallpapered their homes with texts and taverns pasted the Word of God on their bar walls. It was still a time when plagues, famine and disasters in nature were widely thought to be the acts of an angry God. Explanations and solutions for these were sought for and found in the Bible. Magistrates, heads of literate families, teachers were now steeped in the words of the Bible. On her first procession through London in 1558, Queen Elizabeth is said to have 'pressed the bible to her bosom'. When Charles II landed at Dover in 1660, he asserted that he valued the Bible above all else. In the 1640s, battles were fought in Britain that stained the land with blood and challenged deeply rooted order and the Bible in English was in the thick of it.

As the seventeenth century advanced, there was the sense of a gathering storm. Driving it were two forces which were to prove implacable. On the one side, the King's Party, gathered around the Bible of James from which the word 'tyrant' and the king-baiting, status-quo-testing comments in the Geneva Bible had been omitted. On the other were the Presbyterians, rooted in Calvin's idea of the Elect. They had been spurned at Hampton Court but they were too fierce in their faith and too well organised to be dismissed. James I and his son Charles I saw themselves as divinely appointed. The Presbyterians saw themselves as the Chosen People, like the Israelites with whom they identified. It was God versus God.

There was also the Catholic faction, who claimed an ancient monopoly on God. And finally the growing number of moderate Anglicans, frustrated and largely powerless. Presbyterian fervour was to lead to a call for rule by 'Saints', chosen from among themselves. The King's men were well schooled in the Bible and so were the Presbyterians. It was a battle of the book. Within a year or two after the death of James I, a surge of anti-monarchism, which had already expressed itself in the self-exile of the Pilgrim Fathers, began to rise to a tide which was to become a tempest. It began in public sermons quite new in their daring, their number and their learning and ended in a court of law exceptional in that it tried and condemned to death a divinely appointed king.

The arguments were expressed in code and the code was in the Bible. It was taken for granted that the Bible was known thoroughly, often by heart, by a substantial and ever growing percentage of the population. Henry VIII in his last speech to Parliament in 1546 had, with tears in his eyes, railed that the Bible was 'disputed, rhymed, sung and jangled in every alehouse and tavern'. A hundred years later it was disputed and jangled even more widely and more jealously and dangerously. The fortressed kingdom of the Scriptures had been breached and there was no repairing it. The accession of Charles I with his Catholic wife and his Catholic intentions unleashed the Protestant Bible's power.

In the King James Bible you could find defences of the King and his court: 'the powers that be are ordained by God' was written in Romans. You could find justification for the massacre of heathens and idolaters. Idolatry was the 'sin' of the Catholics most hated by the Presbyterians. You could read 'thou shalt not suffer a witch to live'. Bad kings, like Nebuchadnezzar or Jehoichim and Saul, who deserved no obedience, studded the Old Testament. Good kings were few but they were available. Josiah was a rare model of a good and authorised king. There were comments on society: 'often they which are despised of men are favoured by God' (Genesis), and there were the Beatitudes.

It was not new that the Bible played a part in the state. The King James Version had been written with a careful eye on curbing what he saw as rebellious tendencies. But it was the liberating fury of it thirty years on in the middle of the seventeenth century that was new and remarkable both in itself and in its far-reaching consequences.

Charles I, a year after his accession to the throne, married Henrietta Maria, daughter of the King of the second great Catholic power, France. Henrietta Maria was firm in her Catholic faith and determined to haul England back alongside the Roman Catholic mother ship. She was against England's participation in the exhausting 'European' struggle between Catholics and Protestants, which became the Thirty Years War. This provoked an eminent Presbyterian to deliver a sermon quoting from Esther: 'if thou holdest thy tongue at this time, comfort and deliverance shall appear to the Jews out of another place, but thine and thy father's house shall perish.' By 'Jews', in the code of the day, he meant the Presbyterians.

And so the gloves came off. Now that Guy Fawkes Day has dwindled to a social gathering, we forget that in 1605 a Roman Catholic group of what we would call terrorists had attempted to blow up the Houses of Parliament. This, if proof were needed, demonstrated beyond any doubt that the Catholics had not and would not give up their designs on England and needed to be watched, fought and, if necessary, exterminated. It was therefore of no little significance that Thomas Hooker chose Guy Fawkes Day in 1626 to preach a sermon in Essex before a 'vast congregation' in which he called on God to 'set on the heart of the King'. This line comes from the eleventh and twelfth verses of Malachi, which he did not quote but took for granted that this vast congregation would know. They read: 'an abomination is committed . . . Judah . . . hath married the daughter of a strange god. The Lord will cut off the man that doeth this.' The daughter was Henrietta Maria. That man was Charles. That last sentence is an early example of the sentences which would now be laid on the King until his final sentence. The Bible had spoken.

This fed into the growing undercurrent that 'God was leaving England'.

The ill-advised and heedless King decided he could rule without Parliament. Through his archbishop, Laud, he brought back undisguisedly Catholic practices, in particular the reintroduction of graven images: to the Presbyterians this was inflammatory idolatry. This was not what their God wanted. Charles must have known this. The King was unafraid. He attacked through the Scriptures. In a speech he wrote for his trial but was denied the chance to deliver by the court, he declared: 'the authority of obedience unto kings is clearly warranted and strictly commended in both the Old and the New Testaments. There it is said "where the word of the King is there is power and who may say unto him 'what dost thou?' " '

A salient promontory from which attacks on the King were launched was the sermon: most dramatically the Fast Sermons. Fasting became a favoured way of demonstrating religious commitment and sermons associated with these spasms of abstinence appear to have been particularly effective. They were often used to prepare the way for political action. Not only against the King, but also against his ministers. And invariably it would be instances lifted from the Old Testament which would point the finger.

Often these sermons would be calls to encourage the Presbyterian faithful. In 1640, Cornelius Burgess preached a Fast Sermon on a text from Jeremiah: 'let us join ourselves unto the Lord in an everlasting covenant that shall not be forgotten.' He substantiated his sermon with quotations referring to Moses, Asa, and the deliverance from the Babylonians.

'Babylon' was, to these sermons, the state of Charles I's Britain: wicked, damned, endangered, losing God. Why, he asked in that sermon, has God 'not yet given us so full a deliverance from Babylon'?

On the same day in 1640, Stephen Marshall also preached a Fast Sermon, taking lines from Chronicles: 'The Lord is with you while you be with him . . . but if you forsake him, he will forsake you.' Again the argument was in place that it was the true God who should be followed and not the King and his God of the Antichrist. The Bible often said put not your trust in princes but always said put your trust in God. Again, the refrain 'but God may leave England . . . if he goes, all goes'.

The messages grew plainer. Before the outbreak of the Civil Wars, Stephen Marshall, in 1641, preached to the House of Commons on a text from Judges: the inhabitants of Meroz (England) would be cursed by God if they 'came not to the help of the Lord . . . against the mighty'. Horrible violence was not a bar. Not when 'Babylon' was the enemy. Marshall quoted from Psalm 137: 'happy shall he be that taketh and dasheth thy little ones against the stones'. The 'little ones' were the children of Babylon. The Civil Wars were imminent and Marshall uttered a rallying cry from, unusually, the New Testament, and a sentence attributed to Jesus in Matthew's Gospel: 'He that is not with me is against me.'

The pace quickened. In June 1642, William Sedgewick in his Fast Sermon quoted from the Book of Revelation that 'Satan shall be bound and cast into the bottomless pit; and with him this Antichrist malignity.' No one could be in any doubt as to who and what he meant.

The King's treatment of Parliament was resented as unconstitutional. Economic forces worked through to reinforce the deepening sense of divisiveness between the luxuriant party of the King and the growing cohesion of the tax-paying party against him. The organisation of the New Model Army – based on the well-named 'Ironsides' – was a key factor.

The New Model Army won the war and the distinction between Cavaliers and Roundheads has been in our language ever since. It is possible to see the Parliamentary army as the outward and visible force of the revolution. It was a religious as much as a political and military force. Many of its soldiers went into battle with a pocket Bible in their breast pocket and myths tell us that this stopped many a bullet. It was an army that marched on its religion. An army of God. In its ranks were men who had been educated through sermons and interpretations of the Bible and their knowledge was said to challenge that of university men. God's Word was their battle code.

The preachers began to predict victory against the King's forces, although yet again they worked carefully through the Bible. The walls of Jericho fell 'in God's appointed time'. Christ once again came into the argument: 'It is not for you to know the times and seasons.' Job was called up: 'All the days of my appointed time will I wait till my change come.' Which it did at the Battles of Marston Moor and then Naseby in 1645 where the King's army was smashed and slaughtered. Charles I surrendered a year later and there began three years of debate over what should be done with him.

The Bible would continue to be crucial in all this. The King used it to claim he was above the law, indeed on earth he *was* the law. The Parliamentarians, emboldened by victory, their arguments given such a telling voice in the wars, quoted law from the Bible and by law the King was judged. This was a departure from the traditional English method of changing unpopular monarchs – assassination. As such it had a lasting influence on the placing of law in the constitution in Britain and abroad.

The sermonisers were not squeamish. Edward Staunton invoked Isaiah: 'pity to me may be cruelty to thousands,' and he added: 'Could I lift up my voice as a trumpet, had I the shrill cry of an angel . . . my note should be, execution of judgement, execution of judgement, execution of judgement.' In April 1645, Thomas Case quoted from God's instructions to Joshua in Deuteronomy: 'thou shalt smite them and utterly destroy them; thou shalt make no covenant with them, nor show mercy unto them.' Nicholas Lockyer quoted God's instructions to Ezekiel: 'slay utterly old and young.' In the following year, Christ was quoted, from Luke: 'those mine enemies, which would not that I should reign over them, bring hither and slay them before me.'

The country was ripped apart, and the Bible encouraged and even incited that bloody rupture. It was done in the pursuit of a better kingdom to follow, which in some ways it did.

There was rejoicing by the victors as they turned to the trial of Charles 'The Man of Blood'. This phrase was frequently used of Charles in the months leading up to the trial. The Book of Numbers was cited: 'Blood, it defileth the land, and the land cannot be cleansed of the blood that is shed therein, but by the blood of him that shed it,' and Ezekiel: 'if thou be but a man that executes judgement and seeks truth, I will pardon you, saith God, I will turn away my wrath.' The impetus of the war fuelled the Presbyterians' utter conviction of their righteousness and gave to the Presbyterian-Parliamentary forces, *just* (it was a close-run thing), the majority in court to declare the King guilty. This trial empowered the Bible to re-shape the constitution.

His execution in 1649 was thought to open up a time when the new Saints would rule the land, when there would be no more kings and when open debate through the Scriptures would peacefully settle all contentious matters. None of that happened.

After the execution of the King, the army followed Cromwell as he smashed centres of resistance, especially castles, the length and breadth of the country. As well as soldiers, the army nourished statesmen and scholars. Only the ebbing of its authority in the failure and muddle that followed the death of the 'Protector', Cromwell, ended the underpinning of the 'children of the Covenant and the Saints' who for a few years claimed that they inherited the earth.

The gravitational pull of the opposition party was Presbyterianism and its matter was concentrated in the Bible. And that outlasted Oliver Cromwell, the Commonwealth of the 1650s, most dramatically in America.

The Bible, and increasingly the King James Version, had shown its power. It had been used with deadly effect. It was to go on to assume many shapes, one of which was to become the language of the politics and the lawmaking of the day. Though it was in all the churches, in another sense it had left the Church. It was no longer chained to the lectern, it was out in the streets. It was a torch.

What has been quoted from the sermons and homilies is just a sliver of what was said and printed at the time. Not only were these messages hammered home in public oratory, they were alehouse talk, campfire talk, domestic conversation. Although the meat of it was scriptural, the disputatious and judgemental nature of it provided opportunities for wider and bolder discussion which succeeding generations were to build on. Those who learned to read through the Bible – about a million copies were sold in this period – would move on to other literature, wide reading, a shifted horizon of thought.

But the Bible drove the debates and provided the words for thought and the telling images. 'Every valley shall be exalted and every mountain and hill shall be made low' – Isaiah. The idea of levelling and raising bit deeply into the arguments. Certain places carried great meaning: Babylon above all which evoked all wickedness and temptation. Egypt a close second, from whose bondage the Chosen had to make their escape. These two place names, like the notion of the levelling of mountains or the image of the wilderness, occur again and again in the literature of militant Presbyterianism. 'We are all wilderness brats by nature,' wrote John Collinges in 1646.

And the wilderness was contrasted with the garden. 'God Almighty first planted a garden,' wrote Bacon. 'It is the greatest refreshment of the spirits of man.' And the notion of a garden recurs, fenced off from the wilderness, cultivated, protected by God, and on into reams of metaphor. 'True religion and undefiled is to let everyone quietly have earth to manure, that they may live in freedom by their labours,' wrote Gerrard Winstanley, one of the leading thinkers and activists, on what we might call 'the left'. Winstanley, like others, also used the word 'hedge'; in his case he saw hedges as enclosures, against the common good, oppressive to the peasantry, like the Norman yoke. And 'yoke' itself was sought out to be a key word.

These words, like certain names – Moses, Cain, Abel, Abraham, Isaac – drove into the vocabulary of the faith debate and some remain there today. Most have seen their resonance abate in the UK through the secularising of our history, but elsewhere still they carry the meanings drawn from the Bible. America and

Nigeria are prime examples. But they were branded into this nation's discussion with itself which began in earnest in the seventeenth century.

A version of the Bible that had only crept into the public light and stumbled its way to popularity and needed laws to help it gain acceptance, emerged out of the Civil Wars as the dictionary and encyclopaedia of a nation arguing with itself. Its words had aided and abetted massive slaughter. It had nurtured ideas of equality and justice for all. The fact that it was now widely accepted in English made it the nation's book. It assumed a place as the mouth of England's many tongues. It expressed its passion for coherence. It spoke of the country's ancient and cruel divisions, its hopes for a better future, an earthly heaven.

Those Civil Wars and that act of regicide astonished the world. A divinely appointed king had been executed and it had been done through law and the words of the Bible had not only condoned it but urged it on. There was no knowing what might happen next.

CHAPTER EIGHT
THE NEW MAP

Hell had been unleashed on the battlefield and in the pulpit. Carnage had been sanctified by the vengeful God who through Moses had urged on his first Chosen People, the Israelites, to murder all the women and children of the Midianites but to spare the virgins for the troops. Brother set against brother and father against son were not unfamiliar in the Old Testament. In that book of history, poetry, hope and death, life was harsh, God was cruel, punishment was crushing, mercy was rare; loving kindness was saved for and by the New Testament.

Inside the constitutional tension which a king stretched to breaking point was an educated parliamentary class who claimed their rights from the early Middle Ages and, in trace memory and law, from pre-Norman Anglo-Saxon England. They could and would defend them. Inside an economic and cultured insurrection against the traditionally privileged by the aspiring gentry class, there had grown a religious whirlpool whose force had sucked everything into its violent spiral. For most of the seventeenth century, the temper of the times was deep-dyed in religion. It ate up everything it encountered. And the gravitational force of it was focused on the King James Bible.

Intense, often frenzied, interpretations of its words and the actions of its varied cast of biblical characters real, legendary and mythical licensed new liberties and new excuses. Men called themselves 'Saints'. Communism was advocated and practised, as was free love, the preaching by women and the virtue of nakedness. Innocents were murdered, property was razed, all institutions were interrogated.

The Bible was the oracle; the Scriptures were the law. But whose? Who owned the Bible? The British Isles were racked with the effort of attempting to measure every seventeenth-century action against ancient and often corrupted texts written more than 2,000 years before their time. Texts which could be scoured for calming wisdom and moral truths but also texts crammed with extremes of behaviour became increasingly attractive the more bitter the battle became between the King and his enemies. The Bible lit the fire and roared on to feed the flames.

It was a time when religion, through the Scriptures translated in the King James Version, drove kings to believe that 'Kings are called Gods by God Himself because they sit upon God's earthly throne.' James I wrote that sentence. Charles I died for it. It was a time when some Puritans believed that the spirit that spoke within them made them Saints to be counted alongside the Apostles, predestined to rule on earth. It was a time when intellectual rigour went toe to toe with intellectual fanaticism and for many years moderation was the loser. And the soul was on the battlefield more vividly for some than the sword.

After the execution of the King ended the Civil Wars save for a series of vengeful reprisals, the ascent of Oliver Cromwell replaced one make of tyrant with another. But the fight had gone out of the majority. The exiled son of the executed King, a man who claimed no Divine Right, a dandy, a compliant and bankrupt monarch seeking a safe berth, returned to England and landed at Dover.

There he was given a copy of the King James Version, to which instantly he declared allegiance. In London, King Charles II was greeted by cheering multitudes. It appeared that the waters had closed over a riven nation.

By 1660 you could say that the Bible had fought itself to a standstill. Inside that Civil War tangle of arguments and the agitated currents and cross-currents of motivation the plot lay in the Bible. But which version was it to be?

The Geneva Bible was considered subversive by James I and by Charles I and his favoured ministers. Its lower cost and its radical notes made it popular, among the Presbyterians, the Parliamentary Party and the Parliamentary Army. In 1644, however, the Royalists managed to cut off the importation of Geneva Bibles and in that year the final edition of the Geneva Bible was published. It withered away.

Archbishop Laud's argument for this repressive action was that the continual mass buying of imported Geneva Bibles would kill the English printing industry. The crown's lucrative stake in Robert Barker's printing monopoly of the Bible was not mentioned. The Geneva Bible was to be banned and it was banned and the sales of the King James Version, already strong, grew rapidly and would soon monopolise the territory. It would go through several revisions but hold fast to the 1611 version until the misguided decision was taken to recast it in 'modern' English.

Yet the Presbyterians and the Puritans, fed by the conviction that they were the Elect, the Chosen People, would not let go easily. Their Bible emanated from Geneva where Calvin, the source of their rule and discipline, had exercised his form of religious despotism. So versions of the King James Bible began to appear with the Geneva Bible's radical notes. There were at least nine editions produced between 1642 and 1715, most smuggled in from the Netherlands as Tyndale's New Testament had been many years earlier. But it had been convincingly superseded. Yet Geneva went down fighting.

Archbishop Laud was executed in 1645 and the Puritans went into battle to dislodge the King James Version. As A. McGrath describes in *In The Beginning*, they persuaded the Parliamentary Grand Committee to set up a subcommittee. Their attack on the King James Version was cunningly aimed at the veracity of the translations. To secure their preferred version they knew that, even in the middle of a battle, they needed to present a scholarly case.

But surprisingly their cause did not prosper. There was the difficulty, even the impossibility, in proving that the language and translation in the King James Bible was inferior. There was also the difficult fact that John Field, printer, was handed the monopoly on the King James Version in 1656 by the Presbyterian hero, Oliver Cromwell. Field was a ferocious monopolist. This move was to give the King James Version not only Cromwell's authority but a licence which would be best fattened by the crushing of the opposition from Geneva.

By the time Charles II came to the throne in 1660, the rule of the Saints and the Puritans in the Parliamentary cause was exhausted. The Established Church had found some teeth again. The Geneva Bible was effectively outlawed and with sad rapidity rendered ineffective. The Geneva Bible had had its moment and lost it. The Protestants in New England had thought that Cromwell and the Saints would see them marching hand in hand with Old England. That potentially epoch-changing alliance was thwarted for ever. The Atlantic was no longer a connection but a chasm.

And the King James Bible had come through. It would move away from being primarily the source for arguments and pamphleteering to become the buttress of the constitution. It would be thoroughly revised and tenderly corrected up until 1769, when the Oxford Edition became the standard which we still use (or some do) today. This managed the masterful feat of keeping the greatness of the original sound and sense while clearing away extraneous clutter. Out of that Civil War and the rule of Cromwell, the King James Version emerged victorious and, astonishingly, unimpaired. It had achieved and would retain dominance in the English-speaking Protestant world for centuries.

The spirit of enquiry was let loose by the Bible more than by any other book of the age. That spirit of enquiry would turn against the Bible itself. It was grounded in the new arguments which arose out of this civilisation-changing development. It was a new dawn in English-speaking life; this ability for Everyman openly to discuss what to them at that time were the most profound of all matters: the Holy Scriptures. They were at home and secure in their own language. Henry VIII was right to fear the consequences and so were Thomas More and Charles I and many a thousand bishops, aristocrats and autocrats. The walls were down, the Word was out, opinion and interpretation were not solely for priests; each person could now be a judge.

What a difference it made to 'ordinary' people, to be able, as they did, to dispute with Oxford-educated priests and, it is reported, often better them! What an illumination it must have given to minds blanketed for centuries, deliberately excluded from the knowledge said to govern their lives and promise their eternal salvation, minds deliberately stunted! There was, we read, 'a hunger' for the English Bible, for the words of Christ and Moses, of Paul and David, of the Apostles and the prophets. God had come down to earth in English and they were now earthed in Him. It was the discovery of a new world.

It was a treasure chest of sayings, of instances, of teachings. It could be closely read by scholars. It could be memorised and used in daily discourse. Above all, above anything, it could not only be argued about, this Book of Books, it could and did embolden argument *against* itself. The habit of argument was democratised with a speed and spontaneity which indicated how frustratingly imprisoned that capacity had been. The majority had been below the salt of debate for millennia. It was a luxury above and beyond them. It was a mystery they were not allowed to penetrate.

They were literally screened off in the great cathedrals. They had to sit mute for hundreds of years and worship in the Latin they did not understand and believe and act on the diktat of interpreters, priests, bishops, whose agenda was based on the subservience of the congregation. Now they were free. Thanks to martyrs, courageous believers and brave scholars, their minds were liberated in an act even greater than the Pentecostal miracle when the Apostles were said to have been given the gift of many tongues. The English speakers were given the gift of this charismatic, self-contradictory, resonant, historical work. It was drenched in blood. It was enriched by a sacred constellation. The trickle they had only been allowed to sip from became the spring from which they could drink as long and as deeply as they wanted.

There were many forces which began the long haul to democracy in the English-speaking world. But one, perhaps the vital one, was the gift which widespread Bible reading and individual interpretation gave to a literate group of the independent-minded. They knew that if they could challenge what was in the Bible, then they could challenge what was in the constitution. Therefore they could challenge the world they had inherited and make it the world they wanted.

This new power, this build-up of the muscles and sinews of individual questioning, took time partly because they had scarcely been exercised before and certainly not on this scale. Before this tectonic shift, who was to dispute their place in society when God had ordained that place? Who dared speak out when the ruling monarch and aristocracies and the princes of churchly power and wealth were on constant guard to make sure that tongues were stopped? When things remaining as they were consolidated the rich and the powerful?

But the greatest weapon of all had been the ability to preserve ignorance among the mass of people. Illiteracy was authority's best ally. Again and again over the centuries which succeeded the publication of the King James Bible, those in authority would retreat only inch by inch and their argument would be that these uneducated, these peasantry and populace were obedient only as long as they did not know the secrets of the trade of rule. These people did not understand how the mighty forces of the state worked. They did not understand the arts of civilisation and their crude and vulgar intervention would surely wreck the destined and stable order of things.

It was a recurring theme: keep out the majority by characterising them as ignorant and disruptive. Educate them and they would become dangerous. They were to be kept down and, whenever necessary, suppressed. Build an insurmountable wall and call it God's ordering. Democracy eventually clawed its way up and over that high wall as a result of the determination of thousands of individual men and women, who in many instances drew inspiration from the New Testament.

Thanks to the Bible in English, the people, after millennia of repression, could speak for themselves. They had lifted up their eyes. They had found help. And even those who were to abandon the Bible owe their liberation to a book commonly available, in alehouses, in taverns and in homes and in English.

*   *   *

The political routing in Britain of the Presbyterians and other nonconformist groups like the Quakers, who had fought to the last to preserve New Model Army rule, was complete. As Dissenters they sought and found other ways to influence the realm with the most positive results. But within months of King Charles II's coronation, all that bloody biblical warfare seemed to belong to a different world.

By imploding, the Presbyterians judged themselves to have been cast into the wilderness by the Lord and punished for failing to create His Kingdom on earth. They condemned themselves to a pacific regrouping which might take many years. And by accepting the King so warmly, the people expressed above all relief that a familiar order had returned and the Presbyterians were both rejected and snubbed: and disenfranchised.

But though it looked the same, the monarchy was not the same. In the 1680s, James II would attempt to emulate the high-handedness of his father, Charles I. After a brief bloody skirmish he was shunted out of the country never to return. His daughter Mary and her Dutch husband William assumed the throne after a Bill of Rights in what became known as the 'Glorious Revolution'. This confirmed the strength of Parliament's position in the constitution and was regarded as the model of the way in which a nation could bring about fundamental change without much bloodshed. The Bible had declared that the killing of a king could be acceptable: and a king had indeed been executed. His son was exiled. The message was clear. In that regard, the Bible's work was done.

Like a high flow of water which, baulked in one direction, will find another, the King James Version, though it was never to leave the battlefield, moved on. For example, 'All serious English political theory dates from this period,' writes Christopher Hill. 'Hobbes and Harrington, Levellers, Milton and Winstanley . . .

the concept of progressive revelation allowed the possibility of new insights, new interpretations.'

It is remarkable how quickly a country which had fought to the death inspired by the Bible so abruptly and decisively switched its mood. Common sense emerged from the debris. In 1662, John Gardner, a bishop, said: 'Nothing is by Scripture imposed upon us to be believed which is flatly contradictory to right reason and the suffrage of our senses.' A dozen years earlier, if he had dared say that in public, he would have been imprisoned and probably hanged. Now he walked the streets freely to give his views. This liberty raced throughout the culture although censorship was not entirely lifted. Yet the Bible could be mocked by Thomas Hobbes and his ears would not be cropped, his life not threatened.

Yet the Bible could still stir up the law. The nonconformists who preached on the sentence in Hebrews: 'You have not yet resisted unto blood, striving against sin' and Judges: 'the Children of Israel did evil in the sight of the Lord, and forgot the Lord their God and served Baalim and Asheroth' were clapped into jail. References linking Charles II to Nimrod and Nebuchadnezzar and Nero were still made in Bibles printed abroad and circulated underground. But they were now illegal. The fervent, righteous torrent had been quite suddenly reduced to a dribble. Among the intelligentsia believers openly agreed that the Bible could not be infallible given its internal contradictions and, as time moved on, the historical problems it began to pose.

The place of the Authorised Version was now assured and for the next 250–300 years, in the United Kingdom, its congregation was split into two broad groups.

First there were the nonconformists, the Congregationalists and later the Methodists, the heirs and successors of the

Presbyterians of the Civil Wars. This group took the Bible into science, into political thought, into social action, education and areas of the slum cities which would arise and be underserved by the Established Church. It also provided zealous missionaries. Second there were the Anglicans, the Church of England, the state Church, the Established Church, class-bound, state-tethered, still streaked with Roman Catholic practices but at an unbridgeable distance from Rome and popish authority.

This Church of England was to carry on for practically three centuries with its own hierarchy which still aped a system reaching back to the early Middle Ages. Well-bred or wealthy young men would still go to Oxford or Cambridge to be trained for leadership in the Church. They would be parachuted into vast vicarages and plump livings where they would get on with a country life – hunting, shooting, fishing – or pursue a private hobby. They would generally delegate the harassment of pastoral care to their indigent lower-class curates. Lower-class curates would largely be funnelled into the most crowded, newest, least attractive and poorest parishes.

Nevertheless, its adhesion to the King James Bible meant that the Anglican Church was to wield influence, even to stand for the good, despite its social immobility, its political timeserving and its smug hierarchy. It always attracted some men of outstanding talent and enterprise. It joined in the imperial adventure with some positive as well as some negative results. The chief point here is that it was a *force* for better and for worse.

When the second phase of empire began, it was the King James Version which was marched out with British armies across the world. It was read aloud on all official occasions. Military vicars accompanied the troops. In the mission field it was the King James Version which spread the Word. And when primary schools began to grow in number they were Church of England schools. It was the King James Bible which provided the faith, supplemented the curriculum and became the basis of the moral law in the classrooms of the kingdoms. For many observers, this was enriching and ennobling. Many saw it as their unique property, their sovereign book, a book that defined them.

It was not unopposed. The arguments that God was cruel and punitive and corrupted faith by these promises of eternal life found favour among some of the British intelligentsia. But the majority, in these early centuries, including the wealthy and some of the clever, paid lip service to the Church and did not want it rocked. It suited the times. For many years it suited the country's image of itself. It did not impose.

The memory of what had happened when it had been inflammatory took a long time to fade. It bedded in comfortably with a well-organised life of privilege, and a social, familial network. It was a convenient vehicle for snobbery and show. It could seem usefully cohesive. And for some it was a true passion. The Bible's attraction for those in authority still included keeping the potentially militant in their place. That had been weakened but had not died out. The Church of England became a part of the anaesthetisation of England, which many found very comfortable. Its deeper, more hopeful and glorious promises were always there for a minority to fall back on.

As we shall see, the nonconformist strand would take up arms in other struggles. But for about three centuries the authority, the social ordering and the balm of the King James Version of the Church were rarely threatened, not even by steady desertion. Not even by mockery. It was too big and too secure to care.

But the energy drained away from it. Intellectual enquiry moved its tenets elsewhere outside the Anglican walls. It was Dissent that drove progressive thought. There was a new map in the United Kingdom.

But while the kingdoms of Britain were setting out for quiet and regressive times after exhausting and murderous Civil Wars, America was heading for the first Great Awakening, where the King James Version would be the key determinant in the moulding of the character of a new nation.

CHAPTER NINE
THE GREAT AWAKENING

B ible stories had circulated before the publication of the King
James Version. As well as the medieval stained-glass windows,
resplendently illuminating the Bible, the medieval mystery plays
acted out scenes from the Old and the New Testaments. The spec-
tators would know something of the stories of Moses and Noah
and Jonah, of David and Goliath, of Solomon and perhaps of
Salome and Jezebel, of Christ on the Cross, the Virgin Mary,
Ananias, the Three Kings . . . the most pertinent and graphic
stories had studded the minds of largely illiterate Christians for
centuries. The mystery plays were not allowed to be performed
inside the cathedrals or the abbeys. The 'real' Bible had been effectively denied to the many: these few stories were regarded as
somewhere between education and entertainment and they were
tolerated only in so far as they were harmless.

But with the wider development of printing, the rapid increase
in literacy in the English-speaking world and the translations
from the Latin into English, there was a new dynamic – the King
James Bible. In its way, the 'discovery' of America, the newfound
land, matched the uncovering of these sacred Scriptures, the
newfound landscape for the mind. Their laws and proverbs, their
parables' examples and the prophecies became for a long time the

lifeblood of the awakening modern world. The King James Version both in itself and what it led to and inspired was a transfusion which revitalised the consciousness of the post-medieval world.

It was a form of Pentecost for the masses. The Apostles were endowed with the gift of tongues to be able to spread the Word to all people. The King James Version gave tongue to English-speaking people who had been made dumb by deliberate and rigorously monitored silences. The new book broke the silence. And what a remarkable book it proved to be! Even more remarkably, it gave energy to its opponents and even to its enemies.

After the Civil Wars in Britain, the next major move in the voyage of the Bible was the Great Awakening in America.

The notion that life would go on after death is as old as recorded civilisation and the evidence for that belief is regularly unearthed in the most ancient burial grounds the world over. Neanderthal grave goods have recently been unearthed. Some think that the belief in another life is no more than wishful thinking or a mere superstition. To others it expresses something true though currently 'unprovable' save by the Resurrection, itself often doubted. Others believe in it completely. In the seventeenth- and eighteenth-century English-speaking worlds (as in those of many other nations and peoples) there were many people who believed in it completely. The question was – how did you arrive at such a belief? How were we to explain eternal life? The Christian version was layered, tantalising and elaborate, and for millions over the centuries, convincing. It carries what many feel to be an essential probability.

The Christian agenda, for most of the time since the death of Christ, was set by the Roman Catholic Church. It had built its authority on the promise that only through belief in and obedience to the Roman Catholic laws, its bishops and priests and through its churches could eternal life be attained. It claimed direct succession from St Peter the Apostle, the rock on whom Christ built His Church.

Calvinists, at the other end of the Church spectrum, believed that you were chosen and if you were, there was to be eternal life. Some thought you were chosen even before you were born. But there was to be eternal life. The Celtic monks in seventh-century Britain had won over the royal courts and the pagan populace by this promise of eternal life. Indigenous populations of countries conquered by Westerners were expected to have the bitter pill of oppression sweetened by the religion which promised life after death. It was described as the glorious and unique gift.

The faith that went to America from England at the beginning of the seventeenth century was exceptional in its high level of literacy, its emotional intensity, its tenacity and its intellectual certainty. The Chosen, the few Calvinistic settlers, had an influence way out of proportion to their numbers. They lived through faith. To have faith in itself was to be fulfilled. To have the promise of eternal life was to be saved for eternity, a goal so far beyond all others that to live for it and to lay down your life for it was welcomed: and a duty.

In simple terms, eternal life has often been seen as a blessed if illusory hope of release from a life that is nasty, brutish and short. So bad can earthly life be that a life after death becomes not only a hope but a sole purpose. The earthly duty for Christians is to live with a moral rectitude and spiritual devotion which will earn you an eternal reward. This was the message that had to be burned into the minds of the people: the message that would save their immortal souls besides which all else was insignificant. 'True believers' welcomed death in the intoxicated heightening of faith in what they saw as a just cause. Or it was the glad moment, the tranquil glory moment, when your earthly race was run and you were called to meet your Maker and join the heavenly host.

These two factors, the moral faith to see you through this life and the spiritual faith to take you into eternal life were kindling to the fire brought by the preachers who lit the flames of the Great Awakening. This was stoked through the words and messages of the King James Version, which was to go on its most significant and far-reaching voyage, from Britain to America.

As more settlers came to America, not only from England but gradually and increasingly from Scotland, Ireland and Wales, there was a change in the development of the Protestant Christianisation of America.

Fewer of the new settlers wanted to take on the rigours of being one of the Chosen, with its heavy duties of prayer and daily observances which confined them to a scheduled God-centred life.

There was also the issue of the Native Americans. Many died from imported diseases which led to an easy excuse for neglect. This 'proved' they were of inferior stock and therefore God saw it right to let them perish to make room for the Chosen People. There were a few settlers who set out to convert and as they saw it 'help' the Indians by translating the Bible into a dialect of the Algonquin tribe, for instance, or organising Indian 'Prayer Towns' in which the Indians were encouraged to follow a Christian path. But it was all but lost in what soon became a norm of destruction and deceit as the Europeans drove west, robbed the Indians of their lands and trampled down their population and their culture.

Then there were the slaves in the South. Diarmaid MacCulloch points out that 'It was ironic that in the 1640s and 1650s as the English on both sides of the Atlantic were talking in unprecedented ways about their own freedom and right to choose, especially in religion, slaves were being shipped to the English

Colonies in hundreds then thousands. In the early years Protestants did not challenge this any more than Catholics.'

There was often a double standard. The philosopher of liberty, John Locke, in his *Two Treatises of Government*, wrote that to Englishmen 'slavery is so vile and miserable an Estate of man . . . that 'tis hardly to be believed that an Englishman, much less a gentleman, should plead for it.' Yet they did. Including one English gentleman, John Locke himself. When he helped draft the constitution for the new English colony in South Carolina, in that constitution slaves were accepted. At the end of the seventeenth century blacks outnumbered whites in South Carolina. They were essential labour. They were cheap. They could pose a great threat. So were they really God's people? 'Blacks,' as MacCulloch writes ironically, 'were different.' It was very useful for the whites to believe that.

But that began to change, first stirred by white clergymen preaching the King James Version, and then seized on and driven by the slaves themselves. This came about partly because the African-Americans used the language and the stories of that key to the white American mind – the King James Version. They took the words of their enemy and used them to fight and ultimately to overcome him.

It is a strange twist of history that while the descendants of the millions of the Native Americans of the seventeenth century are now a small, dispossessed, disempowered minority, the descendants of millions of Afro-Americans who came as slaves have argued for, fought for and gained parity and grown in number. They have achieved success across the spectrum from Nobel Prizes to the presidency of the United States itself. That 300-year struggle, still ongoing, could be said to have one of its tap roots in the Great Awakening which itself owed a great deal to Methodist preachers, young, idealistic, religious men who, in a running thread in the story, once again came from Oxford.

*　　*　　*

After decades of intense close inspection of the Scriptures and disputation sentence by sentence, sometimes around a single word, it is not surprising that the pendulum swung. There came a moment to throw off the shackles of scholarship and go to the heart of the matter. This, in the first third of the eighteenth century, was what the English evangelicals did. According to Diarmaid MacCulloch they 'sought to create a religion of the heart and of direct personal relationship with Jesus Christ, in consciousness of his suffering on the Cross and his atonement to his Father for human sin'. He observes that 'once more, it was the message of Augustine, filtered through Luther.'

This movement found its natural home among the Dissenters – part of the Presbyterian grouping – who played such a persistent role in missions and conversions. Dissenters were not only outstandingly active in the religious sphere but across society. It was a society whose establishment barred them from most of its ruling heights including parliament, but they were to play a seminal part in education, science, philosophy and philanthropy.

They formed the bedding for the English evangelicals who were spearheaded by Methodism. Methodism began inside the Anglican Church and its founders never wanted to abandon the Anglican Church. But by degrees, due not a little to the sloth and smugness of the Anglican Church, Methodism separated from it and joined the congregation of Dissenters who took the Bible to the people and through the Bible found a vital role.

Initially, the Anglican rejection of Methodism was a cause of sorrow to its leader John Wesley, an Anglican clergyman like his father before him.

Again, as so often in the first centuries of the story of the English-speaking Bible, we have a man who went to Oxford to be ordained as a minister in the inner temple of the establishment and came out of it to rattle the cage of that establishment and change it. Oxford in Wesley's time, in the eighteenth century, was a fastness of reactionary views. Its graduates were expected to be gentlemen and buttress the status quo and perpetuate it. They were admitted to the colleges to be the docile persuaders for the existing authorities. Some of them would become the authorities. Yet it could be and had been the perfect stalking horse for radical ideas. They had taken root there since the fourteenth century.

John Wesley formed an Oxford group which went back to Apostolic practices, feeding and helping the poor, practising regular and passionate devotion – meaning it, in short, unlike most of the other young men who came to the university. Wesley's 'Holy Club' was mocked and given the derisive nickname of 'Methodists'. Like many a clever and derided minority, they took on that nickname as a badge of honour and Methodists they became. Some, however, acknowledging the preaching success and enthusiasm of John Wesley and his brother Charles, who wrote almost 9,000 hymns, called themselves 'Wesleyans'.

Wesley stumped up and down the country like a politician at election time. He mounted the hustings. He spoke with a passion which dismayed both the entrenched conservatives and the new daintily mannered Anglicans. He called out for converts. And they responded. This vulgar method was frowned on by the powers that be. The Wesleys brought rousing music into the churches, they sought and got warm and positive reactions from their congregations who did not follow the Church of England practice of deference, timidity and tepidity. Their hymns exalted the Lord and the congregations alike. The Wesleys lit up feelings which their fellow Anglican priests preferred to be doused down.

Justification by faith, the message of St Paul, taken up by Luther, became a mantra for John Wesley. This was still radical. The waters had closed over the seventeenth-century religious wars and the Church of England, like the Church of Rome before it, much preferred the people to express their faith within its own established customs and practices. Wesley's 'enthusiasm' was disturbing and alien – although a century or so previously it would have seemed commonplace.

On his travels in Britain, Wesley saw that he could reach people in the new industrial cities, then largely unpatrolled by the parish church network of the Anglican Church. That was based in the more pleasant, less crowded rural areas and it wanted to stay put. The cities were dirty, ugly and poor. But there the hungry and hopeless were waiting to be fed and Wesley had the Bible with which to nourish them.

At Oxford, George Whitefield, a fellow Anglican, had joined this Holy Club and he too travelled to preach the Word. He had begun to preach, Christ-like, in the open air, in fields and meadows, partly to accommodate the crowds, partly to counter the efforts of local churches to ban his unsettling enthusiasm. Wesley followed his younger colleague and they struck a golden seam of passionate support from the neglected congregations. Weeping, applauding, casting themselves to earth in ecstasy, these were new industrialised congregations responding to a message which had authority rooted in the King James Bible.

John Wesley organised other itinerant preachers. Charles Wesley's hymns, as Diarmaid MacCulloch points out, 'featured much reference to divine wounds and blood', which the mass industrial workforce knew too well. The Wesleyan message was that life could be changed utterly, even for the poorest, by accepting that Christ had suffered for 'me'. To embrace Wesley's interpretation of the New Testament, for which he asserted clear and strong evidence, was to find the hope that little or nothing else in their lives offered.

The rousing hymns – frequently mentioned and applauded by the poor at the time – electrified these open-air meetings and

Methodism took off in massed singing. Wesley built centres in London and Bristol; local societies gathered funds to put up their own chapels. The sound of the King James Bible rang out across the cities. In the course of this, Wesley, envied and feared by fellow Anglicans, even though he fought to remain an Anglican and called his Church 'a connexion', was levered out and branded as part of the Dissenting Fraternity. His 'enthusiasm' did for him. He was not one of them. He was exiled to what they saw as the margins, much to his sadness and their loss.

Wesley went to America. He only went to America once, but he played a vital role. As the American War of Independence drew nearer, many Anglican clergy left for England and safety. But by 1784, Wesley was so impatient at the Anglican bishops' sloth in encouraging clergy to go and work in the new republic, so he took it on himself to ordain priests. That sensible, legal, useful move was yet another black mark as far as the Anglicans were concerned.

Wesley's teaching and what became 'his' Church sank deep roots in Britain, mostly in England in the growing industrial towns. It became a new tribe in the land and its preachers exercised influence often beyond the reach of Anglicans. It was the Methodists who took the Bible into areas of life ignored by Anglicans – the lower ranks of the army and navy are another example. From their evangelical example were to come many converts all over the world. 'I look upon all the world,' said Wesley, 'as my parish.' As it was. The King James Bible had once again regenerated itself.

Now the time had come for its other great triumph, the Awakening of America. One Englishman, an Oxford contemporary of and heir to John Wesley, George Whitefield, from the age of twenty-two 'as famous as any man in the English-speaking world', played a remarkable role.

* * *

By the end of the seventeenth century the Puritan grip on America appeared to the zealots to be slackening and they were alarmed. They saw the corruption of their discipline after three or four generations of dedication. There was a fear that this New England was slithering towards the state of Babylon which had been their reason for quitting the old England. Jonathan Edwards, a Puritan preacher from Massachusetts and a celebrated theologian, spearheaded what would become a corps of preachers dedicated to reclaiming the people of America. As with Wesley, he went back to what he saw as the core of the matter and preached that all of them would be accepted by God's grace. Grace was the key. Grace was the message.

Meanwhile, in Oxford, George Whitefield was beginning on a similar journey which would take him to America seven times, for periods from as little as six months to as long as four years.

Like so many of these God-driven, Bible-loving, passionate Christian evangelists, he was an odd one. He had clawed his way to Oxford University. To pay his way once he got there, he was a servant to the better-off students. He found the comfort of friendship and spiritual excitement in John Wesley's Holy Club, of which he became an ardent member. He went in for severe self-discipline in his daily readings from the Bible, and through many acts of charity and devotion. He was addicted to self-purification through fasting. At one time it was so prolonged and excessive that it took him seven weeks to recover. His views on what he saw as a gin-soddened, gambling-obsessed, immoral, ungodly, putrefyingly over-privileged, avaricious, unforgivably unjust England echoed the views that Jonathan Edwards held about New England. He was ordained at the age of twenty-two and within months his preaching drew thunderclaps of praise. He 'awakened souls'.

After a successful first visit to America where he preached every day and was hailed as 'the greatest evangelist' he returned to

London to find himself barred from many churches. They feared his 'enthusiasm' which they saw as the gateway to extremism as they did with Wesley. Whitefield took to the fields to bring the blinding light to the people.

He was fearless. For example, he went to Kingswood, an isolated mining area in which bestial conditions had conditioned a fearsome, tribal community who dealt savagely with strangers. There was no church. On the first day he had a congregation of 200 to whom he preached for three hours on the theme that Jesus loved each and every one of them and had been crucified for each and every one of them. Two weeks later, after more sermons, 10,000 attended one of his meetings, a figure that rose to 30,000 a few weeks after that.

By the time he arrived in America for his second visit, in 1739, he was already described as someone who had preached to more people than any man in history. Whitefield, for whom the adjective 'charismatic' seemed to have been coined, and America's Great Awakening to rediscover the faith, were made for each other.

He was always dressed in the correct attire of an Anglican clergyman, a long black gown with a small white cravat, the priestly bands around his neck, and a powdered wig. His voice was exceptionally loud, clear, mellifluous and seductive. We are told that he had a bad squint.

Whitefield knew about corruption and the decay of an immoral, unbalanced society from his time in Oxford and London. He had also seen for himself the unspeakable distress and poverty of industrial England. He seemed to know what the people wanted and he had the King James Version to sate that want. They wanted hope, salvation, a lifting of the burden of life: and some joy, some song, some acclamation with a place for the public ecstasy of the ignored and the powerless: some pride: and a place in the Kingdom of Heaven.

His dramatic renderings of Gospel truths gave them that. He travelled the length of the eastern seaboard of America. He averaged ten sermons a week — some of them hours long. Over thirty-four years he delivered approximately 18,000 sermons.

He preached 'the key test of election to the Kingdom of God is whether you have an emotional experience of conversion.' Gone were the thumbscrew and detailed demands of the hard-line Calvinists and their enforcements. Gone their straitjackets of rules. Gone their displeasure in life. Gone the all but impossible difficulty of making it to heaven. That was gone just as surely as the English-language Bible had thrown off for so many Christians any need for priests and bishops to do their reading for them. You were now free to read the direct Word of the Lord and of Jesus Christ who died on the Cross to take away your sins. And you would now be accepted by the Lord and Jesus Christ if deep inside yourself you simply *felt*, if you experienced conversion, the awakening, the moving spirit.

Whitefield would raise his head and his hands to the skies and speak directly to God and His words came back. 'Become Christian in deed and truth and you will be saved.' Whitefield nowadays is not difficult to mock and reduce to derision or disparagement. But then, among those thousands of mostly desperate people there was a longing for goodness and truth and an acute hunger for a better, different life. His preaching reached their hearts and touched their imaginations. Somehow the music and the Gospel in Whitefield's voice carried messages which struck directly into their experience and enriched them. Who are we to mock that?

The King James Bible from Tyndale on had always aimed to be a preacher's Bible, best when read aloud. Whitefield, it appears, gave it full volume. Benjamin Franklin measured the carrying power of that voice and concluded that in an open space, 30,000 people could clearly hear him. Myths arose that his voice could carry over three miles.

Benjamin Franklin was a rather unlikely supporter of Whitefield. He was a Fellow of the Royal Society in London where he lived as America's Ambassador until the outbreak of the War of Independence which despite his best efforts he failed to prevent. His experiments with electricity had brought him international recognition and acclaim. He was an active rational intellectual and a man of public affairs who was thought to be an ornament to the age in which he lived. His own Christian religion was at best weakly expressed. And yet he took up George Whitefield with a passion.

Among his many activities, Franklin edited a weekly news-paper, the *Pennsylvania Gazette*. He devoted 50 per cent of these issues to Whitefield's activities and especially the public sermons. Franklin was just as captured as thousands of others by the power of this strange man's sermons, by the way he brought the words of the Bible and the story of Christ into the heartlands of the eastern seaboard and re-fortified a fledgling nation. He loved the numerous ways in which Whitefield declared and illustrated from the Bible his conviction that 'All men are equal' and that 'liberty of conscience was the inalienable right of every natural creature'. Huge sermon halls were built simply to accommodate the congregations who travelled great distances to listen to George Whitefield and be converted or born again.

The American evangelists, like their leader Jonathan Edwards, praised him and tried to copy his style and power and failed. He was their standard-bearer. Sarah Edwards, the wife of Jonathan, wrote: 'it is wonderful to see how he casts a spell over the audience by preaching the simplest truths of the bible.' All denominations came to listen – Catholics, Quakers, Presbyterians, Lutherans . . . And he could claim to have been largely responsible for the widespread reinvigoration of the idea that America was a nation chosen by God for a special purpose. The earliest Puritan settlers had come to New England to create 'a city on a hill'. The Great Awakening, driven by George Whitefield and powered by the Bible, led them to that exhilarating summit and profoundly marks the United States still today. It seems fitting that Whitefield died on the east coast of America.

One crucially important consequence of this whirlwind of religious teaching, those vast, singing, praying, crying congregations, was the beginnings of the inclusion of the slaves.

Whitefield was one of the first white preachers to speak to 'the blacks'. The Methodists firmly regarded slavery as sinful and their evangelical determination entered the forbidden territory of slavery. Up to this point the attempts to Christianise the slaves had been few and feeble. Now the preaching of these new evangelicals gave to the slaves not only a dignity they had never enjoyed but the opportunity to use their intelligence on the words and sayings in the Bible.

There was a long way to go. The Great Awakening began as a call to the established white settlers to mend their ways and go back to the roots of their faith, and it succeeded. It called on the more uncertain, more recent white settlers to go along with this and join the flow along the seaboard which would unite them into a chosen state of grace, and that too called in the masses. Soon it was to hit America's deepest nerve.

PART TWO

THE IMPACT ON CULTURE

CHAPTER TEN
THE ROYAL SOCIETY (1660):
EARLY MODERN SCIENCE AND THE BIBLE

The division between religion and science is such a given in most of today's intellectual arguments that it takes a deep breath and an act of imagination to return to a time when they were mutually reaffirming. A useful date is 1660. When Charles II landed at Dover he made a very public show of embracing the Bible authorised by his grandfather James I. Not long afterwards he gave a royal patent to a small group of gentlemanly scholars. This became the Royal Society which still thrives. The poverty-stricken King hoped it would generate great wealth. It did. But in knowledge, not in gold.

Charles gave the society the right to publish its learned papers without censorship, a rare and invaluable gift in that period and one which rapidly gave it fame in both Europe and America. It virtually invented professional scientific publishing. English became a leading language of science. And the Royal Society systematised experiments. Its declared intention was 'for the Promoting of physico-mathematico experimental learning'; its motto 'Nullius in verba' – 'take no man's word for it'. Experimenting was believing. Its experiments aimed to reveal the works of God.

I'll use the words 'science' and 'scientists' here although those engaged in the experiments at the time would have been called 'natural philosophers'.

Some of the greatest experimental scientists were there at the outset. Christopher Wren, Robert Boyle, Robert Hooke, soon to be joined by Isaac Newton, and later Benjamin Franklin, Michael Faraday, Charles Darwin, Paul Dirac, James Clerk Maxwell, Stephen Hawking and, over 350 years, 8,000 more.

What distinguished the pioneers in the seventeenth century was that they were united in a determination to study nature and a conviction that a radical reading of the King James Bible went hand in hand with that aim. Their guiding star was Francis Bacon who had died several decades before the society was formed. He coined the phrase 'knowledge is power'; he called scientists 'merchants of light'. Most of all, however, he asserted that life could be fully understood through two books: the Scriptures and the Book of Nature. Between these two the Fellows of the Royal Society set out to compose a new world.

Both these books had to be questioned. Nature had to be put to the test; 'interrogated' was another word used by the lawyer in Francis Bacon. And the King James Bible, also, had to be put to the test. It bears emphasising that the Bible in English had revitalised the way people saw the world and their own place in it. The Civil Wars had seared it into the minds of men and women throughout the land. The intensity of thought and the extremes of opinion which the Bible both provoked and enabled had probably made more people in the country more actively and consciously religious than at any time in history.

The Protestant notion that you could have personal and direct contact through the Bible, that you, without any intermediary, could make up your own mind on these sacred matters, became an open invitation. Fellows of the Royal Society and like-minded men and women took it to be an invitation to scrutinise the

Bible for evidence that would underpin their science: and vice versa.

Despite what some now see as an unbridgeable rift between the two, in 1660 and for many years on (for some, up until the present day) the King James Bible authorised the work of a substantial number of the finest and most influential early modern scientists. The scientists made increasing use of instruments – the telescope, the microscope and so on – to investigate nature and, equally, in the Royal Society employed a new way of examining the Bible.

This 'modern' period in Western history saw the movement over centuries from one dominating system of thought – Christianity – to what emerged as its successor – science. It was neither a rapid nor an abrupt transition. Medieval scholars like Thomas Aquinas, who attempted to integrate the classical thought of Aristotle and the Christian thought of Augustine, still had a powerful impact on the way in which thought was cast. Oxford University was the seedbed of the Royal Society, as it had been the centre for centuries of the struggle to translate the Bible into English and see it accepted by the crown and Parliament.

Oxford also deserves credit for an intellectual vigour which began in the Middle Ages. In the thirteenth century it had been famous in the Latin-speaking Christian world for its philosophers – Duns Scotus and William of Occam, for instance. The theology they worked on is now largely ignored or discredited. Yet we cannot deny that they were thinkers of the highest order. They worked on the material they had and their processes of thought were strong. This was not an inheritance to be lightly thrown over. Nor was it, as Wycliffe and Tyndale, and then Wren, Boyle and Hooke proved.

There was also in the medieval Church the recorded tradition of intense and what were thought of as mystical experiences of faith. Thinking the unthinkable in a way which might be considered a herald of science. This medieval theology was at that time a bedrock factor in a way that the secular elements in our society today can scarcely imagine or take seriously. But then they did.

Aquinas, for example, the volume and the quantity of whose work is a monument to theological scholarship, experienced a vision towards the end of his life which, he said, brought him closer to an understanding of God than all his scholarship had done. He would not discuss it but the impact it had on him was respected and in some measure understood by those – the majority at that time – who saw faith as innate and as valid a way to understand the world as reason later became. That later medieval world was rooted not only in the Bible but in much classical and preclassical thought that had become entwined in the making and the interpretation of the Bible.

All the key players in the advancement of early modern science – Copernicus, Kepler, Descartes, Galileo, Newton – understood what was at stake in the revolution they were engineering. This was the *place* of the soul. Where did it exist? The nurturing and the salvation of the soul was the fundamental duty and joy of Christians. Newton's proof that all space obeyed the same laws abolished the essential separation and different space for God and the soul.

This separate space had been argued for by Aristotle. The soul, a non-material part of being human, had a long prehistory before Aristotle and a fervent history in Christianity where Augustine and Aquinas were only two of those who constructed systems of thought designed to prove its existence and its essentiality. Now where were these arguments? If there was no special, separate *place* in the universe for God and the soul, where and in what way could they be said to exist? And therefore what to do about God and the soul in the quest for new knowledge?

The Royal Society's way for many years until, in some cases, this day was to hold the faith and through the King James

Version find historical and other proofs. Robert Boyle, one of the original group, a man whose work led him to be called 'the father of chemistry', published an enormous book on the intimate relationship between his admiration for the works of God and the advantages experimental philosophy would bring to religious faith.

Joseph Priestley, another Fellow of the Royal Society in the late eighteenth century and the man credited with the discovery of oxygen, saw a direct link between the right religion (in his case Dissenting Protestantism) and the right kind of natural knowledge. He used his chemical and electrical experiments to promote his Dissenting views about the character of divinity. In the nineteenth century, Michael Faraday saw no gap between his world-changing experiments and his severe nonconformist Sandemanian religious faith. In the twentieth century, Arthur Eddington, another Fellow, was clear about the basic unity of his own spirituality as a Quaker and the principles of modern physics. He argued that mystical religious experience and modern physical science were entirely consistent. Newton saw God as the direct cause of gravity and as for God's place, he argued that space itself was 'as it were, God's sensorium'.

There were others, and among the most distinguished and radically innovative of the Fellows was the botanist John Ray, who wrote *The Wisdom of God Manifested in the Works of the Creation*. James Clerk Maxwell (1831–79), such a seminal influence on Einstein, underwent an evangelical conversion as a student in Cambridge. His biographer wrote that 'he referred to it long afterwards as having given him a new perception of the Love of God – one of his strongest convictions thenceforward was that "Love abideth, though knowledge vanish away".' Even Darwin was sure that his account of speciation with natural selection as one of its engines was not logically connected with atheism.

Lord Kelvin (1824–1907), an important contributor to thermo-dynamics, gave a famous affirmative address to the Christian Evidence Society. Sir Robert Boyd (1922–2004), pioneer in British space science, founded the Research Scientists' Christian Fellowship. Of those still living, Charles Hard Townes won the Nobel Prize in Physics and wrote *The Convergence of Science and Religion*. John Polkinghorne, a prize-winning British particle physicist, is an Anglican priest and author of *Science and the Trinity*. Simon Schaffer, the Cambridge Professor of the Philosophy of Science, believes that there is an aspect of natural theology that characterised the emergent function of the Royal Society. He talks of early modern providentialism.

In 1649, a king had been executed, but only after a trial and that trial had been seamed with references to what was accepted as the ultimate authority, the Bible. If you could execute a king who claimed to rule by Divine Right, what could you not do? But the Bible had been the key to that and it was believed that it would also unlock the new knowledge. There seemed so much in common. The need for science to discover a First Cause, for exam-ple, seems to have been transferred directly from religion into science. Newton's search for an order, a single unifying force in the universe, came from his faith in Genesis. Gravity was God's other face.

In his book *The Bible, Protestantism and the Rise of Natural Science* Peter Harrison has written convincingly on this theme. He writes of the collapse of previous interpretations of the Bible at about this time. 'The Protestant reformers . . . in their search for an unambiguous religious authority insisted that the book of scrip-ture be interpreted only in its literal, historical sense.' He argues that 'the new way in which the bible was read by Protestants played a central role in the emergence of natural science in the 17th century.' And he points out that the majority of those who formed the Royal Society were hard-reading Bible men; Protestantism had a direct influence on the emergence of modern science.

This is a new way of reading the Bible – for its history, and for verification of the science of the day. Moses, for instance, Harrison writes, became 'the father of history', an author and natural philosopher, a historical figure who had written 'a factual account of the first ages of the earth'. He goes on to say, 'the contents of the Book of Genesis attracted new descriptions: "the history of creation"; "scripture history"; "surpasses all the accounts of Philosophers as much in Wisdom as it doth in authority".' Moses was seen as an author and his intentions were taken to be at the very least on a par with those of the Fellows of the Royal Society.

Within this 'history' was to be found all sorts of knowledge including knowledge of the sciences which would reinforce what the seventeenth-century scientists were doing and put them in the tradition of true faith as well as providing a tradition out of which their new science could validly grow.

The Garden of Eden, which in medieval interpretations had been full of allegorical and psychological meanings, was now seen as a particular place on the planet, though there were complaints that not enough information had been provided as to where exactly it was. Seventeenth-century authors tried to remedy that with numerous suggestions as to the precise location. The Bible was being tested in a similar way to that in which the scientists were testing the weight of air or the content of various seeds.

Similarly with Noah's Flood. Out went the charming elaborations of the Middle Ages. The new literalism and the confidence which Bible readers now had led directly to scientific probing. Where was the Flood? Other questions followed. 'Where did the waters come from?' writes Peter Harrison. 'And where did they eventually go? What mutations of the earth took place as a result

of the Deluge? How, wondered the moderns, could the great catalogue of creatures whose lives were to be preserved for the
impending inundation be physically housed in a vessel of the
specified dimensions? . . . How was the craft constructed, how
navigated, by what means did Noah assemble his cargo, where
were the provisions stored, how were fox and fowl kept apart?'
And if they could not quarry the evidence out of the Bible, the
assumption would be that the original author had not wanted to
confuse his largely ignorant readership with too much detail. The
new, modern readers were very ready to supply this out of their
own scholarship. Or it was argued that the gaps were due to faulty
transmission, patchy texts, omissions which again could be
repaired by the moderns.

Some of the scientists, especially among the Presbyterians, were
already well practised in finding their own present in the Bible's
past. The villainous kings of the Old Testament, Ahab, Saul,
Nimrod, Nebuchadnezzar, had been vigorously likened to Charles
I and, in the case of some of the Puritan extremists, with every
other king who had ever sat on a throne.

Yet the balance was kept. The demands on the Bible were not
so fierce as to kill the scientific or natural philosophical goose that
laid the golden egg. Its primary purpose was to teach the most
important matter in this earthly life – the way to attain salvation
and enjoy eternal life. It reinforced and intellectually spurred on
scientific enquiry, but the divergences were already apparent to
those who wanted to winkle them out.

Harrison writes: 'Isaac Newton also believed that the new
discoveries in the sciences were in fact re-discoveries of ancient
truths, traces of which could be found in a variety of texts, including Scripture. The priest-scientists of antiquity, he believed, had
known of atomic theory, the existence of the vacuum, universal
gravitation and the inverse square law.' One task the new

scientists had was, through their experiments on the Book of Nature, to reinforce the respectability of that other book, the Scriptures, passages of which had been lost or adulterated. Newton's belief that the fate of the solar system, following his theory, would bring it to destruction and then restoration was exactly what had been predicted in the Bible. Q.E.D.

The new studies in chemistry which ran alongside a deep interest in alchemy (Newton spent as much time on alchemy as on mathematics) gave some scientists the notion that they would find the way in which God had created the world out of chaos by pursuing their experiments which included efforts to renew life from ashes. Transmutations were everywhere, wrote Lady Ann Conway in 1692: 'Barley and wheat are convertible one into the other; worms change into flies, and the earth brings formed creatures without sex.' Resurrection would be just another transmutation.

The theories of these scientists were criticised and often mocked, especially by scientists in Europe who did not understand or sympathise with this religious strain in Anglo-Saxon science. And since then many of the claims about Moses and Noah and others have been discredited or laughed off the page. Yet there was what Harrison calls 'a phase during which the literal truth of scripture and the theoretical truths of the new science were believed to coincide exactly'. Initially the intellectual energy, social acceptability and moral authority that science gained through such a close association with the King James Bible were undoubtedly of benefit to the scientists.

Robert Hooke, Newton's contemporary, a genius at microscopy, wrote that the more objects were magnified 'the more we discover the imperfections of our senses, and the Omnipotency and Infinite perfections of the great Creator'. John Edwards declared that 'an Insect is an Argument of the Divine Wisdom as well as an animal of the first magnitude.' God was to be found first in nature or nature's Bible. The written Scriptures were then to be examined to provide corroboration.

Christianity assumed that the world was intelligible. So and perhaps, therefore, did modern science. There had to be a first cause because Newton knew it was there: It was God. In the formative years of the seventeenth century it could be said that the King James Bible joined religion and science together in a marriage which has just about held despite massive bombardment.

CHAPTER ELEVEN
LANGUAGE

While Shakespeare contributed more to the word-hoard, the Bible contributed more to the idioms, the catchphrases, expressions now native to English speaking, phrases that have been used and reworked ever since.

In terms of the long-term effect, I think that the Bible has it. Shakespeare has been read and heard by millions: the Bible by hundreds of millions. Shakespeare – who was Bible-bottomed – has infiltrated the imagination of generations, but only relatively recently that of the masses of the people. The King James Bible worked its many effects for centuries, was read in churches and assemblies and in schools and on solemn and formal occasions all over Britain, America, Australia, Canada, New Zealand, South Africa and scores of other countries. Moreover, for much of that time and for many people now, it was not only and not principally a book of fine words but the book of the great faith. Indeed, for millions along the way, it was the Word of God through His prophets and of Christ through His Apostles: language was seen as the subordinate clause of its impact.

By the time of Tyndale the English language was reaping a golden harvest. There was the rock of Anglo-Saxon – still the fundament – the subject-verb-object organisation often of monosyllables that again and again carry rich meaning in brief expression. 'Let there be light', or from Shakespeare, 'To be or not to be' – arguably the two best known quotations from the Bible and Shakespeare. There are thousands of others. Then there was the input of the Norse which freckled the language with tough words and hammered off the encrustations of Germanic grammar. Norman-French brought a bounty of new words and also words which ran alongside the old – 'archer and bowman' for instance, which give the language synonyms, slyness and subtlety, qualities embellished when the more fashionable French of Paris was adopted by the court in London.

Under that was the inheritance of the Latin of the Roman Catholic Church, shards of Greek and, from British seamen, the plunder from foreign languages, fifty of which appear in Shakespeare.

Having survived for about 300 years the stultifying and oppressive domination of the Normans, English re-emerged, enriched and enlarged. It reappeared, regrouped, ready for action, bursting, it seemed, to make its name in the world.

In the early fifteenth century, the hero warrior king Henry V broke with the past and sent home his letters from the battlefields of France not as was customary in the language of the court (French) but in English. Chaucer had emerged, an instant success, as the new voice and father of English literature. Grammar schools began to teach English and halfway through the fourteenth century, the first of the York Mystery Plays was produced – in English – and had a heartening reception.

And the English dialects, the riot and confusion of English spellings were set on the road to coherence by two engines. The first was the Signet Office located in the still existing Great Hall of Parliament. Henry V decreed it should use English. But what English? The variety was profligate: there were dozens of words

¶ The Gospell off
¶ Sancte Jhon.
¶ The fyrst Chapter.

IN the begynnynge was that worde/ãd that worde was with god: and god was thatt worde. The same was in the begynnynge wyth god. All thyngf were made by it/ and with out it/ was made noo thige/ that made was. In it was lyfe/ And lyfe was the light of mē/ And the light shyneth i darcknes/ãd darcknes cōprehēded it not.

¶ There was a mã sent from god/ whose name was Jhon. The same cã as a witnes/ to beare witnes of the light/ that all men through hi myght beleve. He was nott that light: but to beare witnes of the light. That was a true light/ which lighteneth all men that come ito the worlde. He was in the worlde/ãd the worlde by hi was made: and the worlde knewe hym not.

¶ He cã ito his awne/ãd his receaved hi not. vns to as meny as receaved hi/ gave he power to be the sōnes of god: i that they beleved õ his name: which were borne not of bloude nor of the will of the flesshe/ nor yet of the will of men: but of god.

¶ And that worde was made flesshe/ and dwelt amonge vs/ and we sawe the glory off yt/ as the glory off the only begotten sonne off the father.

The opening of St John's Gospel in William Tyndale's New Testament, the first Bible to be printed in English in 1525. Tyndale is the key-stone of the King James Version of the Bible which was published in 1611, seventy-five years after Tyndale was burned at the stake.

Charles I, who came to the throne in 1625, believed in the Divine Right of Kings. He was wholly convinced he was outside and above the law and did not need Parliament.

Trial of Charles I. This trial was conducted through intensive references to the King James Bible on both sides. It became empowered as the book of rebellion.

It was Methodists such as John Wesley who took the Bible into the new British industrial cities. From their evangelical example were to come zealots and converts all over the world.

George Whitfield preaching in America. He addressed literally hundreds of thousands of people and played a big part in changing America's view of the force of its religion for individuals.

The frontispiece to Thomas Spratt's *History of the Royal Society*, 1667. The majority of its Fellows were hard-reading Bible men; Protestantism had a direct influence on the emergence of modern science.

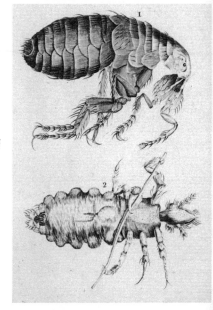

A flea and louse from Robert Hooke's *Micrographia* 1665. Robert Hooke wrote that the more objects were magnified 'the more we discover the imperfections of our senses, and the omnipotency and infinite perfections of the great Creator'.

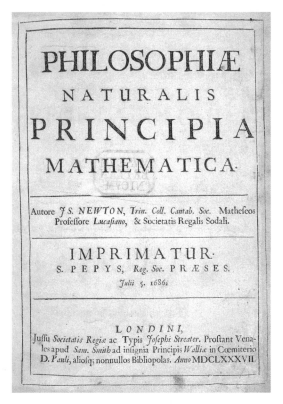

Title page from Isaac Newton's *Principia Mathematica*, 1687. Newton saw God as the direct cause of gravity and as for God's place, he argued that space itself was 'as it were, God's sensorium'.

Michael Faraday, photographed c.1861, saw no gap between his world-changing experiments and his severe non-conformist religious faith.

Joseph Priestley, who is credited with the discovery of oxygen, saw a direct link between the right religion and the right kind of natural knowledge.

The astrophysicist Arthur Eddington was clear about the basic unity of his own spirituality as a Quaker and the principles of modern physics.

William Shakespeare's works include about 1,350 quotes from the Bible.

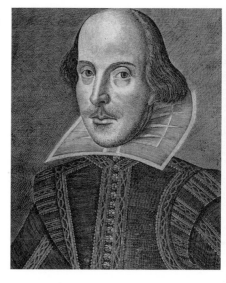

PARADISE
LOST.

BOOK I.

OF Mans Firſt Diſobedience, and the Fruit
Of that Forbidden Tree, whoſe mortal taſt
Brought Death into the World, and all our woe,
With loſs of *Eden*, till one greater Man
Reſtore us, and regain the bliſsful Seat,
Sing Heav'nly Muſe, that on the ſecret top
Of *Oreb*, or of *Sinai*, didſt inſpire
That Shepherd, who firſt taught the choſen Seed,
In the Beginning how the Heav'ns and Earth
Roſe out of *Chaos* : Or if *Sion* Hill
Delight thee more, and *Siloa's* Brook that flow'd
Faſt by the Oracle of God ; I thence
Invoke thy aid to my adventrous Song,
That with no middle flight intends to ſoar

A   Above

The opening lines from Milton's epic poem *Paradise Lost* 1668. His work showed how inspirational the Bible could be.

John Bunyan's *The Pilgrim's Progress* first published in 1679, has since outsold every other book except the Bible.

THE
Pilgrim's Progreſs
FROM
THIS WORLD,
TO
That which is to come
Delivered under the Similitude of a
DREAM
Wherein is Diſcovered,
The Manner of his ſetting out,
His Dangerous JOURNEY,
AND
Safe Arrival at the Deſired Countrey.

By JOHN BUNYAN.

The Third Edition, with Additions.

I have uſed Similitudes, *Hoſea*, 12. 10.

Licenſed and Entred according to Order.

LONDON,
Printed for *Nath. Ponder*, at the *Peacock*
in the *Poultrey* near *Cornhil*, 1679.

Harriet Beecher-Stowe's *Uncle Tom's Cabin* is rooted in the faith nurtured by the Bible and packed with quotations from it.

Walt Whitman saw the 1860 edition of his 'Leaves of Grass' as 'the great construction of the New Bible'.

T.S. Eliot reached back to the King James Version in many of his great poems.

Toni Morrison, the novelist, has brought the world of the deep spiritual adventure of the Afro-Americans into fiction.

An evicted sharecropper reading
the Bible, Missouri, 1939.
The Bible was often the only
book in the house.

A British mother reads Bible
stories to her children in the
1950s.

for church – kyrk, kric, cherche, chorche, schyrche, ssherch. Though it is hard to credit, there were 500 ways of spelling the word 'through' and over sixty ways to spell 'she', but so it was. 'People' went into dozens – 'peple, pepul, pepulle, poepul, puple, pople . . .'. 'Receive' could be 'rasaive, rassaif, rassave, resaf, resaive, resseyve . . .'.

The scribes of the Signet Office took it to the Chancery which was responsible for the paperwork which legislated for the kingdom. The twelve senior clerks, the Master of Chancery, and their twenty-four assistants or cursitors, and *their* clerks and sub-clerks got to work. The work was to regularise the language in such a way that the law of the land would be clear from coast to coast as it had been in Latin. Evidence in court had to have words widely understood and agreed on. Chancery decided that it would be 'such' and not 'sich, sych, seche, swiche . . .'.

The second engine was the printing press: William Caxton, born about 1420, learned the craft in Bruges and came back to London where eventually he set up his press in 1476 and changed the way the world worked and was perceived. One of his first printings was Chaucer's *Canterbury Tales*, which has never been out of print since. By the end of the fifteenth century, English was the language of the state, and increasingly of the law and of literature. Ripe for any purpose. The last fortress it had to conquer was that of the self-appointed, or, as they believed, divinely ordained, keepers of the eternal Kingdom of God, the Roman Catholic Church.

And that Church, with the help of the crown, made it as difficult as it possibly could. The language of the Greatest Authority and His Representative on Earth was Latin and it belonged to them. The Peasants' Revolt in 1381, with its radical call for equality based on biblical slogans, had captured the Tower of London, executed the Archbishop of Canterbury and very nearly toppled the court. This had frightened the establishment badly. The reaction was draconian. The English peasants were not to be armed with the Bible in their own tongue. This was presented as an aesthetic argument – the English language was too coarse and rude to be permitted to carry the Words of God which were already cast in lines of antique beauty.

As the Bible historian Alister McGrath points out: 'In 1407 Thomas Arundel, Archbishop of Canterbury, banned the Bible in English. "We therefore legislate and ordain that nobody shall from this day forth translate any text of Holy Scripture on his own authority into English." ' Translating the Bible into English became a heresy punishable by death: usually death by being burned at the stake. Even as late as 1513, the Dean of St Paul's was suspended just for translating the Lord's Prayer into English.

Yet English would no longer be excluded. When it could legally be read or read aloud, as in the case of Chaucer, it was; when the Bible was banned in English, the Wycliffe translation found its voice in secret locations. The force was with it. One of Henry VIII's advisers noted in 1527: 'the universal people of this realm had great pleasure and gave themselves greatly to the reading of the vulgar English tongue.' Yet in Oxford and Cambridge, even a hundred years later, 99 per cent of their libraries were in Latin.

So when the translation of Tyndale was printed abroad and smuggled in (often unbound in bales of cloth) there was hunger for it. William Malden recollected reading Tyndale's New Testament in the late 1520s: 'Divers poor men in the town of Chelmsford . . . where my father dwelt and I born and with him grew up, the said poor men bought the New Testament of Jesus Christ and on Sundays did sit reading in the lower end of the church and many would flock to hear their reading.'

What the King James Bible was to do was to provide a standard and a stability for what was considered to be the best possible

English literary language. The 1611 translation, after a few uneasy years, became *the* book of English speakers. Its retention of certain already rather archaic forms – 'thee' and 'thou' – gave it an air of important antiquity, the stamp of ancestry, a sense of an emanation from a sacred past. 'You' had replaced 'thou' in educated speech in about 1575. And just as much of the greatest art in the world came about as an unexpected consequence of the religious purpose of those works, so the beauty of the King James Bible came as a by-product of the dedication to accuracy and the determination to do fullest justice to the words of the faith.

Yet Tyndale and others were not afraid to use the full resources of the newly emerged mongrel English tongue to show off the paces of their native language.

When Tyndale learned Hebrew, he said that he found a natural affinity between Hebrew and Anglo-Saxon and certainly the King James Bible is studded with English idioms taken from Hebrew idioms and given the genius touch of memorability. Here are a few. 'To lick the dust', 'to fall flat on his face', 'a man after his own heart', 'to pour out one's heart', 'the land of the living', 'under the sun', 'from time to time', 'pride goes before a fall', 'to rise and shine', 'a fly in the ointment'. And there are so many others, not only from Hebrew sources: 'the mark of Cain', 'a mess of pottage', 'the fat of the land', 'flesh pots', 'to everything there is a season', 'the apple of his eye', 'how are the mighty fallen', 'the wisdom of Solomon', 'spare the rod and spoil the child', 'vanity of vanities', 'grind the faces of the poor', 'a voice crying in the wilderness', 'no peace for the wicked', 'the parting of the ways', 'man cannot live by bread alone', 'go the extra mile', 'cast your pearls before swine', 'wolf in sheep's clothing', 'sign of the times', 'wars and rumours of wars', 'a law unto himself', 'through a glass darkly', 'lost sheep', 'I wash my hands of it', 'of making books there is no end'.

Latin, which had been the monopolist, suffered rather badly in transition to the vernacular. So greatly nationalistic did some scholars become in the second half of the seventeenth century that they attempted to eliminate Latin altogether. The new passion for English – cleverly spotted and exploited by Henry V – is just one, though a very powerful, example of a country or a people (as happened with Afro-Americans) defining itself by how it spoke and what it spoke.

So we get Sir John Cheke (1514–57), the Regius Professor of Greek at the University of Cambridge, a man appointed to uphold and defend the classical inheritance – Greek and Latin – attempting to eliminate both. He translated Matthew and Mark and avoided the Latin 'centurion' (he replaced it by 'hundreder' though this did not catch on); nor did his term 'mooned' replace 'lunatic'. He failed to replace the Latin 'crucified' with his English 'crossed' and we can all be thankful that his 'wizards' did not dislodge 'wise men'. Still, he is a fine, though failed, example of someone who wanted to clear out the cupboard of all inherited goods and spices. Just for balance, the Roman Catholic translation into English – the Douay-Rheims version – kept as strong a Latinate feeling and vocabulary as possible and the result creaks.

On the whole, 93 per cent of words used in the King James Bible, according to Alister McGrath, are native English. This included the retention of what were already becoming archaisms: 'thee' and 'thou' have been mentioned, although 'you' was coming in at that time. This also applied to verbs: 'sayest', 'giveth', although 'gives' was replacing it. Englishness was the benchmark. The older translation and formulations gave it gravitas.

As a book designed to be read aloud, it is reader-proof. Children's voices pipe it shyly in their high clear tones and pick up the music. Adults, however cautious, always feel the urge to step up to the lectern and be at their best and find the rhythmic truth in the ancient, so well and widely heard words. Those who are carried away by their readings in church or assembly from the prophets and the Gospels can fire on seven cylinders and find salvation in a set of syllables. It came out of a time of ardent reborn faith as well as passionate reborn language.

It might entertain you to see what a linguistic scholar makes of the verses. This is very specialised but shows the range of interests this book can provoke. It is from a pamphlet by Dr Lane Cooper, called 'Certain Rhythms in the English Bible' first published by Cornell University Press in 1952.

'If preachers, orators and writers would spend a little time noting the rhythms of [the Authorised Version] they would grow discontented with the sentences that please them now. Consider, for instance, the effect of the long row of dactyls in this sentence: "who hath believed our report, and to whom is the arm of the law revealed?" or the change from iambus to dactyl in the sentence "the sun to rule by day; for his mercy ruleth for ever".' As one example of the use of anapaests, Dr Cooper cites: 'My doctrine shall drop as the rain, my speech shall distil as the dew.' Finally observe the use of cretic feet in the translation of James i,19: 'swift to hear, slow to speak, slow to wrath'.

It is a formidably excavated underpinning to what most readers see as a fluid run of easy sentences. But perhaps it is the lack of that learned sub-stratum which makes all subsequent translation sound flat and tame by comparison.

We tend to think of the Bible in holy terms – initially putting aside the violence between brothers, the lust, rape and slaughter, the unchristian vengeance of Jehovah. Nor do we call to mind 'coarse' language. But it has been found fault with, in its time. Dr Thomas Bowdler, who so successfully 'cleaned up' Shakespeare and Edward Gibbon's *Decline and Fall of the Roman Empire*, gave us a word, a rather derogatory word, to 'bowdlerise', meaning to cut what he saw as matter offensive to ladies.

The influence on orators has been mentioned, most especially on the call to unity of Abraham Lincoln's Gettysburg Address and the call to action in Martin Luther King's 'I have a dream that one day every valley shall be exalted, and every hill and mountain shall be made low, the rough places will be made plain, and the crooked places will be made straight, and the glory of the Lord shall be revealed and all flesh shall see it together.' To *see*, in Old Testament prophecy, was to foretell that something would indeed happen, as Isaiah said in the prophecy on which Dr King drew so heavily for that justly famous speech.

The spirituals, too, found their basic justification in the King James Version, in Paul to the Ephesians 'speaking to yourselves in psalms and hymns and spiritual songs, singing and making melody in your heart to the Lord'. 'Spiritual song' was used in both black and white congregations. The term 'Negro Spiritual' first appears in print in the 1860s by which time slaves had made the form their own, not only in their take on the words and stories from the King James Version, or in the way they intermeshed Methodism with African music, but by the passion and longing and urgency of their sung praise and prayers.

David Crystal is described on his latest book cover as 'the world's greatest authority on the English language'. He writes that the King James Version has 'contributed far more to English in the way of idiomatics or quasi-proverbial expressions than any other literary source'. He cites Lord Macaulay advising Lady Holland in 1831: 'a person who professes to be a critic in the delicacies of the English language ought to have the bible at his finger ends.' He also says, which has appeared in this book but bears repeating for such a source, that 'the good style of the English language has been so influenced by the Bible because of the public presence it had in the 17th century and has had ever since.' A language bred from and carried by a faith.

In his latest book, *Begat*, Professor Crystal takes a few dozen of the best known idioms and demonstrates how they have not only kept their old value but bred, or begat, variations which themselves have entered the language. These idioms have, in fact, been and continue to be a resource for phrasemakers who might have little or no awareness of the spring they come from, let alone the context which gave them their original enduring power. And sometimes they bend and twist the quotation, employing half here and an inversion there without knowing it, let alone acknowledging it: but it's fun and it adds to the word-hoard. The phrases have not only stayed in the minds and the faith of those anchored to the Bible but they have sailed free, roved widely, often wildly.

To take a few examples from *Begat*. From Genesis 'be fruitful and multiply', Crystal's research brings us, among others, 'Be Fruitful' – the National Gardening Association urging its readers to eat more fruit every day: a dietary instruction. 'Be fruitful and flourish' – from the *New York Times* (2008), consumers urged to be fruitful but can sales multiply. On evolution – 'Be fruitful and divide'; and pop groups – 'Be fruitful and multiply (your fan base)'. And there's a recent novel called *Be Fruitful and Multi-Lie*. There are more: they just multiply.

'Let there be light' is another: it's been a film, several songs, a television arts programme, the motto of a university, an episode of *Sex and the City*, and most useful for advertising eye-surgery. An oil find in Israel generated 'let there be light crude'; in Ghana, 'let there be light off the grid'. It is perverted frequently: of airline delays, 'Let there be flight'; of boxing, 'let there be fight'. There's 'let there be height' and 'blight', even, for a vampire show, 'let there be fright'.

'Am I my brother's keeper?' is an example which is rarely used correctly but widely appropriated – as 'Brother's Keeper' in dozens of episodes of television series; as *My Brother's Keeper* in three films and in two pop songs and albums; Dakin Williams's biography of his brother Tennessee Williams is called *His Brother's Keeper: The Life and Murder of Tennessee Williams*. There's 'Her Brother's Keeper' and Our Brothers' Keepers Foundation for HIV/AIDS; and the internet scourings of David Crystal have turned up yet more – *My Mother's Keeper* (a book by the daughter of Bette Davis); and many articles – 'Am I My Brother's Goalkeeper?' and 'Am I My Brother's Gatekeeper?' 'Am I My Bookkeeper's Keeper?' And Crystal refers to the joke about the ape in the zoo reading Darwin: 'Am I my keeper's brother?'

And how many Ten Commandments, or at any rate Commandments, do we have? (The 'Nine Commandments of Travel Writing', *The Eleven Commandments of Wildly Successful Women*.) And how many 'shalt nots': 'Thou shalt not kill, except in a popular video game'; 'thou shalt not upload'. While 'thou shalt not take the name of the Lord thy God in vain' slithers into headlines such as 'Don't take Che's name in vain'; 'US military don't take names in vain.' On we go with 'A Coat of Many Colours', 'How Are the Mighty Fallen!', 'Nothing new under the sun', 'Be horribly afraid', 'Sowing seeds'.

Are there phrases from any of the subsequent versions of the Bible, those which have made a takeover bid for the King James Version, which will dance so usefully through the centuries and give such pleasure? Where are the modern imprints' equivalence of the King James's language, with its wonderful flexibility, its seductive ability to pun and frolic and enlighten in gossip and literature, on the internet, in modern technology and in playground witticisms? Is this not evidence for the durable nature of the King James Version? And if some verses seem a bit difficult now and then a little explanation will clear that up, while regular reading or listening will turn the 'difficulties' into phrases to be cherished.

As a disseminator of Protestantism, the King James Version has been without equal. As a hoarder and breeder of language, it is without parallel in our culture. Why has its begetter, the Church of England, abandoned it?

The cries go up that the new translations are simpler to understand and that Christianity in certain countries, especially in the United Kingdom, is on an inevitable decline due to a multitude of causes and therefore drastic renovations were needed. In my view one cause of the decline is the retreat from the words of the King James Version. Do we tolerate (save for schoolchildren) the dilution and simplification of the words of Shakespeare? People say there is more holiness in a theatre now than in a church and that is largely because the words spoken are the words written, whatever century they came out of.

Not so in our churches now with rare exceptions. We appear to have thrown the King James Bible away on the bonfire of populism. The chief argument is that it is 'difficult to understand nowadays'. Some of it is difficult, but not much, and it is not difficult to explain or to teach. It was always a little difficult and in that difficulty was one of its strengths: it showed seriousness, it expressed depths of meaning, it provoked thought.

The best of what we are – Protestant or not – was grounded in this book. In assemblies and like occasions it was a symbol of community and a reminder of the survival and formation of who and what we are. Surely it has earned a unique place and can be reclaimed as a national book without upsetting others?

And it was written in a language of beauty that is our bedrock. Perhaps the real reason that the Protestant Church here is in decline is that it is now lost for words.

CHAPTER TWELVE
THE BIBLE ITSELF AS LITERATURE

The King James Bible is the book which has most deeply branded English literature, its prose, its poetry and its songs. From Milton to Toni Morrison to John Steinbeck, John Donne to T.S. Eliot, Dryden to James Baldwin, Emily Dickinson, Christina Rossetti, Coleridge, Kipling to Cormac McCarthy and John Updike. It is as present as a watermark in the vocabulary, and in the patterns and rhythms of daily speech. 'You are a human being with a soul and the divine gift of articulate speech,' says Professor Higgins to the uneducated cockney girl Eliza Doolittle in *Pygmalion*, 'your native language is the language of Shakespeare and Milton and the Bible: don't sit there crooning like a bilious pigeon.'

And the most pervasive of these three is the Bible. Albert Stansborough Cook, the Professor of English Language and Literature at Yale University, wrote: 'No other book has so penetrated and permeated the hearts and speech of the English race as has the Bible. What Homer was to the Greeks and the Koran to the Arabs, that – or something not unlike it – the Bible has become to the English.' The Victorian historian Froude wrote: 'it is a literature in itself; and from a fellow historian Lord Macaulay: 'if everything else in our language should perish, this book alone would suffice to show the whole extent of its beauty and power.' Praised and plundered, it became the concept by which for centuries many speakers of English defined their written identity. It gave authority to their language. It has survived parody, ridicule and neglect.

The King James Version is a magnificent work of literature. For some, the religious messages of the prophets, the Apostles, the psalmists are of lesser significance than the sound and song of the words themselves. The crucial fact that it was a Bible designed to be read aloud, a Bible which came from preachers, has given it a tone which rises seamlessly from the page to the tongue. It is worth quoting once more: 'In the beginning God created the heaven and the earth. And the earth was without form, and void; and darkness was upon the face of the deep. And the spirit of God moved upon the face of the waters. And God said, Let there be light: and there was light.'

For a people without science to conceive of such a magnificent metaphor and plant it at the opening of their Holy Book, to call it Genesis and have it translated into such sentences, is to be marvelled at.

And from the Old Testament to the New. John opens his Gospel with the lines: 'In the beginning was the Word, and the Word was with God, and the Word was God. The same was in the beginning with God. All things were made by him; and without him was not any thing made that was made. In him was life; and the life was the light of men. . . . And the Word was made flesh and dwelt among us . . .'

It is not unintelligent (in the context of the time) to see the beginning of life in a breath, to see that there is a relationship between all things, to see a journey from breath to flesh and, in those times, to see a supreme figure initiating all this and, by extension, ruling over it.

We still do not know the origin of matter or the origin of life. Why the soot and sand which is the fundamental dust of the universe turns into our particular planet remains a mystery. It may well be a mystery that physics will eventually solve and mystics be for ever unable to produce convincing evidence, but as a parallel explanation the Bible often has a certain genius made memorable by the poetry of the language.

The poetry in the Bible for me is at its finest in the Beatitudes as laid out in the Gospel according to St Matthew, already quoted. And then there are the Psalms, themselves poems and ever since begetters of more poems. Psalm 23 used to be known of by heart by much of the nation.

> The Lord is my shepherd; I shall not want.
> He maketh me to lie down in green pastures: he leadeth me
>   beside the still waters.
> He restoreth my soul: he leadeth me in the paths of
>   righteousness for his name's sake.
> Yea, though I walk through the valley of the shadow of death I
>   will fear no evil: for thou art with me; thy rod and thy staff
>   they comfort me.
> Thou preparest a table before me in the presence of mine enemies:
>   thou anointest my head with oil; my cup runneth over.
> Surely goodness and mercy shall follow me all the days of my
>   life: and I will dwell in the house of the Lord for ever.

Or from Revelation, chapter 21:

And I saw a new heaven and a new earth: for the first heaven and the first earth were passed away; and there was no more sea. And I John saw the holy city, new Jerusalem, coming down from God out of heaven, prepared as a bride adorned for her husband. And I heard a great voice out of heaven saying, Behold, the tabernacle of God is with men, and he will dwell with them and they shall be his people, and God himself shall be with them, and be their God. And God shall wipe away all tears from their eyes; and there shall be no more death, neither sorrow, nor crying, neither shall there be any more pain: for the former things are passed away.

And he that sat upon the throne said, Behold, I make all things new. And he said unto me, Write: for these words are true and faithful. And he said unto me, It is done. I am Alpha and Omega, the beginning and the end.

For centuries the Bible was the essential, often the only book in the house, and it would be read aloud. These were the houses of the literate and better educated or self-educated, but their numbers were extensive and their effect on education, common speech and authorship was great.

Alister McGrath, in his book *In the Beginning* has written about this impact and points out that the King James Version's 'ability to establish and consolidate norms of written and spoken English . . . became one of the most important yet unintended functions of the King James Bible and gave it power, quite liter-ally, to change the English world . . . to make standard one literary language'. It was published in a land rich in dialects and for many it must have seemed just another variant, albeit privileged and rather antique. But persistent usage, its association with the faith which was firmly held to by many and respected by others, made it the standard. 'It is unnecessary to praise the Authorised Version of the English Bible,' wrote the literary historian Professor Saintsbury, 'because of the mastery which its language has attained over the whole course of English literature.'

Above all the King James Version was an enterprise devoted to God. Like much else in the past – the art of ancient Egypt, the cathedrals of medieval Europe, the mosques and minarets of Islam – its primary dynamic was not directed towards this world but to another. It is a feature of all these that their value in later times – as art, architecture, literature – is an unexpected consequence. Maybe the nature and quality of faith can enable the imagination to reach more deeply into what might be called, by scientists as well as artists, the mystery of things.

The language has caused some controversy. The preface says: 'We have not tied ourselves to an uniformity of phrasing or an identity of words as some peradventure would wish that we had done.' An example already given is the translation of the same Greek verb as 'rejoice', then 'glory', then 'joy'.

It is important to pay full tribute to the Hebrew. It is said by those who know the language that the Hebrew version of the Old Testament is an unparalleled work. Certainly it has lent itself to Greek, Latin and English translations of outstanding authority. Tyndale was captivated by what he saw as the close fit, even a natural affinity, between Hebrew and Old English and his deep study of Hebrew undoubtedly enriched his translation.

This is not to diminish the skill or often the genius of the greatest of the English translators in finding the resonant native word, discovering a rhythm, making it memorable; all this sometimes beyond the call of textural accuracy. Translation has a romance of its own: the early Hebrew texts were begat by even more distant scrolls and before that . . . and before that . . . Knowledge passed on like a baton, meanings more layered than the seven cities of Troy.

Over 90 per cent of the words in the King James Bible are Old English, despite being filtered through Hebrew, Greek and Latin and tinctured with global imports. And, as mentioned in what turned out to be a shrewd move, the language used was rather antique even for 1611. Yet these older terms, once the

Bible had found its place in the hearts of the English-speaking peoples and fastened into the mind were a source of pride. As if in some way they had been there in the beginning, the King James Version had a dignity set apart from the current world. It allowed the faithful to believe that it was in these measured ways that the prophets and the Apostles, even Moses and Christ Himself would have preached.

The high-mindedness of the translators cannot be questioned. But they were also creatures of their time, in ways a coarser time than some of the centuries that followed. In the eighteenth and nineteenth centuries, when the Bible's popularity and general influence was at its height, there was a concern with biblical words which, natural for the age of Shakespeare, were worrying in a later time. The American educator, Noah Webster (1758–1843), responsible for the dictionary that helped establish American-English spelling, was alarmed at 'piss', 'privy member', 'prostitute', 'teat', 'whore' and 'womb'.

Despite this, the prose rode the centuries and matched the changing times. Isaiah xl, 4–5 led directly to one of the twentieth century's greatest flights of oratory: from Martin Luther King, as already quoted, beginning, famously: 'I have a dream that one day every valley shall be exalted, and every hill and mountain shall be made low . . .'

The word 'bible' comes, via the French, from the Latin 'biblia' meaning 'the book' and the Greek 'ta biblia' which means 'the books'. It is both and has also been a prolific generator of other books and a generous treasury of words, phrases, titles, stories, proverbs and arguments.

It was read for its literary qualities after it had embedded itself as the Christian Book of Truth. Which is not to say that its literary qualities were unrecognised early on: they were, however, and for many still are, of secondary importance. Although Christianity came under attack when rigorous scholarly scrutiny in the nineteenth century challenged the historical basis of the books in both the Old Testament and the New, the Bible was not dismissed. It was released into another life. Shelley, the notorious atheist, loved the poetry and the freedom-seeking aspects of the Bible. Matthew Arnold the late nineteenth-century commander of literary culture also valued the style in its poetry and prose. This position was not without its opponents, as David Jasper and Stephen Prickett point out in their close study, *The Bible and Literature*. The poets T.S. Eliot and C.S. Lewis both took issue with the position adopted by Arnold. 'I cannot help suspecting,' wrote C.S. Lewis, '. . . that those who read the bible as literature do not read the bible.'

That the Bible is principally literature is something many now take for granted. In the middle of the eighteenth century, Robert Lowth, a Professor of Poetry at Oxford, reassessed the Psalms, discovered a Hebraic tradition in the construction of those verses, referred that back to the oral traditions in European poetry and opened the door for his contemporaries to begin to claim poetry itself as 'a prophet, a seer, and mediate of divine truth'. It still unlocks windows.

Blake and Wordsworth as poets took on this biblical/mystical mantle and role. When the polemical atheist Shelley also assumed it, the Bible's effect on the English writers of poetry and prose was refreshed ('the distinction between poets and prose writers is a vulgar error,' according to Shelley). More importantly, secular poetry could now claim that it too was heir to the prophets and the psalmists and had access equally to truths hidden from the generality. It is significant that Coleridge, who wrote extensively on the imagination of the poet, spent the last twenty years of his life integrating that with what he called 'the Sacred Book'.

Literature was not only acknowledged in the Bible itself, it was beginning to claim both the literary status and the spiritual reach of the Scriptures. The secular sought to take over the properties of the sacred.

D.H. Lawrence expressed this with his usual vigour. 'The novel is the book of life,' he wrote. 'In this sense, the Bible is a great confused novel. You may say it is about God. But it is really about man alive. Adam, Eve, Sarah, Abraham, Isaac, Jacob, Samuel, David, Bathsheba, Ruth, Esther, Solomon, Job, Isaiah, Jesus, Mark, Judas, Paul, Peter: what is it but man alive from start to finish? Man alive, not mere bits. Even the Lord is another man alive, in a burning bush, throwing the tablets of stone at Moses' head.'

According to Lawrence, '*all* the bible' is is one of the 'supreme old novels'. Writing of how he worked: 'I always feel as if I should be naked for the fire of Almighty God to go through me – and it's rather an awful feeling.' According to Lawrence, the Bible has been taken over and overtaken by secular literature. Others followed his banner. Is it more a historical novel than history? Some argue that case just as they claim that the best way to understand the people in the Old and New Testaments is to consider them as fictional characters. One eminent literary scholar and scrutineer of the Bible reads the Book of Books as part of the literature of imagination (as Coleridge had done) and puts it in the context of 'Kafka, Joyce, Thomas Pynchon and the novels of Henry Green'.

Although he applauded the literary nature of the Bible, the theologian and philosopher Austin Farrer wrote: 'it is a sort of sacrilege to recommend the Bible as culture or amusement. The story of David and Absalom is a better piece of literature than Matthew Arnold's *Sohrab and Rustum*, but that has nothing to do with the reason for which we read the books of Samuel.'

But as the Bible was seen more as part of the general culture than the central and essential book of faith, it was opened up to the sort of enquiry and analysis from which its sacred claims had for so long protected it. The movement for the emancipation of women, to take a striking example, attacked what they saw as an unjust, skewed and unacceptably patriarchal faith. The Bible said that woman was a mere rib of Adam; she was always inferior to men, largely silent, and powerless.

In 1895 Elizabeth Cady Stanton sailed into this in *The Woman's Bible*. One of her examples was Samson, so magnificently honoured in the tale told in the Bible itself and in Milton's equally holy version *Samson Agonistes*. Now that the Bible can be viewed as fiction, its 'characters' can be discussed as characters in fiction but – and this is the extra power charge – they can also be abused for being as they were in the history of 'patriarchal' literature. She wrote:

> Samson was most unfortunate in all his associations with women. It is a pity that the angel who impressed on his parents the importance of everything that pertained to the physical development of this child, had not made some suggestions to them as to the development of his moral character. Even his physical prowess was not used by him for any great moral purpose. To kill a lion, to walk off with the gates of a city, to catch three hundred foxes and to tie them together by their tails, two by two, with firebrands to burn the cornfields and the vineyards – all this seems more like the follies of a boy than the military tactics of a great general or the statesmanship of a Judge in Israel.

We have travelled a long way from the passionate reverence accorded to the Bible as Holy Scripture and the excited acceptance that it could also be read as great literature. It can be mocked.

'Worship' in James Joyce's *Finnegans Wake*, described as 'one of the greatest of all intellectual Biblical "readings"' is now 'washup'. He writes: 'I sink I'd die down over his feet, humbly dumbly, only to washup'.

Given that the Bible has been uprooted and mined it is the more remarkable that it persists still as a source for literature. From the beginning its force field magnetised the style and the imagination of the finest writers in the English language. And it might seem curious, given that the King James Version was published in 1611, just five years before Shakespeare's death, but a case can be made for using Shakespeare as the starting point for this influence of the Bible on writers: and on readers.

CHAPTER THIRTEEN
FROM SHAKESPEARE –
THE BIBLE AND LITERATURE (1)

The King James Bible was published in 1611 and Shakespeare died in 1616. It would seem there was little chance of a direct influence. Yet by an indirect route, we can trace how it did influence Shakespeare. There is also a teasing possibility that Shakespeare worked on Psalm 46.

Shakespeare and the Bible are often twinned. They came out of the same period in the formation of the English language, in the late English Renaissance when, according to the writer of our foundation *Dictionary*, Dr Samuel Johnson, it was 'a golden age', a time that marked the beginning of English 'literary perfection'.

At a time of mutually incomprehensible dialects in the British islands, the Bible and Shakespeare established what would become the standard, and the earthing of the literary language. The plays and poems of Shakespeare are almost as numerous as the books in the Bible and on those two pillars have been built a magnificence of world literature.

We can see how seriously Shakespeare took his church when we go to the Holy Trinity today. On his retirement to his native town he built himself a fine monument which, with his grave and those of his family, is within the altar rails. Nearby is a first edition of the King James Version, from which he might have read aloud in that church.

As a boy Shakespeare would have been obliged to attend the Holy Trinity in Stratford-upon-Avon regularly. The Bible would also have been a teaching instrument in his grammar school, alongside Ovid and Virgil. His work is steeped in it. But from which Bible did his knowledge derive?

The Bible which Shakespeare is likely to have heard in the church which he attended regularly as a boy would have been the Geneva Version. The Geneva Bible, like the New Testament and the first five books of the Old Testament (together with some of the Proverbs), was overwhelmingly Tyndale's translation.

Ronald Mansbridge has proved that the Geneva Version, which was first printed in 1560 (it went through at least 140 printings), was on the whole even more dependent on Tyndale than the King James Version.

A few of his examples, built up from a word count, are:

Genesis xiii: 81.4 per cent Tyndale in the Geneva Bible.
                    85.1 per cent Tyndale in the King James Bible.
Deuteronomy viii: 81.5 per cent Tyndale in the Geneva Bible.
                    79.1 per cent Tyndale in the King James Bible.
Matthew iii: 85.3 per cent Tyndale in the Geneva Bible.
                    82.3 per cent Tyndale in the King James Bible.
Revelation xx: 92.7 per cent Tyndale in the Geneva Bible.
                    92.5 per cent Tyndale in the King James Bible.

From these and other examples offered by Ronald Mansbridge, the total comes to 83.4 per cent Tyndale in the Geneva Bible and 81.6 per cent in the King James Bible. He writes: 'I believe this sample is statistically valid of the whole New Testament and the books of the Old Testament within a margin of possible error of 2 or 3 per cent.'

No wonder that Stephen Greenblatt, in his *Will in the World:*

How Shakespeare Became Shakespeare, wrote: 'without Tyndale's New Testament and Cranmer's Prayer Book, it is difficult to imagine William Shakespeare the playwright.' Shakespeare quotes hundreds of times from the Geneva translation and because of the overlap between the Geneva and the King James it is possible to claim that Shakespeare was influenced by most of what would become the King James Bible. Shakespeare quotes from the Bible about 1,350 times.

The Geneva Bible was the Bible first taken to America, and although it soon became supplanted by the King James Version, the same argument can be applied to its early influence there as has been applied to its influence on Shakespeare.

Professor A.L. Rowse did a masterful study of the influence on Shakespeare of the Bible and the Prayer Book. He points out that 'there are definite allusions to 42 books of the bible.' He notes that 'the story of Cain is referred to twenty-five times, Jeptha . . . in at least seven passages, Samson . . . nine, David . . . six, Goliath . . . three, Solomon . . . nine, Job . . . twenty-five, Judas . . . perhaps twenty-three, Peter . . . seven, Pilate . . . seven, the Prodigal Son . . . nine, Dives and Lazarus . . . seven, the Whore of Babylon . . . seven.' To take one example from so many: in *Richard II*, the lines 'Edward's seven sons, whereof thyself art one/Were as seven vials of his sacred blood' are from Revelation: 'And there came one of the seven Angels, which had the seven vials and talked with me, saying unto me, Come hither: I will shew unto thee the judgement of the great whore that sitteth upon the many waters'.

More importantly, Rowse stresses the effect of an unconscious education. 'He was grounded at church . . . the Bible provided the bed of popular culture . . . it is impossible to exaggerate the importance of this grounding.'

We read of Thomas Hardy as a boy walking two miles to and from school through the woods every day and noting those minute transformations in nature which texture his work; he became a man who 'noticed such things'. That daily trudge in all seasons had become as a university and a bedding for the imagination which would always be expressed through that particular rural landscape. And Dickens, as a boy, on his trek from Camden Town to the blacking factory in central London, and then all over London as a man, unconsciously storing the booming, varied, fractured metropolis deep in his mind. Mark Twain up and down the Mississippi, Balzac in Paris, Joyce deep-dipped in Dublin – on they go, the procession of writers and other artists whose most enduring and most nuanced education came from what they learned unconsciously, from what was absorbed through the curiosity of their own selection rather than being implanted or hammered in by others.

How much more so in the case of a boy, and a youth, who became the greatest master man of words? And 'the greatest mind' as Harold Bloom, the American critic, wrote, 'we shall ever know'. The words of the Bible must have made their own library in the mind of the young Shakespeare; and the rhythms, the abrupt switches of narrative, the contradictions, the high drama, the tenderness and the brutality – all there, read by priests whose chief skill might have lain in reading aloud. And these stories, very likely to be read again alone in his house, one of the few books to which he would have had access and therefore, for that reason, to such a boy, a magnet.

Here are three specific 'borrowings':

Are not two sparrows sold for a farthing? and one of them shall not fall on the ground without your Father. (Matthew)

There's a special providence in the fall of a sparrow. If it be now, 'tis not to come; if it be not to come, it will be now. (*Hamlet*)

Eye hath not seen, nor ear heard, neither have entered into the heart of man, the things which God hath prepared for them that love him. (Corinthians)

The eye of man hath not heard, the ear of man hath not seen, man's hand is not able to taste, his tongue to conceive, nor his heart to report, what my dream was. (A *Midsummer Night's Dream*)

For with what judgement ye judge, ye shall be judged: and with what measure ye mete, it shall be measured to you again. (Matthew)

Death for Death. Haste still pays haste, and leisure answers leisure; Like doth quit like, and MEASURE still FOR MEASURE. (*Measure for Measure*)

As a postscript to Shakespeare and the Bible, there is in circulation one of those many claims in which, by esoteric numerological calculations, Shakespeare is 'proved' to have been someone else entirely, or his works to have cabbalistic properties. In McAfee's *The Greatest English Classic*, he examines the claim that the scholars who put together the final version of the King James Bible called on Shakespeare's help with the Psalms. Not entirely unlikely. His reputation as a poet was very high, higher, in refined circles, than his popular fame as a playwright. Psalm 46 is the most frequently quoted as revealing the master's voice.

The argument is that Shakespeare worked on this when he was 46 years old – that would be 1606. If 46 words are counted from the start of the Psalms you will find the word 'shake'. If 46 words are counted from the end (excluding the word 'Selah' which is considered to have no meaning but be merely a form of punctuation), you come across the word 'spear'.

There is more. Take the number 10. This is 4 and 6 added together. 46 once again! Ten verses into the psalm, you count in 6 words and get 'I am'. Count 4 words on and you get 'will'. If you reverse the 6 and the 4, you get 46 and 'William'! Who could doubt it?

Since 1611, the King James Version has fed quantities of the writing in English of prose and poetry. As the twentieth century developed, other cultures, using English, came into the fold with their own influences – based in India or Africa, for instance, but even in the latter the Bible's influence is often present. But from the beginning of the seventeenth to the middle of the twentieth century, the Bible can be claimed to be unarguably the most pervasive presence in the language and in the literature. And although its religious grip has slackened in some countries, the force of its stories, its imagery, its vocabulary, its moral teaching, its acts of cruelty and villains, and its verses of wisdom even now remain uniquely important.

John Donne, poet and essayist, began work at about the same time as the Bible was published. He shares a Tyndale overlap with Shakespeare. He wrote: 'there are not so eloquent books in the world as the Scriptures . . . we may be bold to say that, in all their Authors, Greek and Latin, we cannot find so high and so lively examples of those Tropes, and those figures as we may in Scriptures . . . The style of the Scriptures is a diligent and artificial style; and a great part thereof is a musical, is a metrical, is a measured composition, in verse.'

His preferences were for the Psalms and the Epistles of St Paul: 'because they are Scriptures, written in such form as I have been most accustomed to; St Paul's being letters and David's being poems.' He believed that 'God's own finger had written the scriptures'.

It will be impossible here to give more than a taste of the total immersion of Donne and other supreme poets in the faith and the language of the Bible. At times it seems everything they write is connected to it. Even an illness is described in high biblical terms. In 'Hymne to God my God, in my Sicknesse', Donne writes:

> We thinke that Paradise and Calvarie,
> Christs Crosse and Adams tree, stood in one place;
> Looke Lord, and finde both Adams met in me;
> As the first Adams sweat surrounds my face,
> May the last Adams blood my soule embrace.

He finds in the Christian story, strata of tenderness and meaning which could seem to outsoar the original save that they are so anchored in it.

In the 'Divine Poems, Nativitie' he begins with Christ in the womb and the holy birth:

> Immensitie cloistered in thy deare wombe,
> Now leaves his well belov'd imprisonment,
> There he hath made himselfe to his intent
> Weake enough, now into our world to come;
> But oh, for thee, for him, hath th'Inne no roome?
> Yet lay him in this stall, and from the Orient,
> Starres, and wisemen will travell to prevent
> Th'effect of Herods jealous generall doome.
> Seest thou, my Soule, with thy faiths eyes, how he
> Which fils all place, yet none holds him, doth lie?
> Was not his pity towards thee wondrous high,
> That would have need to be pittied by thee?
> Kisse him, and with him into Egypt goe,
> With his kinde mother, who partakes thy woe.

Among so much else, the idea of the Christ Child making himself 'weak enough' to come into the world is a marvellous insight into the faith which John Donne, later in his life, would preach from the pulpit.

John Milton, from his adolescence until his death just before the last quarter of the seventeenth century, devoted himself to biblical subjects. He had the King James Version of 1612, and also a Geneva Bible, but his scholar's mind made him familiar with other versions – in Latin, Greek, Hebrew and Aramaic. Yet his chief work builds on the King James Version. At times he threatens to rewrite it.

Milton came out of a classical education into a world of religious and political ferment in which he played his part as a rousing pamphleteer, a champion of liberty and a defender of what he saw as the true, Puritan faith. His greatest works – *Paradise Lost*, *Paradise Regained* and *Samson Agonistes* – are so lavishly doused in the embroidery of a great vocabulary, so much a tapestry of poetic show that they can appear, to our palates, to be over-rich. The high style, I think, was partly to out-bible the Bible, the Authorised Version, to show what an inspired poet could really do. Despite his standing as the second great poet in English after Shakespeare, there can be – a blasphemous suggestion to Milton scholars – a sense that the ornate language and the embossed imagery load it too heavily.

Yet Milton's genius has been too long celebrated by fine poets and scholars to be doubted here and his place, following Shakespeare, is authoritatively sealed. The story of God's work obsessed him. It was as if he wanted to re-imagine the whole of it.

Writing of the beginning, in Genesis chapters 1 and 2, his lines include:

> . . . Heav'n opened wide
> Her ever-during gates, harmonious sound
> On golden hinges moving, to let forth

> The King of Glory in his powerful Word
> And Spirit coming to create new worlds.
> On heavenly ground they stood, and from the shore
> They viewed the vast immeasurable abyss
> Outrageous as a sea, dark, wasteful, wild,
> Up from the bottom turned by furious winds
> And surging waves, as mountains to assault
> Heaven's highth, and with the center mix the pole.

There are those who would prefer the direct words of Tyndale but Milton is undoubtedly magnificent.

He wrote about time, about his blindness, about destiny and character especially in *Samson Agonistes*; he personified Satan in a way so vivid and memorable that famously he made him the most attractive of the heavenly host, and hell more popular than heaven. He wrote political and social pamphlets. But it was the Bible that was the keystone of a body of work so loaded with quotations from it that it can seem not only a commentary but at times practically a parallel universe.

He elaborated continually. For instance the line 'the spirit of God moved on the face of the waters' became:

> . . . on the watery calm
> His broadening wings the Spirit of God outspread,
> And vital virtue infused, and vital warmth
> Throughout the fluid mass, but downward purged . . .
> . . . and earth self-balanced on her centre swung.

Milton's work showed how inspirational the Bible could be, and how deeply you could read into it. His life and dedication confirmed the biblical association. That such a superior poetic and philosophical mind as that of Milton could so passionately take up the Bible was an example which was to be followed. He was a master on whom to model oneself, at least in part, as Wordsworth, among others, was to do. More beloved today of scholars, perhaps, than of general readers, Milton still, in this history, plays a major role. His total acceptance of the faith and his mighty efforts to reimagine and rework what had already been written so memorably were an immense tribute to the power of the Scriptures.

John Bunyan is the first lower-class hero to appear in this story. *The Pilgrim's Progress*, one of his sixty books, has, since its publication, outsold every other book except the Bible. It has been translated into more than 200 languages and been praised by Ruskin, Rudyard Kipling and George Bernard Shaw. It describes the journey of an ordinary, sinful, frail Christian towards salvation. Its storytelling and landscape could be seen as an original compound of religious ecstasy and magical realism. I remember being enthralled by it first in a pictorial edition and later in full print. Bunyan has the great gift of provoking empathy and though his subject matter and the characters might seem to some now to be quaint and outdated, the book remains and will keep. Who knows, as times change again, it may regain its place in the canon of imaginative faith-literature. And he touches the common nerve.

'"Pilgrim's Progress" seems to be a complete reflection of Scripture,' wrote Matthew Arnold. Bunyan wrote: 'I was then never out of the bible either by reading or meditation.' His education was basic. 'My parents . . . put me to school to learn me to both read and write . . . though to my shame I did soon lose that little I learned.'

In the 1640s, aged sixteen, he was conscripted into the Parliamentary Army and would have met the extremes of a brutal war, religious passion and politics: the Levellers, who believed you should only obey those you had voted for; the Fifth Monarchists, who anticipated the imminent return of Jesus Christ; the Diggers, who believed the land belonged to all. Their religious passion appears to have embraced him, but not so their politics, even though in the 1660s he spent two spells in prison 'for holding unlawful meetings' – that is, for preaching. He was a biblical literalist and the story of Christ was, in his view, both a true and a divine history.

Bunyan's prose not so much quoted from the Bible as lived inside its skin. This is as Christian and Hopeful wade into the river of death.

They then addressed themselves to the water: and entering, Christian began to sink, and crying out to his good friend Hopeful, he said 'I sink in deep waters, the billows go over my head, all his waves go over me. Selah!'

Then said the other 'Be of good cheer, my brother, I feel the bottom and it is good.' Then said Christian 'Ah my friend, the sorrows of death have compassed me about, I shall not see the land that flows with milk and honey.' And with that a great darkness and horror fell upon Christian so that he could not see before him; also here he in great measure lost his senses so that he could neither remember nor orderly talk of any of these sweet refreshments that he had met with on the way of his pilgrimage.

McAfee points out:

Christian's two sentences are a mixture of quotation, allusion and imitation clearly intended to evoke the Psalms without ever becoming an exact quotation. His first sentence could easily be mistaken for a quotation, especially as it uses the characteristic refrain 'Selah!', but it is an adaptation of Psalm 42 verse 7 'All thy waves and thy billows are gone over me' and Psalm 69 verse 2 'I sink in deep mire, where there is no standing: I am come into deep waters, where the floods overflow me', while 'the sorrows of death have compassed me about' is nearly a direct quotation from Psalm 18 verse 4. And the 'land that flows with milk and honey' is the land promised to the oppressed and suffering Israelites.

The vocabulary of *The Pilgrim's Progress* is evidence of the literacy of a substantial minority. That literacy was founded and as it were funded by the King James Bible. It was both faith-driven and faith-fed. Together with the Bible itself, Bunyan's work rooted into the English-speaking Protestant reading classes a knowledge of and a loyalty to a particular period and style of Bible language which was reinforced and made sublime by Shakespeare and to some extent Milton. These three, Shakespeare, Milton and Bunyan, point the different but conjoined ways in which the Bible will be used by writers over the next four centuries. From its publication, the King James Bible did not walk alone but gathered around it three champions whose own writings fortified the English Scriptures of 1611 and helped the genius of that translation not only to endure, but to be quoted, and looted, ever since.

To list every writer whose work owes debts to the King James Bible would be to write another book and several have already been written. In this book which looks at its overall impact and its penetration into many aspects in the history of English-speaking Protestants, there is not the space for many mansions. Even so, this and one other chapter will be needed . . .

John Dryden (1631–1700) was a political pamphleteer as well as being a satirical poet. His most famous poem, the epic *Absalom and Achitophel* is an attack on Charles II's bastards and a denunciation of the politics of that time, of what was called the Exclusion Crisis. He is prime evidence of the elasticity in the legacy of the Bible. In his hands it is an instrument of political torment, beginning with his scarcely veiled comment on the public promiscuity of Charles II: apparently applauding it:

> In pious times, ere Priest-craft did begin,
> Before *Polygamy* was made a sin:
> When man, on many, multipli'd his kind,
> Ere one to one was cursedly confin'd:
> When Nature prompted, and no Law deni'd
> Promiscuous use of concubine and bride;
> Then *Israel's* monarch, after Heaven's own heart,
> His vigorous warmth did variously impart
> To wives and slaves: and, wide as his command,
> Scatter'd his Maker's image through the land.

Daniel Defoe (1660–1731), is the father of the English novel according to Valentine Cunningham, who has written convincingly of Defoe's close kinship with the Bible. He was 'a lifelong Dissenter. He was brought up from the age of two in the "gathered" congregation of the Reverend Samuel Annesley,' which his parents had joined in 1662. Daily Bible reading, meditation, copying chunks of it out in shorthand, Defoe at one stage was set on a career in the Presbyterian ministry before he went into business. The Bible permeated everything he wrote: pamphlets, *Moll Flanders*, *Robinson Crusoe* all draw on a 'huge repertoire of direct quotation'. It was ingrained in him whether claiming that Moses gave the world its first knowledge of letters when he brought the tablets down from Mount Sion, or having the narrator of *A Journal of the Plague Year* open the Bible with apparent casualness to light on a quotation which would arm and uplift him for the fight. As for the plague itself, there are two explanations according to Defoe. It is certainly the will of God. But it also arises from the 'natural causes' which 'Divine Power' has put in place.

Everything is explained and excused through God by this writer, who was also acclaimed for bringing the news of his times into vivid and enduring fiction. *Robinson Crusoe*, for instance, is shot through with religion. Cunningham takes up the matter of the barley:

> Famously, some barley unexpectedly springs up, to be rationalised as all at once completely providential and completely natural. When Crusoe first sees the shoots of English barley he supposes it God's miraculous provision. Then he remembers he had earlier shaken a 'little bag of corn that had been reduced to Husks and Dusty by rats' and this natural explanation abated 'my religious thankfulness to God's Providence'. But then he had a further thought that 'it really was the work of Providence as to me' in that the rats must have left 'ten or twelve grains of corn' unspoiled in the bag and he happened to shake them out in a place where they would flourish.

Jonathan Swift, apart from his satires which included at least one work of genius, *Gulliver's Travels*, was a devout clergyman. Whatever his mockery, he, not unlike Defoe, held closely to the faith and to the way in which it was expounded. In *A Letter to a Young Gentleman* in 1720, he explains how seriously a sermon should be undertaken, how carefully prepared and delivered. Of his own sermons, it was said 'they emit hardly a breath of his fabulous spirit and are surely unadorned in respect of wit and fancy.' The wild and rude riot of some of his writing, like that of Dryden, runs in apparently comfortable harness with a solid Anglicanism. And in his case too it could be argued that one reason for his rage against the world is because of its failure to live in the morality of the New Testament.

William Blake in his engravings and paintings, his poems

and commentaries, is a man wholly immersed in the King James Bible. He is also in a perpetual argument with it. He has, as it were, surfing on it, his own meditative, even mystical philosophy which spoke directly across the centuries to the 'hippies' of the mid-twentieth century for whom he became a poetic guru. Allen Ginsberg, the American poet and a big cylinder of the hippie engine, seems to have worshipped him. He became a T-shirt, a pop icon. What travelled down the years was to do with his spiritual implacability quarried out of the Bible.

He recreated the first lines of Genesis in *The Book of Urizen*:

> Lo, a shadow of horror is risen
> In Eternity! Unknown, Unprolific,
> Self-closed, all-repelling: what Demon
> Hath form'd this abominable void;
> This soul-shudd'ring vacuum? Some said
> 'It is Urizen.' But unknown, abstracted,
> Brooding, secret, the dark power hid.

And in his 'The Chimney Sweeper' he would write of a child left weeping in the snow by parents who have gone to church:

> And because I am happy, and dance and sing,
> They think they have done me no injury,
> And are gone to praise God and his Priest and King
> Who make up a heaven of our misery.

And then he could write the hymn of the Women's Institute of Britain, a hymn that seems to capture the yearning of many who want to be anciently anchored in a place, a church and a faith by imagining Christ in their own land.

And did those feet in ancient time
Walk upon England's mountains green?
And was the holy Lamb of God
On England's pleasant pastures seen?

Blake shows yet another side of himself when, in a letter to a friend, he writes: 'Why is the Bible more Entertaining and Instructive than any other book? Is it not because they are addressed to the Imagination which is Spiritual sensation but mediating to the Understanding or Reason?'

It was beginning to seem that a well could be sunk in the Bible at any point and it would find energy for any view. It was available across the waterfront. Women poets at this time, Mary Robinson and Charlotte Smith, also sought a voice in what appeared to many women to be a monopoly of patriarchs past and present. But Mary Wollstonecraft, like Defoe a Dissenter, would draw on her Bible reading to energise her campaign for women's rights. In the Romantic Revival (which overlapped the Englightenment!) the most influential woman living in England in the Romantic era was Hannah More, whose radical pamphlets have pushed her religious literature into the background. In 1782 she published *Sacred Dramas*. She writes about 'David and Goliath', 'Belshazzar' and 'David'.

In the drama *Moses in the Bulrushes* she brings together women both Hebrew and Egyptian and gives them common qualities. In this and other instances she is a key figure in bringing women on to the page. Her transparent faith exemplifies the religious nature and the learning of the women writers to come. For many of them, the Bible and other religious works were their only way to get an education and find a source which could give them the chance of literary equality.

The Romantic poets sought answers and questions in nature as much as in a biblical God. Wordsworth wrote:

> She has a world of ready wealth
> Our minds and hearts to bless—
> Spontaneous wisdom breath'd by health
> Truth breath'd by cheerfulness.

And, much more ominously:

> One impulse from a vernal wood
> May teach you more of man,
> Of moral evil and of good,
> Than all the sages can.

The Old and the New Testament both put briskly aside! All the history and storytelling grandeur of the Old and the morality of the New deleted in a simple quatrain. Yet Wordsworth's pantheism often seems to merge with Protestantism:

> Not in entire forgetfulness,
> And not in utter nakedness,
> But trailing clouds of glory do we come
> From God, who is our home.

Without at least the inheritance of a religious sensibility it is doubtful if he would have written his greatest poetry. *The Prelude* is shot through with a sense of the divine.

Lord Byron wrote: 'I am a great reader of those books [the Bible] and had read them through and through before I was eight years old; that is to say, the Old Testament, for the New struck me as a task but the other as a pleasure.'

We know that Byron was iconoclastic, at the very least sceptical. In *Childe Harold* he writes:

> . . . Religions take their turn:
> 'Twas Jove's – 'tis Mahomet's – and other creeds
> Will rise with other years, till man shall learn
> Vainly his incense soars, his victim bleeds.

Again, though, as often happened, the effect of the King James Bible was felt by believers and unbelievers alike. Byron dug deeply into the Bible, often taking the Old Testament stories at their own value. 'Jephthah's Daughter', 'Song of Saul Before his Last Battle', and others are faithful to the original story. Even in *Childe Harold* and *Don Juan* in which there are many references to Adam and Eve and the Fall, though there is mockery there is relish in the knowledge. The Bible continued to be a necessary resource. George Gordon Brown in his essay on Byron says of the 'dust and clay metaphors' that each of them appears well over a hundred times in his poetry.

As the centuries rolled through, the Bible's literary and historical wealth often grew detached from its spiritual mission. Yet it remained no less powerful in the influence it maintained among great writers.

There is an extreme example, at the beginning of the nineteenth century, in the work of the atheist, Percy Bysshe Shelley. He had studied carefully much of the Old Testament, especially the Book of Psalms, Job and Isaiah. *Queen Mab* is given as one example in which Ahasuerus, the Wandering Jew, tells the Bible story in detail only available to a close reader.

Coleridge is the apotheosis of the Romantic movement, even though he bowed to Wordsworth as the greater poet. He was born in 1772 and before Coleridge was three he could read a chapter of the Bible. 'He continued to read both Testaments all his life, and read them in the hope that they would reveal, and help create in him, the being of Christ. He valued the bible above all other books.' Coleridge himself wrote: 'the words of the bible find me at greater depths of my being.' We are told that 'when you read *Hymn Before Sunrise in the Vale of Chamounix* you may as well be reading the 19th Psalm.' He said: 'intense study of the bible will keep any writer from being vulgar in point of style.'

His philosophical works, which have been a steer in literary criticism, are also suffused by his belief in the Bible as a source for both faith and literature. 'Only a Man is capable of ideas . . . and as far only as he is capable of an Ideal . . . is man a *Religious* being. But neither the one nor the other is possible except through the Imagination.' Imagination for Coleridge is the key to a sense of the divine as well as a guide to a perception of beauty. He had a mission as determined as a Wesley. 'This is my aim,' he wrote, 'to bring back our faith and affections to the simplicity of the Gospel Facts, by restoring the Gospel facts to their union with the Ideas or Spiritual Truths therein embodied or therein revealed.'

Coleridge's intellectual religious passion existed alongside an appreciation of the powers of nature, especially in its extreme manifestations. He, like Wordsworth, can be seen to be at a turning point. The Bible still infused much literature but other primary inspirations were coming into view. The greatest of these was science, what Francis Bacon in the early seventeenth century had described as the 'Book of Nature'. It threatened to eclipse Scripture but not for a surprisingly long time and, even recently, not for some key writers.

Coleridge was contemporaneous with Jane Austen, not generally much thought of in the context of the biblical consensus. But her concerns with honouring parents, with the sin of pride, the obligation to care for the weak, as well as her interest in the social and domestically political place of the Anglican clergy in the society she portrays, bring her into the orbit of what might be called the tradition of Anglican-Protestant literature. Her grasp of the

Bible was sure and her grip on the value of good deeds can be tracked back to the Beatitudes and other teachings in the New Testament.

Jane Austen represents another layer – the moving of the religious content from the foreground into the background of literature. Once again, there are exceptions. But as we roll through some of the giants of the nineteenth century, there is some sense of an ebbing tide, and yet it has not left the shore.

Charles Dickens frequently uses phrases from the Bible to make a dramatic moment swell even larger with spiritual and emotional significance as when in *Bleak House* little neglected, starved Joe lies dying. A friend teaches him the Lord's Prayer as he sees the Light coming. It was at the time thought to be of one of Dickens's most affecting scenes, and it is still very moving. It evokes deep feeling and through religion it gives it even greater depth. While *A Christmas Carol* is a masterpiece of biblical Christian art.

For all that, the Bible is not at the forefront of Dickens whom some claim as England's greatest novelist. Yet his books are always morality tales, a mix of New Testament Christ-ness and Old Testament vengeance. Who is good and who is bad is determined, fundamentally, by what Christ preached. Who will be punished and how savagely, by the acts of Jehovah. But the specific biblical instances and the use of the stories which are dominating in earlier writers have started to slide away. The Bible remains, however, as a resource, a hope and as a warning. There is salvation in Dickens, but it is as often in marriage as in heaven. Dickens would be appalled not to be included among the Christian writers – but the blunt and total embrace of John Bunyan is no longer in the great fiction of the day.

George Eliot, another novelist whose admirers claim her as 'the greatest', is as inevitably and dynamically related to the Bible as any other of her countrymen and women but, again, she is an agent of change. She was a distinguished biblical scholar whose engagement with the German biblical textual analysts of the day led her to abandon her belief in the literal truth of her original faith. But rather than move away altogether, she took the standpoint of a cultural commentator on this deeply embedded phenomenon called Christianity which rested its case on unassailable revealed truths. She saw much in it that was good, morally, socially and even intellectually. Her novels are perhaps the last in the line of the novelist as genius to embrace closely the religion – its morality and spirituality – described in the King James Version, in such resonating language.

She moves from the false simplicity of *Silas Marner* – practically a straight addition to Christ's own parables – to the moral imaginative amplitude of *Middlemarch*, often using discrete dramatic devices from the Bible. George Eliot is forever resting on and taking nurture from her young pre-scholarly years of open belief as well as her reconsidered post-faith position.

Dorothea Brooke, the heroine of *Middlemarch*, explains her point of view in a chaste early love scene which is imbued with Christian sentiment:

'. . . by desiring what is perfectly good, even when we don't quite know what it is and cannot do what we would, we are part of the divine power against evil – widening the skirts of light and making the struggle with darkness narrower.'

'That is a beautiful mysticism – it is a——' [says Laidlaw]

'Please not to call it by any name,' said Dorothea, putting out her hands entreatingly. 'You will say it is Persian, or something else geographical. It is my life. I have found it out, and cannot part with it.'

And his great novel closes with words from the Old Testament: 'in their death they were not divided'.

It would be possible to embark on a long run of nineteenth-century English novelists and poets. And Scots too. There are few books as darkly saturated in the King James Version as James Hogg's *The Confession of a Justified Sinner*. And of course alongside there were those for at least a couple of centuries who did not take much from the Bible and followed classical or non-religious models.

But its soul went marching on. Charles Kingsley was a minister and a Christian Socialist more likely now to be included in a chapter on social change but his novels, such as *The Water Babies* and *Alton Locke* were wildly popular in his day and were heavily banked on biblical quotations. His intense Bible reading went directly into books that changed attitudes and manners.

All three Brontë sisters were schooled in the Bible and the evidence is there in their novels. Charlotte Brontë's *Jane Eyre* is the outstanding example: David Norton, author of a textual history of the King James Bible says of it, 'In *Jane Eyre*, Romantic Religion and the King James Bible come together to create important artistic effects and the result is sometimes an insight into the King James Bible.'

The novel, published in 1847, is distinguished, according to McAfee, by 'the ease with which the King James Bible was able to slip into Brontë's novel without announcement'. He cites Rochester analysing and describing Jane Eyre's character. 'Strong wind, earthquake, shock and fire may pass by: but I shall follow the guiding of that still small voice which interprets the dictates of conscience.' An allusion to the vision in 1 Kings.

Like John Bunyan, she quotes from the Psalms – in one case the same Psalms 42 and 69 – as he had. After the broken wedding, she writes: 'That bitter hour cannot be described: in truth, "the waters came into my soul; I sank in deep mire: I felt no standing; I came into deep waters; the floods overflowed me."'

This is not a direct quotation but an adaptation, yet the quality of it, by eliminating the linking words, heightens the effect and justifies McAfee's large claim that she gives 'an insight into the King James Bible'. Her own prose in 1847 takes up the prose of the King James Bible from 1611 seamlessly: the Bible has again spliced with literature.

Finally, to a poet who all but rounds off the century: Alfred Tennyson (1809–92). Dr van Dyke a Bible scholar writes that 'we cannot help seeing that Tennyson owes a large debt to the Christian Scriptures, not only for their formative influence on his mind and for the purely literary material in the way of illustrations and illusions which they have given him, but also for the creation of a moral atmosphere, a medium of thought and feeling in which he can speak freely and with an assurance of sympathy to a very wide circle of readers.'

As with all the other King Jamesian writers, there are many references – over 400 – spread through the poems. In his elegy for the death of his friend Arthur Hallam, *In Memoriam*, he uses the resurrection of Lazarus:

> When Lazarus left his charnel-cave,
> And home to Mary's house return'd,
> Was this demanded – if he yearn'd
> To hear her weeping by his grave?

This brief sweep through English literature in Britain spanning 300 years, from Shakespeare to Tennyson, has, I hope, shown how deep, varied and persistent has been the impact of the King James Bible on English literature. It will be seen at work again when American literature and the twentieth century are discussed and in both cases, I think, the impact is every bit as deep even into our alleged secular times. It seems that the Bible's essential poetry and the beauty of its prose carried into literature even when the main matter, the religious content, waned in importance or was challenged or doubted. It became a unique living thing in the language and in the books it bred.

This is from Tennyson, on the story of Moses striking the rock so that water will flow.

> O living will that shalt endure
> When all that seems shall suffer shock,
> Rise in the spiritual rock,
> Flow thro' our deeds and make them pure,
>
> That we may lift from out of dust
> A voice as unto him that hears,
> A cry above the conquer'd years
> To one that with us works, and trust,
>
> With faith that comes of self-control,
> The truths that never can be proved
> Until we close with all we loved,
> And all we flow from, soul in soul.

CHAPTER FOURTEEN
AMERICAN LITERATURE AND THE TWENTIETH CENTURY – THE BIBLE AND LITERATURE (2)

When the King James Version was shipped across the Atlantic and landed on the eastern seaboard, it was an event which was to play an immeasurable part in shaping the modern world, the American world.

American English is bred from the Jacobean-approved translation of the Word of God. American books – both literary and popular – drew from and dredged the Bible. In the construction of Hawthorne's *The Scarlet Letter* and in Harriet Beecher Stowe's *Uncle Tom's Cabin* equally, the Bible is in the beams and in the joists. In *Uncle Tom's Cabin*, for instance, direct reference occurs in thirty-eight of the novel's forty-five chapters and the book is rooted in the faith nurtured in the Bible. There seems little doubt that Uncle Tom's passionately convinced embrace of American Protestant Christianity made the novel not only a bestseller but a book that changed the opinions of hundreds of thousands of readers. It worked as benign propaganda and brought them to an abhorrence of the evils of the slavery Harriet Beecher Stowe described so movingly.

One way to gauge the effect of the Bible is to check the impact it had on writers. As we saw with the small selection from the enormous number of 'biblically' literate writers in the previous chapter on literature in Britain, this Book of Books has spawned innumerable books. The writers knew that their references would be picked up. They knew they could illuminate and fortify a point by apt or jarring biblical reference. They knew their readers. And the readers knew their Bible. It is impossible to name any single book in the English-speaking world which has had and still has anything approaching that congregation of a readership. And as it was also a preachers' Bible there were listeners, too, scarcely literate, some of them, but surely intelligent and earnest enough to want to hear the truth of the Word of God and its progeny.

Professor Mark A. Noll writes persuasively on the dimension of the Bible's presence in America's early history. He points out that the first English book published in North America was commonly known as *The Bay Psalm Book*. Thomas Jefferson, the third President of the United States, thought the miracle stories were 'a ground work of vulgar ignorance . . . superstitions, factitious, fabrications'. Yet during his first term as President, he prepared his own editions of Jesus's sayings (in Greek, Latin and French) and read the Gospels daily for the last forty years of his life. Towns were named from the Bible. So were children. It was a totem as well as the Word of God. In Philadelphia in 1844 when the Roman Catholic bishop tried to persuade the city officials to let Catholic children hear teachings from the Douay-Rheims translation instead of the King James Version, there were riots and the Protestants tried to burn down the Catholic churches.

It took some time for the Bible to be printed legally and profitably in America. The monopoly of the London printers held hard and across the ocean they went, these sacred cargos, Bible-bound boats. The Bible in America was translated into German, Spanish and several Native American languages before the War of Independence released the new states from the printing monopoly of London. The flow of new American-printed Bibles after an initial slow start (not unlike its publishing history in London) quickly became a flood. The American printing presses sent their Bibles down the great rivers, and across the plains and the mountain ranges into every corner of what became a Christian continent.

We're told there were almost one hundred presses printing copies of the Bible and the New Testament in America in the last twenty years of the eighteenth century. Just after 1800, a travelling Bible salesman wrote to his publisher: 'I tell you this is the very season and age of the Bible. Bible dictionaries, Bible tales, Bible stories, Bibles plain or paraphrased, Carey's Bibles, Collins's Bibles, Clarke's Bibles, Kimpton's Bibles, no matter what or whose all, all will go down – so wide is the crater of public appetite at this time.' And underpinning all of them was the King James Version. New translations flopped. Even the version of Noah Webster, the phenomenal bestselling dictionary compiler and educator of American children in their spelling and pronunciation, failed to touch the King James Version.

The American Bible Society was founded in 1816. By 1830, it was printing 300,000 Bibles a year at a time when the population was 13 million. By 1991 that had gone up to 2,283,000 in a population of 252.8 million.

There was so much new and daunting about the American experience, so much heroic and cruel, violent, severe and unexpected, that it would be rash to claim too much for a book in this often wild landscape. But substantial evidence is there, in the multitude of the small churches, in the roving preachers and the often rabid prayer meetings. There is widespread proof that the Bible was cleaved to for its confirmation of a faith often profoundly felt and followed, a source of wisdom and morality. But also it provided a justification for the very opposite of what Christ stood for. The devil's work was given scriptural authority

too. It could and it did champion the causes of two wholly opposite sides in the most bitter conflicts – as it had done on the Civil
War battlefields of Britain and would do so over and again around
the English-speaking empires. This was nowhere more vivid than
in the arguments and often vicious struggles over slavery which
has a chapter of its own.

The main point here is that the King James Version both ate
into and fed American society from slaves to entrepreneurial
emperors of capitalism. The writers of the time were often as
much part of that movement as the society they wrote about. In
hymns and constant new settings of the Psalms, in sentimental
music hall, in popular sheet music, in biblically inspired ballads
printed in their hundreds and thousands, the Bible was present.
The most frequently requested sheet music title was 'My Mother's
Bible'.

This Bible sowed and reaped much of the culture of the first
centuries of Anglo-America. The writers affirmed all of that in
their scriptures of poetry and fiction.

'Call me Ishmael.' This, it could be argued, is the most dramatic
opening remark in fiction. He is named Ishmael after the son born
to Abraham and the slave girl Hagar who is exiled by Abraham's
wife Sarah after she herself gave birth. Every reader of *Moby-Dick*
would be expected to know who Ishmael was. Herman Melville's
epic adventure is open to the double and entwined interpretation
as a re-telling of the Old Testament story of the Ark and the
pursuit of evil by good men; and also the key myth of this new
country's view of itself – forever pushing on, ceaselessly seeking
Canaan, finding the promised land, and when that ran out, on still
to conquer the ocean and, finally, space itself.

Billy Budd, in my view Melville's finest work, can be interpreted as a Christ-like figure set on his own path to crucifixion.

The story of Christ's birth, journey and death has engaged writers for centuries and it still does. It has been woven into hundreds of stories, adapted, used, abused, an apparently endless seam for re-imagining. Sometimes this story is used approvingly; sometimes with mockery or criticism.

Melville saw the Bible in another seminal American author, the author of *The Scarlet Letter*, Nathaniel Hawthorne. 'Certain it is . . .' Melville wrote, '. . . that this great power of blackness in him derives its force from its appeal to that Calvinistic sense of Innate Depravity and Original Sin, from whose visitation, in some shape or other, no deeply thinking mind is always wholly free . . . Perhaps no writer has ever wielded this terrific thought with greater terror than . . . Hawthorne.'

The Scarlet Letter is taken from the story of David and Bathsheba in the Book of Samuel. And within the novel, Hester and Dimmesdale closely parallel Adam and Eve. There is sin, suffering, expulsion and the awareness of damning Knowledge.

It is sometimes difficult to know whether the writers who so freely 'use' the Bible do so for opportunistic or devout reasons. Is the Bible convenient or is it so mythic and full of such spiritual possibilities and unconscious forces that it is a magnet for writers? Are they being ironic as well as re-expressing what is boldly stated as 'true' in the Bible?

The words quoted from Melville that most intrigue me are 'from whose visitation, in some shape or other, no deep thinking mind is always wholly free'. The Bible is seen to provide the ultimate insights into life: by implication it soars above philosophy as an explanation of what obtains in the world. It is not only a prime source of stories and proverbs and moral wisdom, its followers believe that it holds the ultimate, if as yet unprovable key to why we are the way we are.

Its influence stretches from the stern and literary work of

Melville and Hawthorne to equally biblically grained books largely unrated by the critics but taken to their hearts by millions. A good example is General Lew Wallace's *Ben Hur*, in 1880. Wallace received a letter of thanks from the White House, Sears and Roebuck alone printed a million copies, touring dramas took it to the stage, chariots, horses and all, and the twentieth century dug two blockbuster films out of it.

It was simplistic and bombastic and sentimental but it told part of the Christian story with verve and excitement and for that it was loved. This book/film/drama and others like it have been accused of being vulgar – and so they are, if by 'vulgar' we mean tailored to mass appeal, even a lowest common denominator. But there is plenty of appeal to the lowest common denominator in the New Testament. And there is no evidence that the non-vulgar are, morally, any 'better' than their so-called 'inferiors'. *Ben Hur* is not Hawthorne nor is it Melville nor can it ever be given the intense and layered respect or interest of those two classic authors. But it had its impact; it rode the Bible and it shows us how ready so many are to be as seduced by biblical fiction as they are by the Gospels themselves.

William Faulkner, Nobel Prize winner, is ambivalent and ironic about the biblical stories he uses. *Absalom, Absalom!* is based on the story of Absalom, son of King David. Absalom murders his half-brother in order to seduce his sister Tamar. As well as this dramatic context, critics have pointed out that the book is packed with biblical references, from Adam and Eve to David and Goliath to a mirroring of the Creation story. Faulkner's prose, which could sometimes be said to play off the King James Version like jazz, is, I think, a clinching factor in the appropriation of the Bible stories. *A Fable, The Sound and the Fury, As I Lay Dying* – these and others of his books take off from biblical drama. Faulkner needed this to unlock the contemporary drama he described.

The King James Version united American and British writers, underpinning a wide and often rather unexpected cast of writers. 'From earliest years, right into manhood,' wrote D.H. Lawrence, 'like any other nonconformist child, I had the bible poured every day into my helpless consciousness, till there came almost a saturation point. Long before one could think or even vaguely understand, this bible language, these "portions" of the Bible were *douched* over the mind and consciousness till they became soaked in, they became an influence which affected all the processes of emotion and thought.' This is a perfect description of the experience of hundreds of thousands educated in Christian schools over the last 150 years.

Lawrence, perhaps more than any writer since John Bunyan, had the Bible under his skin. But whereas Bunyan had devoted himself to it and walked in its path, Lawrence was forever attacking and tearing it down. He could not let it alone. He mocked the stories, he dismissed God, he assailed the morality of Christ, he played games with it, he was apocalyptic and sometimes he was tender with it. Perhaps he wrote more truly than he knew when he wrote that it had 'soaked in'.

The power of some of his prose, as in the long opening passage of *The Rainbow*, is spellbound by rhythms which are extracted from the best of Tyndale. And not only the rhythms. The sense of a life of devotion and worship. Even though the devotion and worship is to the land and to work it carries, to me, echoes of and achings for the fraternity of the Chosen. Yet there is also a paganism there, a note which may show the influence of Nietzsche and the anti-Christian thinkers to whom he gave head room. Lawrence confessed that one of the 'real joys of middle age' was 'coming back to the bible' and putting it back into 'its living connexions . . . as a book of the human race instead of a corked-up bottle of "inspiration"'. And there was certainly throughout Lawrence a sense of the sacredness of life and the holiness of all living things which must find its roots in the anointing with words to which the boy Lawrence was subjected so persistently in the black pit village set inside the glorious Edenic countryside which was his escape.

The following comes from the opening chapter of *The Rainbow*, with a vision which, without the King James Version, would not have been possible:

> So the Brangwens came and went without fear of necessity. Working hard because of the life that was in them, not for want of the money. Neither were they thriftless. They were aware of the last halfpenny, and instinct made them not waste the peeling of their apple, for it would help to feed the cattle. But leaves and earth were teeming around them, and how should this cease? They felt the rush of the sap in the spring, they knew the wave that cannot halt, but every year thrusts forward the seed to begetting, and, falling back, leaves a young-born on the earth. They knew the entrance between heaven and earth, sunshine drawn into the breast and the bowels, the rain sucked up in the daytime, nakedness that comes under the wind in autumn, showing the bird's nest no longer worth hiding. Their life and inter-relations were such; feeling the pulse and body of the soil, that opened to their furrow for the grain, and became smooth and supple after their ploughing and clung to their feet with a weight that pulled like desire, lying hard and unresponsive when the crops were to be shorn away . . .

And on Lawrence would go until the end of his brief life. Almost at the very end he wrote about the nonconformist preachers in the coal-mining chapels of his childhood, of their possession by the Lord, their joy in the Book of Revelation, their use of the language of the Bible to explain and to rant and rail, for power and for pity.

It is argued that the power of the King James Version was broken, like much else, as a result of the First World War, and certainly there was a sea change. Yet the pulse of its language and the incantation of a seductive mystery still moved in the poetry. Alfred Noyes wrote, drawing on the Book of Revelation:

> When the great reveille sounds
> For the terrible last Sabbath,
> All the legions of the dead shall hear the trumpet ring!

David Jones, with Isaac Rosenberg the greatest of the First World War poets, in his magnificent book *In Parenthesis* based on his own experiences in the war, writes simply how:

> The official service was held in the field: there they had spread a Union Jack on piled biscuit tins, behind the 8 in siege, whose regular discharges made it inaudible, the careful artistry of the prayers he read.
>
> He preached from Matthew text, of how He cares for us above the sparrows. The medical officer undid, and did up again, the fastener of his left glove behind his back, throughout the whole discourse. They sang 'Onward Christian Soldiers' for the closing hymn.

Between 1914 and 1918 it's been calculated that about '40 million religious tracts, prayer books, bibles and hymn books were distributed to British servicemen'. There were many stories of Bibles in breast pockets stopping bullets as in the Civil War. Despite the carnage and the powerful sense of an uncaring or indifferent or a cruel God, the Bible stayed in the front line. Edmund Blunden, Edward Thomas, Ivor Gurney, Robert Graves and Wilfred Owen are just some of the poets using, raiding the

Bible for stories to help illustrate what they saw and felt, to give undercurrents of religion – whether supportive or critical.

The Bible was used to notably subversive effect in the Wilfred Owen poem based on Abraham and Isaac (Genesis xxii, 1–18):

> So Abram rose, and clave the wood, and went,
> And took the fire with him, and a knife.
> And as they sojourned both of them together,
> Isaac the first-born spake and said, My Father,
> Behold the preparation, fire and iron,
> But where the lamb for this burnt-offering?
> Then Abram bound the youth with belts and straps,
> And builded parapets and trenches there,
> And stretchèd forth the knife to slay his son.
> When lo! an Angel called him out of heaven,
> Saying, Lay not thy hand upon the lad,
> Neither do anything to him, thy son.
> Behold! Caught in a thicket by its horns,
> A Ram. Offer the Ram of Pride instead.
> But the old man would not so, but slew his son,
> And half the seed of Europe, one by one.

It might have been thought that after the carnage of the First World War and the evil of the Second World War, writers might quit the Bible. Its transcendental promises and its Psalms and proverbs could seem to be redundant. Yet out of the slaughter in Flanders, the mass deaths and the Holocaust, came not only questionings and angry disavowals, but still the Bible was used as an affirmation. John Steinbeck is a prime example.

I read John Steinbeck in my early teens. I think I began with *Cannery Row* and *Of Mice and Men* – books which could not then be read often enough. I was coming towards the end of a childhood and adolescence of intense Christianity, soaked in guilt, but also alert to a goodness in life that surely ought to win through. *The Grapes of Wrath*, the novel that clinched Steinbeck's Nobel Prize, all but hypnotised me. It revealed, in imagination, both characters and a situation with which I could totally identify. It also, I realised then, carried a Christian socialism which brought grave charges against the operating powers in society.

The title is taken from 'The Battle Hymn of the Republic':

Mine eyes have seen the glory of the coming of the Lord:
He is trampling out the vintage where the grapes of wrath are stored;

But there is a deeper reference – to the Book of Revelation:

> Thrust in thy sharp sickle, and gather the clusters of the vine of the earth; for her grapes are fully ripe. And the Angel thrust in his sickle into the earth, and gathered the vine of the earth, and cast it into the great winepress of the wrath of God . . .

There is a direct reference to this at the end of chapter 25 as the poor, flailing to cross the dust bowl of America, begin to starve.

> And in the eyes of the hungry there's a growing wrath. In the souls of the people, the grapes of wrath are filling and growing heavy, growing heavy for the vintage.

J. Paul Hunter has published a detailed analysis of *The Grapes of Wrath* in relation to the Bible. The connections are numerous. They demonstrate that Steinbeck believed in the biblical stories as an effective and profound enabler of his fiction. He believed they would give his own story a far wider resonance. He must have thought also that some of his readers would recognise the references and be moved on a different level to that obtained by non-religious, non-spiritual fiction.

Hunter points out that the novel is in three parts, like the Exodus account of Israel: Captivity, Journey, the Promised Land. The Joad family is yoked to that of the Hebrews – to the degree that there are twelve of them (the twelve tribes of Israel) embarked on a truck (their Ark) for the journey across the wastelands. 'The rest swarmed up on top of the load, Connie and Rose of Sharon, Pa and Uncle John, Ruthie and Winfield, Tom and the preacher. Noah stood on the ground looking up at the great load of them sitting on top of the truck.' There are allusions to Lot's wife (Grandpa's character), to Ananias and Moses, and to Jim Casey as a Christ figure.

In his novel *East of Eden*, there are even more parallels. The story of Cain and Abel in Genesis is the key: 'And Cain went out from the presence of the Lord and dwelt in the land of Nod on the East of Eden.' The correspondences between Cain and Abel and Steinbeck's Caleb and Aaron are undisguised and numerous.

One of the bold and moving characteristics of these books is that Steinbeck sees the sacred figures of the Old and New Testaments in the life of the poor, often what would be called the 'white trash'. He sees the divine in the ordinary and in the dispossessed and he has no hesitation in plunging into that association. His Christianity and his socialism both feed his fiction and they are intermingled.

Rather more unexpectedly, F. Scott Fitzgerald's masterpiece and a work of genius, *The Great Gatsby*, has been analysed in Christian terms.

Gatsby is seen again and again as a Christ-figure. 'He was a son of God – a phrase which, if it means anything, means just that – and he must be about His Father's business.' Much play is made of Gatsby's wedding with the parable of the wedding feast in the

Bible and the lack of guests. The narrator writes of the strangers at Gatsby's wedding, called in to make up a crowd, people Gatsby did not know. His funeral, too, is, like the death of Christ on the Cross, attended only by two women.

Another Nobel Prize winner, William Golding, was a classicist and something of a pagan, but the Bible infuses what for me are his two strongest books, *The Spire* and *Lord of the Flies*.

The Spire is the story of the building of a medieval cathedral. It is based on the construction of Salisbury Cathedral. Golding taught in Salisbury Cathedral School and lived for much of his life within easy driving distance of that tremendous slender spire, such weight and elegance raised on such treacherous ground. Golding takes the business of the building, the technical problems, the ingenuity, the labour, and reinforces it with the primitive faith of his protagonist, who sees it as a sign for God, a miracle in stone. If this great mass can be raised on such unsuitable marshland, then God exists. It becomes a test of the power of God and the novel is as passionate about direct prayer and the probability of its being answered as any of the Old Testament prophets.

The title *Lord of the Flies* is a literal translation of 'Baal-Zebub', the old Canaanite god of evil. Though there are no direct connections, *Lord of the Flies* contains echoes and parallels which come from a Bible which Golding knew well.

The island itself is a Garden of Eden until the fall of the formerly innocent – choirboys in this instance – brings evil into the human equation. There is a 'snake-thing', a parallel with the snake that tempted Eve. Simon, the boy who is killed by the other boys, is a representation of Jesus Christ. And Golding's use of the word 'beast' is rooted in the Book of Revelation. Golding 'uses' the King James Version to layer his novel, and uses parts of it which are more from the New Testament than the Old. It is still sufficiently potent in the mind of this often despairing classicist. He reaches out for it. In that sense it remains a support, even a necessary foundation.

From Walt Whitman, who saw the 1860 edition of *Leaves of Grass* as 'the great Construction of the New Bible', to John Updike, who takes on Protestant rigour, ambition and guilt in many of his novels, to Cormac McCarthy's *The Road* almost 150 years later, the King James Bible has not ceased to play a major part in American and much of English-speaking literature. It would be possible to rummage around and find so many other examples: C.S. Lewis, Emily Dickinson, Dylan Thomas, Gerard Manley Hopkins, Christina Rossetti, G.K. Chesterton, Oscar Wilde, Elizabeth Bishop, Rudyard Kipling, Margaret Atwood, Wallace Stevens, Mark Twain. These writers take what the Bible said as sufficient, if not gospel, as words and possibilities if not prophecies and certainties, but are still beguiled, even a little bewitched by it. Or they use it – to challenge as well as to affirm, full of ready-made subjects with the convenience of being widely known. Even if, as in Thomas Hardy's *The Oxen* it is at a meditative, wistful distance, a trace memory.

> Christmas Eve, and twelve of the clock
> 'Now they are all on their knees,'
> An elder said as we sat in a flock
> By the embers in hearthside ease.
>
> We pictured the meek mild creatures where
> They dwelt in their strawy pen,
> Nor did it occur to one of us there
> To doubt they were kneeling then.
>
> So fair a fancy few would weave
> In these years! Yet, I feel,
> If someone said on Christmas Eve,
> 'Come: see the oxen kneel,

In the lonely barton by yonder coomb
Our childhood used to know',
I should go with him in the gloom,
Hoping it might be so.

And for the poet regarded as seminal to the twentieth century, T.S. Eliot, and the novelist who has brought the world of the deep spiritual adventure of the Afro-Americans into fiction, Toni Morrison, both Nobel Prize winners, there is still a felt truth. Despite generations of sound and fury against the King James Version and despite the disproofs and pinpoint dismissals, the Bible to them is still the Word of God.

T.S. Eliot, American poet-philosopher, is an extraordinary tribute to the lasting influence of the King James Bible and his private embrace of Anglicanism. He stationed himself in London for the greater length of his life, where he worked as a banker and then as a publisher. His heroes included the committee, especially Launcelot Andrewes, who had finally steered the Bible into the harbour of the King James Version.

T.S. Eliot is regarded as an icon of modernism. Somehow, the poetry of such a man ought to be post-religious, not as utterly steeped in the King James Version and in Anglicanism as is much of the work of T.S. Eliot. And his great rival, W.H. Auden, was no less devoted to the Anglican Church and its book.

Eliot was a true believer and an explorer of the spiritual meanings to be gleaned from Christianity. He came from New England nonconformist stock. He converted to Anglicanism and became a regular churchgoer in his adopted city, London. In 1934 he became Warden of the Church of St Stephen, a post he held until 1959. He supervised the collection during Mass. He went on retreats, confessed his sins and received absolution. How strange this must have seemed to many of his contemporaries – increasingly secular, indifferent or atheistic – and to his increasingly secular successors that Christianity and the Anglican religion and its sacred language and Catholic practices played such a crucial part in his life and in his imagination.

Surely this great twentieth-century Modernist poet could not be bound up in it in the same way as John Donne, a poet in whose lifetime the King James Bible was published? To continue in that vein in the sceptical, war-worn, scientifically triumphant twentieth century seems such an anachronism. Yet far from being an anachronism, T.S. Eliot was and remains the sounding poet of the century, his 'message' as relevant to the age as his techniques and essays which have helped substantially to shape its literary style and tone.

He reached back to the King James Version in many ways: for words and sentences, for images, but above all, I think, for the meditative melancholy he found there, for the room to brood over mysteries without being mangled in the new philosophy. It might be more simple. It might be that he sincerely believed in Christ, in the Trinity, in the Resurrection, in a life eternal, in an Almighty God – and used his great gift to celebrate, explore and attempt to describe it. The fact and the results of his faith need to be reckoned with.

At times, in *Ash Wednesday*, *Four Quartets* and in *Little Gidding*, it seems that everything he writes – however powdered with past cultures – glides on a current of Anglicanism. As if all of it was composed in an English country churchyard, the graves, the few tilting tombstones and the ancient and sturdy little church were the perfect, in truth the only, context.

A seemingly simple example, 'Journey of the Magi', is in a rather different category but it serves to illustrate two points: Eliot's unstrained commitment to the story of the Three Wise Men, and the ease with which he played it into the musings so characteristic of him.

He begins in such a practical way that you could think – you *are* to think – that this was a well-reported, historically accurate journey and what is being said is a matter-of-fact, trustworthy account.

> 'A cold coming we had of it,
> Just the worst time of the year
> For a journey, and such a long journey:
> The ways deep and the weather sharp,
> The very dead of winter.'
> And the camels galled, sore-footed, refractory,
> Lying down in the melting snow . . .
> A hard time we had of it.
> At the end we preferred to travel all night,
> Sleeping in snatches,
> With the voices singing in our ears, saying
> That this was all folly.

'Realistically' grumbling, tentative, there is neither vanity nor vainglory – Eliot leads us expertly into this story from the Gospels of Matthew and Luke and makes it new without yielding a centimetre of its flat factual truth.

A few lines later, the voice of the poet changes

> . . . were we led all that way for
> Birth or Death? There was a Birth, certainly,
> We had evidence and no doubt. I had seen birth and death,
> But had thought they were different; this Birth was
> Hard and bitter agony for us, like Death, our death.

It is impossible to think that Eliot was simply 'looking for a subject from the Bible' as so many others, legitimately, had done down the centuries. The King James Version inspired his prose: the faith it denoted inspired his thinking: the story of Christ and what He promised inspired some of the finest poetry of the century.

He even, like Milton, rewrote the very opening of Genesis in his chorus *The Rock*.

> In the beginning God created the world. Waste and Void.
>   Waste and Void. And darkness was upon the face of the deep.
> And when there were men, in their various ways, they
>   struggled in torment towards God.
> Blindly and vainly, for man is a vain thing, and man without
>   God is a seed upon the wind . . .

Like T.S. Eliot, Toni Morrison won the Nobel Prize for litera-ture. Her prose comes, in part, from the Gospel tradition begun in slave-America and turned into song both in the singing and in the speech. *Song of Solomon* seems an inevitable title for a novel by Toni Morrison, as does *Beloved*: 'this is my beloved son in whom I am well pleased.' In Morrison's *Beloved* the son becomes a daugh-ter, resurrected into the life that had been ripped away from her, reincarnated and 'seen' and accepted back in her home after the long absence.

There is actual Bible preaching in the book, the unmistakable Bible preaching/talking honed by the slave experience and the liberation from that experience. Souls join up and inhabit the bodies of those who are in a mutual circle of holy love. There is an omnipotent aura of the mystery of things and a belief that the key to that is to be discovered in biblical language. It all but beggars belief that after all the pounding it has taken, the King James Version is still a source for such great imaginative writers today.

CHAPTER FIFTEEN
THE EIGHTEENTH-CENTURY
ENLIGHTENMENT

The 'Enlightenment' traditionally describes a time when thought is considered to have come out of medieval religious darkness. This new thought is generally taken to be driven by reason, motivated by scientific enquiry and in its early stages dedicated to throwing off what were seen as the shackles of religious bondage. This Enlightenment, among a small number of scholars, was in place in the British Isles by the end of the seventeenth century: soon afterwards it was present in intellectual circles in America and throughout what we now know as Europe.

Despite being apparently vanquished in the Enlightenment century of tournaments of competing systems of thought, the Bible survived. In many ways it was even more influential in the nineteenth century than ever before and still today it is not without intellectual and artistic significance. Moreover, it was against the Scriptures, as revealed to the English-speaking world from the King James Bible, that these competing systems had to fight in order to flourish.

In that sense, the Bible served a vital purpose. It was the whetstone and the essential opposition. Where would the Enlightenment have been without it? It enabled arguments to be developed and provoked them because its domain was so vast and self-contradictory. A new orthodoxy of thought, reason, gained a purchase on thoughts and systems which its apostles considered to be not only superior to the Bible, but to supersede it and render it obsolete. At the very least the Bible provided an essential negative dynamic for the birth and progress of the Enlightenment.

Moreover, though the Enlightenment is now considered to have swept away any intelligent claims for the Bible that has not proved to be the case with everyone. Great congregations still attend churches and chapels and meeting houses and prayer meetings unfazed by the news from the intellectuals on high that the day of the Bible is doomed. Theologians, artists, teachers, philanthropists, politicians, men and women in many professions, including the sciences, and ordinary people in their millions continued to keep faith and draw intelligent comfort as well as spiritual satisfaction from the ancient Scriptures.

Yet the Enlightenment did change the landscape in which, for centuries, the Bible had been supreme and unchallenged. It had been the sum of the human knowledge of the human condition, its history, its eternal promise and its purpose. By the sixteenth century, Christianity had long ago gathered monopolistic strength through the Roman Catholic Church. It had absorbed paganism, tamed, though not eradicated, superstition, and in holy crusades savagely and bloodily defined itself against what it saw as heretics or non-believers or followers of other threatening, competitive creeds.

The Roman Catholic Church covered its territory under a canopy which was as pervasive as the atmosphere. Some see this as a time of darkness, bigotry, ignorance, injustice, prejudice, cruelty, authoritarian excess and enforced intellectual stagnation. Others find great beauty there, deep comfort and occasional ecstasy, an order of things and people which makes perfect sense in what they see as a spiritually purposed world. They see the Roman Catholic supremacy, despite its failings, as an era of truth, the one Church as a keeper of the keys to salvation, unflinching at the harshness of the narrow path to that glorious destination.

There had been disputes within the Roman Catholic Church, and later with and inside the Protestant Church. There had been divisions and revisions. But little to compare with the force of change and threat brought in by the Enlightenment with its insistence on a totally new world: a world based not on faith, not on good works, not on ancient Scriptures but on the unchallengeable power of reason.

In his book *'Religion' and the Religions in the English Enlightenment*, Peter Harrison claims that it was in England, in the seventeenth century, that 'the groundwork was laid' for the Enlightenment. 'The Religious upheavals of the 16th and 17th century,' he writes, 'meant that Englishmen enjoyed a freedom of religious experience which was matched nowhere in Europe with the possible exception of the Netherlands.' And, as the philosopher Locke wrote, the kings and queens of post-Reformation England had been 'of such different minds in point of religion that no sincere and upright worshipper of God could, with a safe conscience, obey their several decrees'.

In the sixteenth century, under Henry VIII you were expected to be a faithful Roman Catholic and after his divorce an Anglican Protestant; under King Edward VI, a Protestant; under Queen Mary, a Roman Catholic; under Elizabeth I, a Protestant; under James I, a Presbyterian in Scotland and an Anglican in England; under Charles I, an Anglo-Catholic; under Cromwell, a Presbyterian; under Charles II, an indifferent Anglican; under James II, Roman Catholic. So where was guidance from the monarch?

One starting point is once again with the lawyer, politician, essayist and natural philosopher, Francis Bacon. The fruitful and scandalous last phase of his life was contemporaneous with the publication of the King James Bible. He spoke of the two books of life – the one to be read in nature, the other in the Scriptures. 'The one, that which springeth from reason, sense, induction, argument, according to the laws of heaven and earth; the other, that which is imprinted upon the spirit of man by inward instinct, according to the law of conscience.'

As Pope was to write in the eighteenth century: 'The State of Nature was the State of God'.

Both nature and the Scriptures were to be tested. As the centuries rolled on, nature proved increasingly boundless, enlarged and empowered by being tested: the Scriptures were found increasingly vulnerable and frail, needing more and more faith. But the space for faith was still defended.

It was a time of major shifts in society in the English-speaking and other worlds. The Reformation introduced the astonishing and liberating idea that the Bible could be read by an individual who could have their own 'discussion' with it. The Bible in the vernacular – German, Italian, French, but, as it proved, most influentially, English – meant that control had passed out of the power of the priesthood.

The Renaissance retrieved classical learning from Greece and Rome which had achieved glories without Christianity. The navigational compass and an urge to trade brought other religions firmly on to the scene. How were they to be dealt with? Was Christianity the major, the supreme religion or just one of many? Were the others Saved? *Could* they be Saved?

The blunter young bloods of the new experimental sciences whetted their mental appetites on crunching the Bible. It was a tempest: looking back, the Middle Ages seemed an inland lake of calm compared with the storms out on the high seas of the new knowledge. For some English speakers the King James Bible was the Ark, for others it was the wreckage.

The questions intensified. What did religion itself come from? The Greeks believed it had begun in man's fear. Fear was certainly core to the Catholic project. Sin and be damned. What is sin? We will decide. Dare it be suggested that it was man-made? Voltaire, the epitome of the eighteenth-century French Enlightenment, asserted that 'if God did not exist it would be necessary to invent him.' The two arguments brought in to support religion were reason and nature: reason which grew in authority in this period was increasingly thought to be on the side of nature. Yet, in its fight to hold its ground, the Church scholars in England in the seventeenth century and subsequently held to the words of the theologian Benjamin Whichcote that 'Reason *discovers* what is Natural; and Reason *receives* what is Supernatural' (my italics). The supernatural still had its place.

Whichcote hailed back to Plato who wrote that reason was man's highest faculty *because* it corresponded to divine reason. For Defenders of Faith in the King James Bible this was a classic knockout to petty post-Platonist opponents. Plato was the great fountain of philosophy and to be able to call on him was to have a majestic ally in the battle to save what the guardians of the faith saw as the survival of their God-given Scriptures.

Then there was the mire of whether those of faiths other than Christianity should be allowed to enter the Kingdom of Heaven. Culverwell, a contemporary of Whichcote, wrote: 'I am farre from the minds of those Patrons of Universal Grace, that make all men equal in propinquity to salvation, whether Jews or pagans or Christians.'

He points out the privilege of the Christian that 'God planted thee in a place of light, when he shut up and imprisoned the world in palpable darkenesse.' Once again the King James Bible was used as a shield to protect the Protestant believer from the spears of the gathering hordes.

And as the Protestants were driven back, they still found what they believed to be sure footholds. Their innate faith and the God-given conscience were argued to be superior to deduction. The traditions and authority which were being so battered by the growing attacks on the accuracy of the Bible and its relevance to the natural world were still claimed to have greater authority than all that reason could offer.

Protestants who saw themselves as the saviours of the faith were well capable of rational argument but in facing this onslaught from the Enlightenment, they found their redoubt in the idea of inner strength. This was the strength of a belief which was beyond examination but available to the senses: an experience rather than a thought, felt and not, finally, wholly available to reason.

The Bible, long regarded as the sole and perfect history of humankind, was beginning to buckle. The greatest of all the Fathers of the Church, St Augustine, in 'The City of God', in the fifth century, states that the 'fable . . . of the Antipodes' as 'on no ground credible'. That 'it is too absurd to suppose that some men might have taken ship and traversed the whole wide ocean', and that Scripture is never wrong. But by the mid-seventeenth century, it was embarrassingly apparent that Augustine was wrong on both these claims. The sacred text was not infallible. And what did the discovery of America and its Indians say about the story of Adam and Eve, the enclosed Garden of Eden, when over a vast ocean men had discovered another sort of paradise – inhabited?

Harrison quotes Hans Frei who, he says:

correctly characterises the different role which biblical history was to assume in the 18th century when he observes that 'It is no exaggeration to say that all across the theological spectrum the great reversal had taken place; interpretation was a matter of fitting the biblical story into another world with another story rather than interpreting that world into a biblical story.' There were other worlds now, there were other stories, other religions; the great book of faith for the English-speaking peoples was under siege.

Its use and its purpose could appear to have come to an end. The weapon of destruction, of course, was a book, by the leading star in the constellation of the Scottish Enlightenment, David Hume. In 1757, he wrote *The Natural History of Religion*. Hume seems to put the cap on it. All religions, he implied, were no more than made or socially constructed artefacts based on acceptable superstitions. For Hume, there was no primary religious sentiment or predisposition.

He went back to the early Greeks who saw religion as best accounted for by the need to explain natural phenomena: thunder, lightning, storms, famine, plague, death – all, in days of limited natural science, most satisfyingly explained by imagining gods 'up in the sky' venting their wrath and, less often, displaying some kindness at the antics of mere humans. Hume wrote that 'polytheism was the primary religion of man'.

Reason, Hume argued, played no role in the development of religion. The origin of religion could be explained fully in 'natural', non-religious instincts – primarily fear and the 'universal tendency among mankind to conceive all beings like themselves, and to transfer to every object, those qualities with which they are familiarly acquainted, and of which they are intimately conscious'. In short, God was no more than a human father blown up to gigantic size and significance by fallible human beings who, at that stage, needed a simple explanation for complicated phenomena.

For many intellectuals religion was all over. Yet, in a quite extraordinary comeback, the full power of the King James Bible was yet to be unleashed.

The slow-motion crunch of ideas which rolled through Europe and America from the Reformation until the French Revolution was a time when thought and belief and society's view of itself began on a journey of constant change which continues to this day. The King James Bible played many parts. It would be thought to be the stopper in the spring which, once removed by Hume and others, let flow a waterfall of liberated ideas. It could also be seen as a chameleon, forever changing its shape and its character to the demands of the time, or even the good shepherd, still guiding the new flocks though often unseen by them.

It was not only an intellectual debate. There were the deeper economic causes for the growth of the Enlightenment which would become seismic when a cluster of unschooled men largely in the north of England invented what could be claimed to be the greatest of all the world revolutions – the Industrial Revolution. All these men were nonconformist Bible believers.

But there were always strong intellectual currents as the peoples of Europe, particularly in Britain, and then in America, saw the well of humanist scholarship. This inspired opposition from the Christians. New Christian literature was opened up: esoteric writing from hermetic books, Neoplatonic writings and the Jewish Cabbala attracted the minds of those who saw another route by which the mystery of life could be apprehended.

It was optimistic. Newton, among others, spent as much time and energy on Cabbalistic and other esoteric lore as he did on the study of mathematics. It was an awesome rearguard spectacle: this attempt to dig out the rare minerals from the past, not lose them, but turn them into gold while at the same time staring at a rational future head-on, both amazed and half blinded by what the sum and the sun of it promised.

The importance of the Jews and Judaism to all of this is great. Were there several routes to Enlightenment? The old Book of Books was their book first. Their scholars refined their minds on disputations on the Pentateuch and the prophets; their poets on the psalmists.

In 1492 the Jews suffered what has been described as their greatest single disaster since the destruction of Jerusalem in AD 70 when they were expelled from the Iberian Peninsula. Settling in different countries, forging their own communities, some converting to Christianity for survival, others stubborn and magnificent in their fidelity, they were always a strong presence. This was most clearly seen in the work of Benedict de Spinoza, son of a Portuguese Jewish merchant in Amsterdam who, according to Diarmaid MacCulloch, had by the age of twenty-three 'already questioned some of the basic principles of all Judaic religions: the prospect of immortality for human beings and the intervention of God in human affairs'. For this, in 1656, he was expelled from his synagogue in Amsterdam. But his ideas spread across Europe: he spoke for a new time. Sacred texts to him were 'human artefacts', writes MacCulloch: 'venerable religious institutions were "relics of man's ancient bondage". The whole argument of the work was disposed to promote human freedom.'

'The supreme mystery of despotism,' wrote Spinoza, 'its principal story, is to keep men in a state of deception, and with the specious title of religion, to cloak the fear by which they must be held in check, so that they will fight for their servitude as if for salvation, and count it no shame, but the highest honour, to spend their blood and their lives for the glorification of one man.' A later Jewish writer would describe religion as 'the opium of the people'.

The beat of liberty was strengthened and that became part of a mix in which, ironically, the King James Bible played a major role. It is one of the remarkable properties of this book that it was at one time a supporter of grim and cruel authoritarianism and at another a key begetter of democracy, a flagship for liberationists.

Spinoza's work is considered to be one of the leading causes of the recent widely publicised re-emergence of atheism.

Thomas Hobbes, at about the same time as Spinoza, brutally attacked the Holy Trinity, undermined Christian doctrine and demolished the claims of the clergy. His work, too, went into the melting pot of a theological battle of ideas which was to determine the character of the modern age.

It is useful to emphasise both how important the Bible was throughout the Enlightenment but also how comprehensively it was attacked. Perhaps the latter fortified the former. Did its enemies give it strength? In 1719 there appeared in print a pamphlet written thirty years before, but considered too outrageous to allow to be read by a wider readership. Called *Treatise of the Three Impostors*, it claimed, wrongly, to have been written by Spinoza. It certainly plagiarised his ideas and those of Thomas Hobbes. It indicted Moses, Jesus Christ and Mohammed as the three 'impostors'. All three of their faiths were condemned. It said: 'there are no such things in Nature as either God or Devil or Soul or Heaven or Hell . . . The Religious . . . are all of them except for some few ignorant dunces . . . people of villainous principles, who maliciously abuse and impose on the credulous populace.' A view sometimes echoed today and in no less strident terms.

The author might have been an exiled French Huguenot. As well as radical Jews, some of the Huguenot thinkers were in the vanguard of the attack on the roots of religion. What is new here, in *The Three Impostors*, is that Judaism, Christianity and Islam are being lumped together in order to be dismissed with one blow.

All the 'Children of Abraham' were impostors and so were all their works. But it was Christianity and especially the Protestants who took most exception to this attack.

As MacCulloch points out this was part of the 'long process of moving Christian doctrine and practice from the central place in European life which it had enjoyed for more than a millennium, and placing it among a range of personal choices'.

'Choice' was an operative word. The English and the Dutch, in the late seventeenth century, began an exceptional climb to a more general wealth. Their fleets brought back goods from around the world. Manufacturing grew. Prosperity began to be democratised. Having things, possessing luxuries once the preserve of a few aristocrats, and enjoying leisure enabled the ever rising and expanding middle classes to make choices never before available to so many. The Church had been the sole provider of so much: now it was only one of an increasing number. Devotional music, for example, was now performed outside churches and cathedrals and even written to be performed outside the Church – Handel's *Messiah* began life in a Dublin concert hall in 1742. The words, from the King James Bible, still stir millions riding on the music they inspired.

The Protestant Church, like other Christian Churches, appeared to be losing its grip on society and on thinking about society. John Locke, who examined the problems of consciousness, wrote that since the mind 'hath no other immediate object but its own Ideas . . . it is evident that our knowledge is only conversant about *them*' (my italics).

Using the King James Bible, the Protestants fought back. They asserted and through the Scriptures set out to prove that the philosophy which could be sifted from their Bible was fully capable of entering the lists against the rationalists. There was and remains an obstinacy about the truth in the Book of the

Word of God, a truth whose transcendent claims are thought to be 'proven'.

Its history has been devalued; its prophecies proved wrong; its morality contradictory and the abuse of its powers scandalous. Yet, despite the philosophies of Locke and Spinoza, Hobbes and Descartes, despite the German scholars of the nineteenth century's assault on the credibility of the Scriptures, the faithful held to the notion of revelation, the experience of a sensation which will not be explained save by faith. Given the assault of the Enlightenment, the Scriptures, like the core of an army which refuses to surrender, retreated. They were to regroup and return, in the nineteenth century, with greater force than ever before.

And they were not without philosophical allies. Immanuel Kant, for instance, argued that there were vital 'Ideas' beyond the possibility of experience: of these there were three – God, Freedom and Immortality. Not to be reached by reason, he asserted, but through conscience. 'I had to deny knowledge,' he wrote, 'in order to make room for faith.'

Perhaps the truly remarkable thing about the Enlightenment is not that it swept away for ever the King James Bible and all it stood for but that it failed to do so.

CHAPTER SIXTEEN
THE MATTER OF RICHARD DAWKINS:
THE NEW ENLIGHTENMENT

Richard Dawkins is a popular figure in the New Enlightenment – today's continuation of that eighteenth-century movement. He has introduced me to some of the scientific details of the world in a learned and exhilarating manner and I am in his debt. His book *The God Delusion* uses some of that knowledge but takes his Darwinian proselytising zest into the world of religion. The range of his reading deserves respect and his central argument – the case for atheism – is well made. His lack of faith is convincing. His commitment to evangelising his atheist message verges on fundamentalism. He is out for converts. He can be seen as an extension of the Enlightenment, taken to the extreme.

Richard Dawkins takes on virtually all religions from all ages and attacks the root, purpose and meaning of religion itself. *The God Delusion* sets out rational proofs that God never existed and is not necessary. Dawkins's concerns may seem too wide for the subject of this book. How can a mere 400 years in the history of one Bible, the book of one modest vessel of merely one of the world's religions, haul up alongside the Dawkins Armada?

He dwells in epochs and in thousands, sometimes tens of

thousands of years. He swoops into neuroscience, calls up his encounters on the television documentary trail, quotes from a pack of fervent allies – admired and eminent writers, comedians, psychologists and other fellow scientists – acolytes all. A praetorian guard! An alpha team of atheists who, mentioned several times by Dawkins, are from the educated elite of our society and therefore to be looked up to in his implicit intellectual hierarchy.

He preys on anecdotal evidence, often as insubstantial as some of the miracles, and he rather worships statistics with a touching trust in their authority. Now and again he brings us the delight of his primary skills as a world-class populariser of zoology.

For many readers today, Richard Dawkins is the 'noise' about religion. His atheist fundamentalism has set an agenda. Others are hopping on his bandwagon. God and the Bible are once again in the stocks.

In the process, many of the achievements which owe their origins to the King James Bible (achievements alongside its basic purpose of spreading the Protestant religion) have been diminished, or bypassed, or denied. There is now a very fashionable version, some might say a distortion of its history and its impact, which flows from the current ideology of atheism.

In the furious effort to raze religion from the surface of the earth much else – that is to say much that religion generates which is not itself primarily religious – is being unjustly downgraded or ignored. The just and the unjust are lumped together. The only colours are black and white. It is oddly reminiscent of the most crude passage in the Old Testament.

Dawkins has claimed today's religious weather. There is his rather touching faith that all the problems in an area of life probed for meaning for millennia are now and for ever more solved by this new blinding light of atheism. And in the process the earth around those ancient congregations of knowledge has been scorched. I think Dawkins has made himself part of any and all religious debates and discussions, including the impact of the King James Bible.

Einstein, approvingly quoted in *The God Delusion*, wrote: 'I believe in Spinoza's God who reveals himself in the orderly harmony of what exists, and not a God who concerns himself with fates and actions of human beings.' I agree with that, as with his more direct 'The idea of a personal God is quite alien to me and seems even naïve.' But also with 'I am a deeply religious non-believer. This is a somewhat new kind of religion.' I am also impressed by Darwin's statement that his great idea of speciation did not discount the notion of a Creator. And there is still the big unanswered question: where and what was the specific *origin of life*, the first act of replication?

There is also the persistent pursuit of a First Cause which still appears to be elusive. It may be discovered in the tabernacle of mathematics and physics. But at the moment that is not a racing certainty.

Then there is Martin Rees, former President of the Royal Society, Astronomer Royal, and distinguished author of books on astrophysics. He is a believer in the eternal fact that there are mysteries we shall never solve, things we shall never know. I agree with that, too, as with his religious observance. Martin Rees says that he goes to church 'out of loyalty to the tribe'.

Richard Dawkins's total lack of faith is far more straightforward. I sometimes feel that my lack of his lack is little more than an anchor of nostalgia. Is my respect for some of the aspects of Christianity little more than regret for days long gone? Is it 'only' a gravity pull of apparently inexpungable childhood memory and longing? But perhaps the child *is* father to the man and maybe that is even more significant than we give it credit for. What if there *are* things we see and feel and even 'know' in childhood that have truth, are insights that we cannot yet grasp, but fade away as the flesh ages and changes? The words 'perhaps' and 'maybe' must irritate the scalpelled Dawkins. But sometimes the world does seem more 'real' when it is fuzzy. I suppose I always come back to the belief that there is so much that we do *not know* that to close any door is a little hasty.

My chief unease about Richard Dawkins is rooted in his own words. In the section 'Childhood Abuse and the Escape from Religion' he writes about the recent exposures of child abuse in the Church. 'The Roman Catholic church,' he writes, 'has borne a heavy share of such retrospective opprobrium. For all sorts of reasons I dislike the Roman Catholic Church. But I dislike unfairness even more and I can't help wondering whether this one institution has been unfairly demonised over the issue, especially in Ireland and America.' He continues:

> I suppose some additional public resentment flows from the hypocrisy of priests whose professed life is largely devoted to arousing guilt about 'sin'. Then there is the abuse of trust by a figure in authority whom the child has been trained from the cradle to revere. Such additional resentments should make us all the more careful not to rush to judgement. We should be aware of the remarkable power of the mind to concoct false memories especially when abetted by unscrupulous therapists and mercenary lawyers . . . there's gold in them long gone fumbles in the vestry.

I cannot understand how he can or why he does rush away so lightly from the well-documented, widespread, proven and horrifying crimes of child abuse by Roman Catholic priests. It was covered up for years and clearly responsible for the ruin of lives, the pain and trauma visited on young boys and girls raped by the Catholic clergy. Of course, 'the psychologist Elizabeth Loftus' as he explains, has documented 'how easy it is for people to concoct memories that are entirely false'. But surely that is not the main point here. He offers no evidence whatsoever of that being the case with the victims of child rape.

I fear that he wants to deny the full scale and horror of these rapes to raise up his own argument that the Catholic religious vision of hellfire causes more 'long term damage'. He has said the words in the Bible taught to children constitute 'child abuse'. On the same scale as criminal and violent rape? This equalising is worrying. It reveals his lack of understanding at a common-sense level, his lack of proportion – evident elsewhere in his book – and even his lack of basic sympathy. These are relevant to a mind so set against faith. Were these assaults nothing but 'fumbles in the vestry'? An unworthy and insulting snigger from a safe, smug vantage point.

But the most important sentence I pick up in that passage is his assertion: 'I dislike unfairness even more.' I think he is unfair to religion throughout his book.

He is unfairly dismissive of ancient religions, totally fails to contextualise them, shows no historical respect and merely scorns them from our present pinnacle of knowledge (which will surely pass in its time). For instance, writing of the Australian Aboriginal tribes: 'on the one hand aboriginals are superb survivors under conditions that test their practical skills to the utmost.' He is quoting, with approval, Kim Sterelong. Richard Dawkins (in his own words, I presume, as there is no indication they are a quotation) goes on to write: 'the very same peoples who are so savvy about the natural world and how to survive in it simultaneously clutter their minds with beliefs that are palpably false and for which the word "useless" is a generous understatement.'

It is worrying that he does not understand what is really going on. A people, without a tittle of the banks of knowledge available to us now, without access to the information in Newton's generation, in that of Avicenna, the Romans, the Greeks, even as far back as the Babylonians, felt compelled to construct systems which explained the world to them. What now seems to Richard Dawkins, dismissively, as useless 'clutter' was an elaborate fabric based on dreams, intuitions, experiences and hopes – all of them literally stabs in the dark that lay about them. But the dark was what they had. And they made an intricate web of explanation out of it. So it was with so many civilisations who struggled to make sense of the world in times that were without a twig of scientific knowledge. Some of their metaphors were sustaining, ingenious, admirable.

We may, if we want to feel superior, merely scoff at them now. It is not difficult, given our current constellations of information, to dismantle those ancient systems. It is, though, grossly unfair and a lack of intellectual energy and respect to fail to attempt to understand them. Nor would a little sympathy have come amiss.

So – trees were worshipped as were double-breasted mountains, roguish and tyrannical deities feasting in clouded-capped hills and certain animals were declared to be sacred. The ocean was worshipped and so – and most of all – was the sun. Practices naïve to us, in their time served a purpose. It is the purpose which is at the heart of it. Why was it so constantly pursued? Why did it matter so much to peoples to find ways to understand the world? Those are the questions.

Is it all to be written off with a 'clutter' and 'useless'? Is all prehistory just a trivial prologue to what is here presented as the ultimate rather supremacist creeds of atheism and science? If so, the argument needs to be made with rather more than a sideswipe and a sneer. There were questions out there and our ancestors tried to address them with the material to hand.

Where did plagues come from and why? What was death and birth? What came before us, what was to come after us? Why were we here at all? Did thunder mean the anger of the gods and rain their benison or, depending, their drowning fury? I see them as bewildered but brave. Every bit as intelligent as us where it most matters: survival. They would live where we would starve. Should the Aborigines not be venerated for that and their, let us call it religion, accepted for what it was: their explanation?

In an uninterrupted succession, Christianity follows in that tradition. It is itself a compound of many traditions, almost an anthology of religions. It came into history when belief was at least the equal of observed evidence and while that can now be repudiated I see no reason why it cannot be respected and examined for what it was. It was a desperately needed explanation. It provided the essential satisfaction for humankind's innate and intractable rage of curiosity – to know the workings of the world. And obviously very annoyingly for Richard Dawkins, it still does so for many people.

The Aborigines and others like them deserve more than derision, more than hilarity, more than easy superiority, an easy dismissal. They were at a stage: they were us, back then. They flailed around; unlike us, of course.

What happened was that in many cases – in ancient Egypt most spectacularly, but also in Christianity – these imaginings and guesses and profound longings for an answer became institutionalised. The faith system which was often the spine of the knowledge system became the body of the state, the principality, or the monarchical system. The Church turned consoling convictions into stone. The powerful saw another window of opportunity for the exercise of power and moved into the Church. The faith systems were colonised by the engines of societal ambition. The very innocence of faith made it malleable.

But unfair, I think, to mock those early gods and goddesses and saints. The number of Our Ladies (of Fatima, Lourdes, Guadeloupe, Akita, etc., etc.) are roundly scorned by Richard Dawkins. They were real to some people once. Probably people not educated enough to be atheists but still human beings trying to make sense of life or come to peace with it. Yes, they became exploited. And no, their miracles did not take place and their place in an unproved heaven is a chimera. But I think merely to deride and dismiss them is again unfair: rather like stamping on those who cannot defend themselves. A bit like deciding that certain casts of mind are simply not in the same league as that of the alpha-educated atheist and therefore to be ignored. Why not attempt to understand, and point out how new knowledge has made this questionable or obsolete? And why not let people get on with the old ways unsneered at, if they want to, if it's harmless?

In the very paragraph after his gleeful knocking of the Ladies of Lourdes and so on, the author writes: 'How did the Greeks, the Romans and the Vikings cope with such polytheological conundrums? Was Venus just another name for Aphrodite, or were they two distinct goddesses of love? Was Thor with his hammer a manifestation of Wotan, or a separate God? Who cares?'

If anyone ought to care it is a man who has received a brilliant and privileged education, inherited and been encouraged to develop a fine mind, and been deservedly successful in his chosen field: Richard Dawkins. He ought to care about the gods and goddesses of the Greeks, the Romans and the Vikings, if only because all three cultures had a vital and lasting impact on his own civilisation – in language, thought, technology and science. They cared a lot about their gods. All three peoples saw their gods and goddesses as integral to their civilisation. But another swipe is all they get from our twenty-first-century mega man.

The God Delusion is particularly good on the brainwashing of children. But I have a problem here. If parents think that the better way for their children to thrive in their world is to become familiar with that world and be prepared for that world, then what he calls 'brainwashing' can become politic parental guidance. Certainly Richard Dawkins's youthful immersion in Anglicanism to prepare him for a successful Oxford life and an English career appears to have done him no harm at all. He easily cast it off as so many do. Yet he may have picked up some useful tips about the establishment of his day, how to work the system. He may have found his prose improved by contact with the King James Version – Anglicanism might even have left the young Dawkins enhanced.

My book wants to look at what has been neglected: a history that no longer dares to speak its name. A history of positive achievement catalysed by the King James Bible and the Protestant movement.

Richard Dawkins scarcely mentions these. You could argue that in his broad sweep there was not the space for such a diversion as positive thinking. Or that he was writing a polemic, and the gusto and pace of that must not be allowed to stub its toes on stubborn contradictions and awkward facts. And he could say that he did, indeed, refer to the lasting value of the language of the King James Version, but he would, I hope, be honest enough to admit he shovelled it in hurriedly and made no great play of it.

In fact the language is only one great play, only one lasting and enriching unexpected consequence. Would it have appeared without men and women prepared to die for that Bible, to see it burned and to be burned for it, to spend a lifetime's hoarded scholarship on its shape and sentence, would it have happened without that?

These men and women believed in a Sky God, in Eternal Life, in Purgatory, in the Resurrection, in the Virgin Mary. And these men produced the King James Version. Perhaps the one could not have come about without the other and at the very least that should be acknowledged and its root causes investigated carefully.

Then there is the crucial role in the development of democracy, in the abolition of slavery, in the relief and education of the poor, in large-scale philanthropy and the evolution of social equality. Why do these – and other – positive factors so rarely if ever feature on the Dawkins scorecard? The positive record is there to be seen as much as the negative.

There are those who respect Richard Dawkins's lack of faith but wonder why he is so intolerant of their lack of his lack. Is atheism the final conclusion, the end of all thought about religion? Is everything about everything that preceded it of no more account? Are we now living on the summit of human achievement? I doubt it.

He is convinced that the indoctrination of children is entirely to be deplored and I agree with him: it can be wicked. But what if that 'indoctrination' is a form of teaching that helps children lead a happier and fuller life? What if it is a rather lackadaisical, half-hearted sort of tolerant 'indoctrination' as it certainly was in my experience? Those of us in the boys section of the church choir were as susceptible as any other boys to tales of hellfire, but we did not take it then all *that* seriously. They were about the same as ghost stories, not as frightening as the atom bomb, less worrying than the teacher with the cane, not as scary as the school bullies. We made up our own minds and found our own ways through.

The consolation of religion gets short shrift with Dawkins, but to need it is no small yearning for some people. He appears to have little or no empathy for the utter desperation people find themselves in and the comfort which the depths of the Bible's promises can bring. What is the full meaning of comfort? Is it only for the under-educated and therefore not worth examination?

There is the bizarre paragraph about medieval cathedrals. 'A mediaeval cathedral could consume a hundred man-centuries in its construction, yet was never used as a dwelling or for any recognisably useful purpose.' That is one way to look at it. Another is to think oneself into a period when prayer was considered 'useful', when 'worship' of God was considered 'useful', when the glorification of the Creator was considered 'useful', often by educated men and women. All these uses were part of a religious society which in some countries has come and gone but it was like that here once and among brilliant folk too.

People sometimes cleverer than us were living in that age of belief and if asked the questions posed by Richard Dawkins they would have had little problem in answering him. And one unforeseen consequence, one impact of this 'usefulness' was the construction of supreme works of art. So often the greatest works of art have been the by-product of religion. Surely it is worthwhile to investigate what, if any, the connection might be.

We underestimate the intelligence of the past at the peril of misunderstanding the past. Context is key. To take a rather extravagant example. Richard Dawkins has great fun with 'the Four Choirs of Angelic Hosts, arranged as Nine Orders: Seraphim, Cherubim, Thrones, Dominions, Virtues, Powers, Principalities, Archangels (Leaders of all hosts) and just plain old Angels, including our closest friends, the ever-watchful Guardian Angels'. He goes on to say: 'It is shamelessly invented.' Quite. Just like science fiction, perhaps? Or the brilliant novels of a close Dawkins ally, Philip Pullman?

Why could it not be the amusement of clever monks and nuns?

They were confined to a small patch of knowledge-acreage compared with what we have today. But they held on to their right to be inventive; to amuse themselves, to elaborate the heavenly life which they must have seen and sensed as beyond their present grasp. They charged at the impenetrable for sport, a sort of gallant, witty stab in the dark. Could that be an explanation?

About certain matters I think he is badly off track. Now and then he is just plain wrong, and so wrong it undermines his historical credentials. He writes: 'It is surely true that black slaves in America were consoled by promises of another life which blunted their dissatisfaction with this one and thereby benefited their owners.' Leave aside how he can possibly know that 'black slaves were consoled by promises of another life'. All of them? Some? Which ones? Where's the evidence? As often, it is partial, anecdotal or altogether absent, as here.

It is insulting to the African-American slaves to treat them as objects – as their slave owners once did – and see them as so docile, unintelligent, and without spirit that they simply obeyed their masters and took religion as opium. Many of the slaves were not like that. They were often remarkable, brave and intelligent people. Records prove it. Dawkins is so very wrong about them.

The fact is that access to the King James Bible gave to the many different tribes of slaves a common language, a common religion and an inner force often experienced through their appropriation of Bible stories and messages for their own purposes. It gave them access to politics and strategies for a future. They took it and made it their own. They made it essential in their long, courageous struggle for liberty. This happened again and again, as I point out in a later chapter.

There is much chaff, much that is bad in religion and Richard Dawkins seizes on it often with glee. There is also, as manifested in the King James Version taken up by the slaves, good wheat to be found, and good guidance to be unearthed. Far from 'blunting their dissatisfaction' with this life and benefiting their owners, the Bible as an education and as a cohering force raised their expectation, nourished their anger and fired what became, under the most terrible conditions, revolutionary hope. If Richard Dawkins had searched harder he might have found a more accurate Darwinian message in the survival and advancement of the African-Americans over the last four to five hundred years.

It is clear that he has not studied the Bible's effect on slavery. As a scientist he would never allow himself to be so remiss in such a comparably crucial area. So why here? It is embarrassing and raises questions about the authority and trustworthiness of other points he makes. All those other sweeping dismissals – what hard evidence does he have? How carefully is it weighed?

His Google search engine, so nimble at racing along and picking up statistics and quotations which hammer nails in what he sees as the coffin of religion, has a curious defect. One example will do. He is very fond of quoting and at length the unacceptable ravings of the extreme evangelicals in the Mid-Western Bible Belt in the United States. Yet, though declaring himself a friend and an admirer of Richard Harris, former Bishop of Oxford and a distinguished author, his Google engine seems to have sought out none of his books. Why not? Would a positive Christian intelligence have weakened his case? Is it so weak it can't bear such an intervention? Would it have spoiled the fun he has in taunting the telly preachers? Is this another example of Dawkins being unfair? As again when he quotes the Bible where it embraces slavery but omits all the quotations that deplore it.

Richard Dawkins writes: 'I am not a dualist,' and then goes on to explain why. He quotes from Paul Bloom who puts dualism most squarely in the minds of young children, though he concedes that this condition persists in some adults. Dualism is defined here as 'a fundamental split between matter and mind'. But is there another way to look at this differently, that does not demand a split between mind and matter? Is there not another intriguing 'split': in the mind itself which can inhabit two or more places simultaneously?

For what about imagination? When Einstein was asked what was the most important factor in his work, he said, 'Imagination, above all, imagination.' When Samuel Beckett wanted to signal the end of things he wrote: 'Imagine dead. Imagine.' Knowing that we could not. And when we look at men and women who leap as it were to new thought worlds, it is imagination that takes them there, that conjures words out of the air, as Shakespeare said of the poet's gift, and gives them 'a local habitation and a name'. What does that tell us?

Children move easily into other worlds. A game of football or cricket as a boy often involved us taking on the names of our heroes: 'I'm Denis Compton; I'm Jackie Milburn.' (Long-gone stars of respectively cricket and football.) As Richard Dawkins points out, they can have imaginary friends; they can go to see a film and when they come out for some time they can 'be' one of the actors they have seen.

I think it is mistaken to think that this faculty does not persist throughout life. For example, the late Brigid Brophy, a fine novelist, wrote an article on the subject: 'The Novel as a Takeover Bid'. And so, for many of us, it is. We receive from an author of fiction, most often someone who is a stranger, these infinite combinations of the alphabet. Generally in solitude we translate these intimate revelations into our own experience and they become 'us' and we become 'them'. We are 'wrapped up' in them, 'spellbound' by them, 'carried way' by them, 'hooked'. Is this not living another life, even lives? And if so does it not have something to say about hitherto 'unproven' possibilities of other lives?

These fabricated people stand outside us. We not only bring them inside, we are also perpetually aware that they stay 'outside'. In short, we have experience of what is both inside and outside of us. The notion that there is a being, spirit, essence, entity, force, pulse, emanation, otherness 'out there' is part of how we experience the world. Without this faculty we would not be able simultaneously to operate on the many levels we do.

The evidence that we are apparently encoded with this leads me to conclude that the long catalogue of 'worlds out there' and all manner of 'otherness' is part of our world. It is not psychic or weird but normal. Not to have imagination may be a cause of insanity. The King James Bible provides us with a blazing instance of that majestic and opaque 'other worldness'.

Finally, is reason, as Dawkins believes, the only way to understand ourselves and our predicament? 'The heart has reasons which reason does not know' – a cliché but like all clichés well worn because found consistently useful. Perhaps, as Francis Crick a co-discoverer of DNA believes, or rather asserts, we shall come to a time when every jot and tittle of every move we make, every step we take, every impulse we feel, every thought we form, every sensation we experience, every sight we see, sound we hear, taste we take will be accessible to mathematical formulations described in minute and inescapable detail. That is a certain outcome, if a wholly rational universe is postulated.

But what about those other words that we have found to describe the state we are in? What about romantic or wholly inappropriate, unsuitable, dangerous, foolish love – could that be broken down into reasonable particles? If not, does it not suggest that there may be more than one path to the top of the mountain? And the sway of music, does that come out of reason? And unexpected pleasure – 'surprised by joy' – is that in the same arena as logical thought? What about those artists and inventors and lovers who have 'defied reason' and taken imagination (as Einstein did: as Shakespeare did) and arrived at conclusions unexpected? Were they serving reason all along? This is not to suggest a heaven or hell or any form of reincarnation: it is however to suggest that something is going on for which, as yet, we have no satisfactory explanation – and perhaps we never will – and therefore there are still open doors.

The biologist J.B.S. Haldane whom Richard Dawkins admires greatly, wrote (quoted in *The God Delusion*) in *Possible Worlds*: 'Now, my own suspicion is that the universe is not only queerer than we suppose but queerer than we can suppose . . . I suspect there are more things in heaven and earth than are dreamed of, or can be dreamed of, in any philosophy.' Or even, one might add, in the philosophy of atheism.

Dawkins's non-religious Enlightenment is a place which has little or no flexibility. The eighteenth-century Enlightenment, to which we return, found benefits in plurality.

CHAPTER SEVENTEEN
MARY WOLLSTONECRAFT AND
WILLIAM WILBERFORCE

It is too easy to see this story in terms of 'movements'. The Englightenment is one example of several – the Reformation, the Counter-Reformation, the Civil Wars and so on. It is tempting to see and over-emphasise the effect of these movements with the neatness of hindsight. It was all more stumbling, more fractured, more human than that.

Because the overwhelming majority of the population led lives unchronicled until very recently, we have only a small pool of examples to choose from if we wish to put a face, a documented human being, on to these movements. So much of the face of our history is of kings and queens, aristocrats and archbishops: the mighty, who had the time, the wealth and the chroniclers to make and keep records of their lives.

To illustrate how effective individuals were in this story of the impact of the Bible, I have picked out two people whose actions rather than their ancestry raised them into their history.

Mary Wollstonecraft is credited with being a key early voice, even, by some, a founder, of the movement which became feminism. William Wilberforce is credited with being an essential voice in the long struggle to abolish first the slave trade and then slavery itself. Both came out of the late eighteenth-century

Enlightenment when rational, distinguished and brilliant intellectuals had pronounced that the Bible was dead, or not much more than mumbo-jumbo. Yet both Mary Wollstonecraft and William Wilberforce were profound Christians and it was their Christian belief, nourished through intense study of the King James Bible, which drove them on.

Their impact – based on their Christianity – came out of the eighteenth-century parallel with the Enlightenment (of which it could be argued it was in its way a fine example). It swept at first slowly but then irresistibly through the nineteenth century and it can still be seen clearly in the fabric of society today.

Mary Wollstonecraft's immersion in the faith came by way of reason, what was considered to be divinely originated reason: that of William Wilberforce came through revelation. There were elements of reason in Wilberforce's conversion, though no evidence of revelation in the Protestantism of Mary Wollstonecraft. Both reason and revelation had been denied to Christianity by some of the Englightenment thinkers. Reason, it was thought, had no place in the unreasonable world of belief. Revelation, it was argued, had no place in the logical world of scientific investigation. But here were two individuals, two of many, who showed not only that a movement – such as the Enlightenment – can miss the exception but that the exceptional individual can have an effect greater than a movement.

Mary Wollstonecraft's book *A Vindication of the Rights of Woman* was published in 1792 and, revised, in 1793. It can fairly be called the first feminist tract. Wollstonecraft sought, in her words, to 'persuade women to endeavour to acquire strength, both of mind and body, and to convince them that the soft phrases, susceptibility of heart, delicacy of sentiment and refinement of taste are almost synonymous with epithets of weakness'.

To today's feminists hers would seem a rather timid voice.

There was no frontal attack on patriarchy, no demand for women's votes. But, in her time, she was radical and hounded down for it but what she wrote and what she did planted a seed on fertile soil. People live in their own historical period: for her time, Mary Wollstonecraft was, and was seen to be, revolutionary and dangerous.

She believed that education was the key. Education, she argued, was to be as available for women as for men. She wrote about love, passion, sex, society, fashion and marriage, but the bedrock was education. Her own had been patchy.

Her father inherited a small fortune and squandered it in a drunken attempt to become a gentleman. He was violent with his wife, the mother of his six children, and Mary's youth was scarred by confrontations with him to protect her meek Irish Protestant mother.

She found ways to get the beginnings of an education with the help of the kind parents of her friends and her strong habit of reading. She became a lady's companion. She began to write for the cheap populist publications on what was known as 'Grub Street'. It was rapid-turnover journalism, hack-work, but she had a flair for it and the guts to survive in a man's world.

Mary was a regular churchgoer, and it was her church which, in her young womanhood, gave her the education she needed to succeed as she wanted to do. Through the church she found a bookseller, Joseph Johnson, who published her first book '*Thoughts on the Education of Daughters*' and her first novel *Mary: A Fiction*. Through Joseph Johnson, she fell in with a congregation of English radicals, Dissenters who had embraced the idea of equality emerging from the newly independent America. Dr Richard Price, the Unitarian minister of a beautiful plain church, which still exists, in Stoke Newington in east London, took Mary into his congregation and it was there that her yearning for an education was fulfilled. Nonconformists and other Dissenters were forbidden to go to university so they set up their own equivalents in their churches or in their homes. Their achievements in many fields – especially in the sciences – often outstripped Oxford and Cambridge.

Price was a formidable polemicist and his impact on Mary was galvanising. In 1789 he set off the fuse which was to lead to her great work. He preached and then published a sermon congratulating the French Assembly for the new possibilities of religious and civil freedom offered by their revolution. In this sermon he developed this Christian idea of 'perfectibility': that the world could be improved through Christian human effort. Mary took up that idea.

Dr Price's sermon provoked one of the great intellectual battles in English history. Edmund Burke responded fiercely with his *Reflections on the Revolution in France* which argued that traditional authority could not be sacrificed for ideas of liberty. Thomas Paine replied to Burke with his magnificent *The Rights of Men*. Mary rushed into the battle with her own version, *A Vindication of the Rights of Man*. This was soon followed by *A Vindication of the Rights of Woman* in 1792 – dashed off and revised in 1793. She argued passionately for the God-given (as she saw it) rights for women of civil and religious liberty.

Her argument was that human beings have 'natural rights' validated by God's will. And 'virtue', she also argued, like 'wisdom', both to be found in her King James Bible, were the keys to the kingdom currently occupied only by men. Because of that, she wrote: 'if the present constitution of civil society is an almost insuperable obstacle, [to women] then the implication here seems very clear: the present state of civil society must be changed, if we are to progress.' She proposed a revolution, on Christian principles.

Mary Wollstonecraft's Anglican faith never left her. It drew on the radical elements of Christ's teachings in the New Testament which pointed the way to equality and a society released from traditional hierarchies. It also became plaited with the more secular revolutionary ambitions of Thomas Paine, with whom she enjoyed a platonic friendship and mutual admiration. Nor can her own personal frustrations with her education and her experience of a violent father be ruled out of the entwinement of ideas and ideals which became her voice.

Yet at the root of it was a Protestantism based on the King James Bible and shaped by the Dissenters. It was they, the nonconformists, who kept her reputation and her works alive in a nineteenth century which turned its back on her because of the perceived shortcomings of her private life.

That rejection points to another aspect of Protestantism: its capacity for pettiness, judgementalism and hypocrisy.

Mary's adult life was irregular. In London she had a wild affair with the artist-as-public-genius, Fuseli. In Paris to meet the French revolutionaries, she met and fell in love with an American, and went through what she thought of as a marriage. It was a sham. She had a child. It turned out to be illegitimate. Her American lover abandoned her. She made two attempts at suicide.

Her next marriage was to the radical agitator William Godwin. When she died at the age of thirty-eight, he published an honest memoir on her which openly detailed what appeared to many commentators an immoral life. As the revolutionary mood changed to repressed piety during and after the French wars, Mary, who had been a radical heroine in revolutionary Paris, was thought to be too dangerous. Her ideas were feared to have been contaminated by the French connection and were even more unacceptable because of her apparently licentious and uncontrolled life. To take up the work of Mary Wollstonecraft was to forgive what were seen as her sins and that was beyond most of her successors, save for Dissenting women writers. They kept the faith.

Thanks partly to them, her work prevailed. First in mid-nineteenth-century America, then in Britain and now across the world, she is acknowledged in ever more secular circles for what she was: a bold, fearless Christian radical whose work fed the early flickerings of feminism.

Mary Wollstonecraft came out of one English Protestant Christian inheritance. William Wilberforce out of another. Both were tutored by the King James Bible. Both had a resounding impact on the character of the world we now live in. She emerged into her wider world through the route of divine reason. In that way she can be seen as widely allied to the many debates which grew into the Enlightenment Project. He emerged through conversion, a state of transition into Christianity reported on from the time of Jesus Christ Himself and most famously recorded when the young Jewish Saul of Tarsus on the road to Damascus met his sudden conversion to Christianity.

In a sense, Mary Wollstonecraft's Christian route could be seen as a new progression and one capable of further development in an increasingly scientific, questioning, analytical world. William Wilberforce's conversion took root in the deep past, in the origin of faith itself. Both cases seem to prove that whatever victories the Enlightenment won, snuffing out the reforming zeal and intellectual vigour of Bible-based Christianity was not one of them.

Wilberforce's greatness lay in his success, over many years and despite often violent and virulent opposition, in leading forces which eventually pushed through the Parliament at Westminster an Act which abolished the slave trade in 1807. His continuing work and iconic place in Parliament meant that he was also a major instrument in the abolition of slavery itself a generation later.

It was widely acknowledged, not least by Wilberforce himself, that he was by no means alone in leading this campaign. Nor was he the originator. In England, men like Clarkson – a key anti-slavery campaigner – had begun to work for the abolition of the slave trade several years before Wilberforce's interest was enlisted. And the final abolition of slavery itself, though it formally began in the London Parliament, needed the efforts of many in the United States and the West Indies, including many influential former slaves.

Yet Wilberforce played a unique and an essential role. There had to be that Act of Parliament to get the movement going. He did it out of a passionate Christianity. One of his religious disciplines was the daily reading of the King James Bible.

He was born in 1759 into a secure and long-established trading family in the port of Hull, in Yorkshire in the north of England. His family was wealthy but not aristocratic. Their substantial home was in the middle of the city's energetic business quarter with trading ships moored literally at the end of the garden. A narrow, teeming High Street was directly outside the front door. The Wilberforce family tree had long Yorkshire roots and claims were made that it had played a valiant part in the Battle of Hastings. He was the third of four children, two of whom died in childhood: and he too was feared for. He was and was to remain fragile, his eyesight was always poor, his full adult height was five feet four inches. From an early age his melodious speaking and singing voice was applauded.

He went to a superb grammar school in Hull and then, after the unexpected early death of his father at the age of thirty-nine, he was housed with relations in the south, near London. He was hauled back north a couple of years later by his mother and packed off to a mediocre boarding school like most boys of his background and class. From there to Cambridge University. This saw the beginning of a life of luxury, profligacy and idleness which moved to London when, at twenty-one, through money and oratory he acquired a seat in Parliament and became the Member of Parliament for Hull.

Mary Wollstonecraft struggled and then fought her way through a petticoat world that dismayed and devalued her. Hers was a landscape in which the best she could hope for was to be a companion to a rich lady or a governess to a rich family's children. She saw polite society through spoiled women whose lassitude angered her and the rest of society through degraded women whose plight angered her even more. She saw the arrogance of privilege and the abyss of poverty.

Mary finally managed to balance herself somewhere between the two, finding fulfilment in the public arena. She worked hard and read hard and met men (it was mostly men), whose manner of thinking was affiliated with the more extreme direction of Enlightenment thought. So although her circumstances taught her of a country ruinously and ruthlessly divided and riven by class, wealth and birth, her lifeline – her rational Christianity – and her companions – Dissenters and radicals – enable us to see her as part of that tide of enlightened religion.

Wilberforce's England was spectacularly unenlightened. It festered with inherited wealth and position, pagan in all but tokenistic outward observances, squalid, riotous, publicly immoral, gaming, drunken and almost insanely extravagant.

As a youth at Cambridge and particularly in London, he came up against an Anglo-Saxon version of Sodom and Gomorrah. The aristocracy and the industrial nouveau riche were bloated with treasure which their younger element seemed bent on losing at gaming tables. Fortunes which had been accumulated through generations were lost on the throw of dice. And the poor were not only oppressed but only just finding enough air in the gutters of a polluted metropolis.

Like several of the most passionate and effective converts to Christianity, Wilberforce before his conversion lived in, even basked in, a world he would later regard as sinful, slothful, unjust and intolerable.

The Anglican Church had returned to the indolent and corrupt practices of the Roman Catholic Church which the Reformation had attacked. The King James Bible was often little more than a convenient calling card. For the upper classes and the lower aristocracy a pious, even a counterfeiting public observance and the swearing of oaths got you on to what would later be called a 'gravy train'. It was a way in to more wealth for those who came from wealth but were not fortunate enough to be the eldest son – who would inherit the entire estate – or the daring son – who could be bought a commission in the army or the navy. The Church was fat with cash from the strictly enforced tithing tax (10 per cent of income) from truly massive land and property holdings and from the flow of endowments. Be well born. Go to Oxford or Cambridge. Enjoy all that could be bought. Get any old degree and the Church was your oyster.

There were exceptions. There were those of good family who were of good faith. There were valiant parish priests, scholarly bishops and upright archdeacons. But that was not the character of the Church that Wilberforce would have seen. He had enjoyed a taste of the other Church, the Methodists, when, as a boy, he had stayed with his uncle and aunt in Wimbledon near London. There he had seen the strict piety, the rule of Christian conduct, the practice of a deeply held faith; but his mother had hauled him out of that. She was afraid that he might be permanently stained by this lower-class Methodism and therefore unable ever to take his place in society. Ironically, her intervention enabled him to become a Member of Parliament where he did his great work.

Wilberforce, though, would be more likely to know and to be, by class and inclination in those days, at ease with the likes of the Beresford family, for example. William Hague points out in his biography of Wilberforce that one of the Beresfords 'had cumulatively received £350,000 from his Church living' (i.e. £350,000 in eighteenth-century money – multiple millions today); 'another lucky member of this not notably religious family received just under £300,000, a third £250,000 and a fourth, with four "livings" simultaneously, £58,000. In total, through eight clerics, this entrepreneurial Anglican family obtained £1.5 million [in eighteenth-century money] from the Irish [Protestant] Church.' It was money that could have built a city.

One relative of the Prime Minister Lord North gained the see of Winchester and received £1.5 million over his lifetime and secured thirty livings for other members of his family. The work in the parishes was done by lower clergy who would receive a shilling a day and supplement this by farm work, teaching or any other way they could. This was widespread. The Church of England was a smug, unassailable scandal which dressed itself in establishment respectability: many of its leading figures were no better than scoundrels primped out as benefactors.

Jane Austen gives us a glimpse of this. Later in the nineteenth century, Trollope was to manufacture an enjoyable satirical world out of these corruptions. The Church remained for the well-off just another way in which to get richer. In his wild oats young manhood, Wilberforce saw none of that: indeed he went along gaily with the huntin', shootin' and fishin' clergyman whose rectory often dwarfed the village church. The execution of holy office was as much theatrical as theological and had very little to do with preaching on the shores of Galilee.

We are all coloured by the company we keep and Wilberforce's metropolitan clique circled around the fashionable gentlemen's clubs. William Wilberforce belonged to the Goosetree, perhaps the most exclusive. The chief occupations were drinking and gambling, gambling above all, night and day. In one uninterrupted seventy-two-hour session, the famous politician Charles James Fox, twenty-five, and his younger brother lost £32,000. Young aristocrats lost their entire estates through this fashionable addiction to gambling which for a time besotted many of the aristocracy and the wealthy. Walpole wrote: 'the young men lose five, ten, fifteen thousand pounds in an evening. Lord Staverdale, not one and twenty, lost £11,000 last Tuesday but recovered it by one great hand at Hazard.' They would gamble on anything and clubs kept a Betting Book for the more outrageous and bizarre bets.

This was the Enlightened world of the young William Wilberforce. Tempered, it must be said, by political company including William Pitt, his closest friend, a man very soon to become the youngest ever Prime Minister. But for most of them, political discussion appears to have been the diversion in the intervals between the serious business of hedonism.

This was made more gaudy and uncontrolled by the prevalence of prostitution in the capital – about 50,000, many of them children, lining the streets in regiments outside the gentlemen's clubs. Add to that number the recorded assortment in 1796, of 'Thieves, Pilferers, Embezzlers ... Cheats, Rakes, Burglars, Highway Robbers, PickPockets, River Pirates, Swindlers and Dealers in Base Money' and you have over 15 per cent of the London population engaged in crime, most often starved into depravity. It was 'Babylon'. But Wilberforce had experienced an alternative London.

Wilberforce had a crucial childhood experience of the kind and dutiful face of Christianity in Methodism in an outer London suburb. Though his mother as she saw it rescued him from a

Methodist fate (which, she thought, would have made him an outcast in high society), there was always an attachment to the industry and godliness of the people of that childhood time in the south of England. But when he was taken back north to his home, as he wrote: 'as much pains were taken to make me idle as were ever taken to make anyone else studious.'

The establishment thought Methodism lower class, but its fear was that it would take over. Its distaste for Methodism lay in an abhorrence of enthusiasm. An example of this is a sentence from the Duchess of Buckingham, who said of the Methodists: 'It is monstrous to be told that you have a heart as sinful as the common wretches that crawl upon the earth. This is highly offensive and insulting and at variance with high rank and good breeding.'

The turning point came when Wilberforce was a roué of twenty-five. He set out on a Grand Tour of Europe with his mother, his sister, two sick cousins and a remarkable scholar Isaac Milner, whom Wilberforce took along as a companion and tutor. Isaac was the younger brother of the headmaster who had taught so success-fully for two years in Hull Grammar School. He had lost his place in Hull society and his job in the school when he declared himself to be a Methodist.

Isaac, son of a journeyman weaver, went to Cambridge where he became the first Jacksonian Professor of Natural Philosophy, and, according to some, it was believed 'the university, perhaps, never produced a man of more eminent abilities.' He was not a rich man and Wilberforce's offer gave him the unexpected chance to see Europe. Over weeks of travel, their conversation appears to have been an education for Wilberforce. When he persuaded Milner to discuss religion, it became a revelation.

Wilberforce came across a book by Philip Doddridge – *The Rise and Progress of Religion in the Soul*. Milner told him: 'It is one of the best books ever written. Let us . . . read it on our journey.' Many years later, Wilberforce wrote to his daughter: 'you cannot read a better book. I hope it was one of the means of turning my heart to God.' Doddridge based his work on that of Richard Burton, an English Puritan minister in the seventeenth century, who saw the Bible as the source and strength of life.

Wilberforce went back to Tyndale's Greek translation of the New Testament and then he turned to the King James Bible. He suffered agonies not as it seems of doubt but of guilt and strain as he fought to slough off the old skins. He emerged as a devout, rigorous student of the Bible, a disciplined Christian. From what we read of his illness it had symptoms in common with a severe nervous breakdown.

He consulted others. John Newton, the slave-ship owner turned priest, author of 'Amazing Grace', and William Pitt his friend, who supported him in this unexpected but implacably serious endeavour. Eventually, he saw his way through and he wrote: 'surely the principles as well as the practices of Christianity are simple, and lead not to meditation only but to action.'

It is impossible to locate the impulse for the reconstruction of character and the exceptional release of energy undergone by Wilberforce. I sketched in the society in which he had immersed himself to show how far he had to move and how deep was the slough out of which he had to heave himself. It was his own version of Bunyan's *Pilgrim's Progress*. It also brought to him the energy and the compulsion to act. His newborn Anglicanism was dynamic. A key element was a disciplined daily reading and study of the King James Version which seems to have given him such strength that he turned against the morals and the manners of the age in which he lived and set out to change them.

He helped organise the Bible Society and spoke at its first meeting in 1804 and stayed in the society until his death. He helped found the Church Mission Society. He forced the rich, mighty and arrogant East India Company to change its charter, in law, so that it would provide for teachers and chaplains for missionary work. He supported the work of the Society for the Suppression of Vice. His correspondence was mountainous; his workload prodigious. It is the contemporary fashion to provide psychological explanations for such a change but Wilberforce himself and his contemporaries had no doubt whatsoever that he had seen the Light and found God. Thereby he had found the way to a true Christian life, in faith and in works.

His first cause was nothing less than to mobilise the whole country against vice. He saw moral improvement as the only way to redeem and fortify the country and he founded the Proclamation Society for the Reformation of Manners. He enlisted the Prime Minister, the Archbishop of Canterbury, the King, the Queen, several bishops whom he visited in their distant dioceses, ten peers and six dukes. He was satirised by Sydney Smith and William Hogarth but this remarkable release of Christian zeal would not be easily stoppered and his Proclamation Society ploughed on. To the astonishment of many observers, it became a force, eventually, in helping to move the licentious Hanoverian society to the sober and more civic-minded Victorian. Perhaps his success helped impede the recognition of the worth of Mary Wollstonecraft.

He is remembered and honoured for his opposition to the slave trade. The historian G.M. Trevelyan wrote that it was 'one of the turning circumstances in the history of the world'. Wilberforce needed to be persuaded of his fitness for the essential role which he would be required to perform. This was to become the parliamentary spokesman and public leader of what, at the outset, seemed even more hopeless than reforming the manners of the people. This time his success had an impact which rang around the world.

Between 1600 and 1800 about 11 million slaves had been transported from Africa to the Americas. The trade had a long line from the Arab slavers who brought the slaves across Africa to the west coast, to the African traders who bartered with the European traders, the Spanish, Portuguese, British, French and Dutch who carried the slaves across the Atlantic to the American traders who bought them and used them and their offspring as property with no rights.

By the end of the eighteenth century the commercial sea power of Britain, with the armoured protection of the world's most powerful fleet – the Royal Navy – put it in the dock as the key culprit in that long line of abuse, violence and injustice. British cities and industries and traders benefited greatly from the slave trade. Other countries did too but Britain's overall booming post-Industrial Revolution wealth made it the target, then and since, often the sole target, for criticism and obloquy. All the more dangerous, though, for someone to take up arms against what was seen as a vital pillar to the economy. All the more need to do so, some thought. A movement began in the last quarter of the eighteenth century which would seek and find the only way to stop the trade – to secure an Act of Parliament for which they needed a champion. Wilberforce became their man.

His opening speech on the subject is still considered to be among the greatest acts of oratory recorded in the Houses of Parliament. It was a speech that lasted four hours in a packed House of Commons in 1789. It impressed parliamentarians and public alike. Yet it was not until 1807, after eighteen years of embattled persistence during which his life was threatened, he had to hire bodyguards, his name spat on by among others Admiral Nelson, that he succeeded in getting the British Atlantic slave trade abolished. Moreover he got the British navy to enforce this. From a starting point at which the idea of abolition was unthinkable, he won through. Many had worked for that day. But it was Wilberforce, through his speeches in Parliament, the crucial forum, who won the day.

His arguments in that four-hour speech were grounded in the morality of Christ's teaching in the New Testament. His research and his passion gave a picture of horrors which no Christian could support. 'Let us put an end to this inhuman traffic – let us stop this effusion of human blood.'

'The true way to virtue,' he said, 'is by withdrawing from temptation . . . wherever the sun shines, let us go round the world with him diffusing our benevolence . . . total abolition is the only cure for it.'

Wilberforce drew on all his resources. His wealth went into the campaign as did his contacts in society from the court to the Prime Minister. His ease in the fashionable world opened up the cause. The small group of dedicated and politically suspect nonconformists (who could not sit in Parliament) who had initiated the movement would never have had the necessary social clout to roll up the influential support which Wilberforce brought in. There were the expensive Wedgwood brooches, for instance, depicting African slaves with the words 'Am I not a man and your brother' which became advertisements as well as ornaments fashionably worn by young women.

It would be a long trek to the abolition of slavery itself. But after the 1807 vote, the Atlantic trade was abolished by the United States in 1808, and by 1838 throughout the British colonies. There still remained the matter of slavery itself. Wilberforce just lived to see it abolished in the British Empire in 1833. The planters were unbelievably richly compensated by the British government and turned their hand to developing what became a thriving internal slave trade in America itself.

But a new dawn had arrived. 'Thank God that I have lived to

witness a day in which England is willing to give twenty millions sterling for the Abolition of Slavery,' Wilberforce said, three days before he died. It is impossible to imagine he would have done all that without his conversion to Christianity and his faith in the words he knew so well in the King James Version.

But slavery and the King James Bible and the American people still had an account to settle. The final outcome would reshape America and change the perceptions of the world.

PART THREE
THE IMPACT ON SOCIETY

CHAPTER EIGHTEEN
SLAVERY AND THE
CIVIL WAR IN AMERICA (1)

One of the greatest blots on American history is slavery. One of its greatest triumphs is the liberation of the slaves. Their progress through American society, from enslavement to full equality, is the triumph of humanity and courage over prejudice and savagery.

The slave trade between Africa and America and the treatment of the slaves in America tested the King James Version to its limits. The sickening story of horror and brutality has been often told. That it ended in triumph is every bit as remarkable a story. That such victory should come from such beginnings in the sixteenth and seventeenth centuries would have seemed unimaginable.

The captured or kidnapped slaves were treated as things. No rights, no release, neither family nor liberty allowed. The 'Middle Passage' – the journey across the Atlantic on barbarically crowded ships prone to disease, subject to malnourishment, resulted in death at sea for many. It has been described and revisited many times from the graphic speech of Wilberforce in 1789 onwards.

The slaves' existence on many of the plantations was often made even more unendurable by the deployment of iron face masks, shackles, mouth clamps, and other instruments of torture. Their accommodation was bestial, their food minimal, their exploitation total. The purpose of the slaves was to reap harvests of cotton, sugar cane, tobacco, rice and other goods, much of which would go back to the European countries on the boats which had shipped them over from Africa.

If strongest proof were needed of the crucial role played by the Bible in modern English-speaking history, it is here in the American experience of slavery. It was coupled with the integral part the Bible played in the American Civil War which became a battleground for the liberation of the slaves.

The Bible in the debates over slavery and democracy was overwhelmingly the King James Version. Would other versions have had the same impact? To some extent, in the first half of the seventeenth century, the Geneva Bible did have a strong impact. But the overlapping of Geneva and King James has been noted. More importantly, as the seventeenth century progressed, the King James Version became the sovereign book. It was *the* book of the English-speaking nations. It achieved the status of being a holy object. The unequalled number of copies, the growing literacy (mostly through the study and reading of the King James Bible) and the veneration for what this version had achieved gave it an unrivalled authority. In the key developments of the argument on slavery and democracy, it was from the King James Version that people drew their examples and ideas.

Slavery seems to have been embroidered into the tapestry of civilisation. The Babylonians had slaves as did the Jews; the Assyrians had slaves and so did the Indian and Chinese warlords; the Greeks had tens of thousands of slaves; the Romans had, it has been estimated, more than 2 million. As did the Arabs. The Vikings and the Anglo-Saxons had slaves, as did the Africans. Christians kept slaves in the Roman Empire and after the fall of that empire, Christians were enslaved by the Moors in the Middle

Ages. Slavery reveals an exceptionally early and profound division of opinion in Christianity. St Augustine in the fourth century was a supporter of slavery. A few generations later there was St Patrick who opposed it.

The Afro-American experience stands out as the apotheosis and the nemesis of the slave trade. Perhaps because it was so heavily documented, certainly because it was on such a scale, it showed plainly then and now the evils of that practice. The unshackling of slavery and the success of the Afro-Americans in enduring, defying and destroying the system that had enchained them is a beacon to the world.

There *can* be change, the Afro-American experience tells us, and it can be on a deep and global level if the spirit and the strength of the cause are relentlessly determined. In this case they were. In the end, the slaves and the ex-slaves themselves ended slavery. But nothing comes of nothing and along the way there were allies – like Wilberforce, like Harriet Beecher Stowe, like the black Baptist preachers; and there was always the lantern, the guiding light, the Book of Books, the King James Version.

In both the Old and the New Testaments, slavery is taken for granted. It is difficult now to retrieve and imagine that state of mind: but to own slaves was seen as commonplace as in later ages it was to employ servants and in more contemporary times to rely on 'helpers'. Slavery was simply and unquestioningly part of the daily lives of many of our ancestors for centuries.

The Bible reflected that. But it also provided lines of help to the slaves. The Bible could be read as both pro and anti slavery. Noah cursed Canaan, son of Ham, and all his offspring to slavery. Muslim and Christian slave traders took that as their validation: thereby they stood on holy ground. The fatal shift was when the fact of slaves, among religious Christians and Muslims, became bound up with the fact of being black. The Canaanites cursed by

Noah were not black. Many slaves in the first millennium AD were black. It became the ignorant opinion of the slave traders that the black 'race', as they saw them, were born to be slaves.

This convenient ignorance might have died out after it had run its commercial course but it became registered in what was considered to be acceptable scholarship.

Diarmaid MacCulloch points out that 'the link between blackness and slavery reached the Christian West late and it was ironically via Judaism.' Isaac ben Abravanel, a Portuguese-Jewish philosopher, suggested that Canaan's descendants were black. Therefore, under the curse of Noah, all black people were liable to be enslaved. Genesis gives no support to this, but it proved extremely convenient for some Christians, Muslims and Jews.

Another pseudo-scholarly but nonetheless accepted as authentic reading of the story of Cain declared that black people were descended from Cain when God punished Cain for killing Abel, his brother. The 'mark of Cain' was to be black. This baseless scholarship was a boon to the Christian and Muslim slave trade. These interpretations were to be lethal.

So began the battle of the verses. Every bit as deadly as the verses used in the mid-seventeenth-century Civil Wars in the British Isles and the verses to be used with just as much fatal effect in the American Civil War.

A useful starting point in the American experience occurred in the public apology of Judge Samuel Sewall who had behaved disgracefully and unforgivably. When he was in authority during the Salem Witches trial innocent citizens were persecuted and sentenced to death on the hysterical evidence of adolescent girls whose murderous 'visions' were taken to be from God.

The Christian judge took a course of action since widely followed and sought forgiveness or public favour in a belated apology. However, in his self-serving grovelling, he brought up a line from Exodus which became an important rallying cry for the abolitionists in America. 'He that stealeth a man and selleth him,' it read, 'or if he be found in his hand, he shall surely be put to death.' In short, anyone enslaving anyone else ought himself to be punished by death.

That would seem to be a clinching argument. But the grip of slavery was so deep in the minds and customs of people that the argument would not be settled anything like as easily as by a single quotation from Exodus, however faithfully the words of Moses (who it was thought had written Exodus) might be revered. There were others. Timothy lists 'men-stealers' with the 'lawless and the disobedient'. In Colossians 'Masters: give unto your servants that which is just and equal, knowing that ye also have a master in heaven.' Jesus condemned the withholding of wages from hired workers. In Galatians 'there is neither Jew nor Greek, there is neither bond nor free, there is neither male nor female, for ye are all one in Christ Jesus.'

The Enlightenment project in Europe in its eager and passionate pursuit of knowledge through scientific investigation began to study different 'races' and, in the prevailing intellectual climate, found some inferior to others. That this contradicted the Old Testament declaration that there was a fundamental equality in humankind because all of it was necessarily descended from Adam and Eve was thought to be all to the good. But there was a party in the Enlightenment which wanted to contradict the Bible at every turn.

The Bible-loving Quakers in America were the first organised religious group to petition against slavery, which they did in 1688, a century before Wilberforce brought his bill into the House of Commons. A movement grew – small, probably unnoticed by the majority of people and thought of no consequence by the minority who kept track of these matters: but it grew.

Correspondence and pamphlets sailed to and fro across the Atlantic. There was a chipping away at the monolith of received and ingrained opinion that slavery was God-sanctioned. A few white individuals were united in conscience and in determination. All this while at the same time among the slaves themselves, organised opposition and acts of great courage built up what would become the ready army of the oppressed.

In England, Granville Sharp, an Anglican gentleman, nurtured a great hatred of slavery informed by his correspondence with a Pennsylvanian Quaker. He scoured the Bible for anti-slavery evidence. His landmark success, however, was to support an English lawsuit in 1772, Somersett's Case. McCulloch explains: 'In his judgement of this case, Lord Chief Justice Mansfield found in favour of an escaped slave, James Somersett, against his master, a customs officer of Boston, Massachusetts. Mansfield refused to accept that the institution of slavery existing in 18th century England could be linked to the legal status of serfdom . . . recognised in English common law: logically, therefore, *slavery had no legal existence in England*.' Therefore only a decision in Parliament could legalise it: therefore a decision in Parliament could ban the trade in it. The scene was set for one of Sharp's fellow evangelicals, William Wilberforce.

There was some room, thanks to Somersett's Case, for what proved to be a helpful though hypocritical dimension to the argument in Britain. It was a country which would not tolerate slavery on its own land: there were 20–30,000 blacks in the country at the end of the eighteenth century. It was also a country which in all but legal form was 'enslaving' in its first-stage Industrial Revolution, hundreds of thousands of men, women and children in the bondage of factories and mines. It was also a country that shipped scores of thousands of slaves from Africa to America every year.

Yet out of that came a phrase which the descendants of enslaved Africans are surely tired of hearing: the judgement of the Victorian historian W.E.H. Lecky. He wrote that 'the unwearied, unostentatious and inglorious crusade of England against slavery may probably be regarded as among the three or four perfectly virtuous acts recorded in the history of nations.'

But for all that, the real battleground for the abolition of slavery itself was to be America. The battle was fought with Bibles on the plantations in small churches built by the slaves, with bullets on the battlefield and finally on the streets of twentieth-century America.

Slavery began in North America with indentured white slaves. In the 1660s, the demand for labour grew and the English tobacco growers in the southern states followed the South American and Caribbean example and began to ship in men, women and children from Africa.

In the first hundred years, there was little effort to convert the slaves to Christianity. The chief task was to control many different tribes and tongues with their many beliefs which were barely comprehended by the whites and feared as the possible seeds of rebellion. This control was exercised by cruelty, by torture, confinement and the imposition of inhuman divisions in families and in tribes. In the early years the unquestioned notion was that slavery was a natural part of the way in which society was organised.

The words of Jefferson Davis, President of the Confederate States of America in the nineteenth century, reached back across two centuries of belief in the South that 'slavery was established by decree of Almighty God . . . it is sanctioned in the Bible, in both Testaments from Genesis to Revelations . . . it has existed in all ages, has been found among the people of the highest civilisation and in nations of the highest proficiency in the arts.'

In the slave-owning, slavery-dependent southern states, education was organised through the Bible. The formal school system was patchy. It was the Sunday schools and home Bible reading that educated the people. They were guided, in the churches, by preachers who from their pulpits taught the inevitability and the righteousness of slavery. It was difficult for those thus directed to assume anything else. That view was always shored up by references to the King James Bible, where people were sold into slavery, captured as slaves, used as slaves. That those references were open to challenges would become part of the later war over the Word, but for generations of slave owners there was no guilt and no doubt.

Eventually two streams of history merged into each other to start the flow of what was initially called 'slave religion'. The Great Awakenings, especially the Second Great Awakening, reached out to the slaves. Methodism was particularly effective. The Quakers were stern in their anti-slavery stance; other evangelicals began to carry the message across the races – to Indians as well as to Africans. And individuals, English and in increasing numbers Americans, began to see the slaves as potential converts. They could be redeemed. Their colour was immaterial, it was their souls the evangelicals wanted to capture. You could argue that it was the determination of the revivalists to leave no soul untouched that helped set off a conversion process which eventually grew into a coherent political force.

Alongside this the 'slave religion' developed its own internal dynamic, its own teachers and preachers and its effective organisational skills. In the face of barbaric and imprisoning opposition from the white Christian masters, there grew up a black Christianity which absorbed many African beliefs and practices. Common faith and community were expressed in gospel songs and spirituals; visions Christian and African were intense. There were physical expressions of exaltation and hope. The King James Bible was a source for language as well as for faith but above all it was a source for the stories around which the African-American slaves created their own new culture. These stories fed the imagination and portrayed other possible worlds. This religion drew deeply on two cultures, transplanting the traditional African spirituality and transforming the traditional Christian. Eventually it became central to the unique identity of America.

It was the stories that gave the black religion its spine. Daniel in the lions' den; Moses rescuing the Israelites; Jonah, David, Mary, Jesus: and the stories were turned into songs that steeled the resolution of what became a new nation within the United States. For years it was invisible to most of the whites. They ignored its churches which flourished beside the swamps and in the dark forbidding ghettoes. But the slaves had found a way, a footing, and the story of their long stony march to liberty was to be voiced in their own King James Version.

There were, then, three different versions of the same 1611 Book of Books in America. One which was claimed by the abolitionists to support their cause; one which was claimed by the pro-slavery South to support theirs; and the Bible as claimed by the slaves. It has always been a book for all seasons but rarely as dramatically as in what would become a bitter civil war shot through with racism, idealism, religious prejudice and zeal and widespread biblical literacy. Going into that war the American peoples, whatever their background, were already predisposed to strong religious passions. Coming out of it they were, as in part they still are, even more tightly sealed in their compact with God through His Word in the Bible.

It took time for the sides to assemble their forces. In the eighteenth and early nineteenth centuries there were many small signs. The Society for the Propagation of the Gospel in Foreign Parts, (known as SPG) was formed in London in 1701 after a report that the Anglican Church in America had 'little spiritual vitality'. The fact that the SPG itself got much of its funding from the Codrington Plantation in Barbados – which employed slaves – was characteristic of the muddle and the confusion over this issue. The roots of slavery were so deep that to tear them out was to rip open the ground on which you stood. The SPG did not give up its slave holdings until after the 1833 Act in the British Parliament which abolished slavery.

Despite attempts at conversion it is vital to acknowledge that it was the slaves themselves who reached out, through the Bible, for a religion which in some profound way satisfied their past, dignified their present and gave them both hope and a goal. For example, there was, from the beginning, an intense identification not only with Jesus Christ but also with the Hebrew slaves.

This had two crucial elements. They read the Bible as history and saw that the Hebrew slaves had eventually been liberated by God. Why should God not do the same for them? Second: God was now their master, not the plantation owner. Just as the Presbyterians in the British Civil Wars in the middle of the seventeenth century had found in the Bible that God was superior to any king and therefore a king could be overthrown with God's blessing, so the slaves found an intellectual and emotional wedge to prise away the authority of their 'masters'. They could see them not as masters but subjects of the same God as they were – and equal in the eyes of that God. They were just as vulnerable to being dislodged by the One who sat in judgement over everyone. This realisation was, as it was for the Presbyterians who tried and executed a king, a decisive and seminal first step on the road to freedom.

It was the black preachers of black Baptist and Methodist Churches (such as the African Methodist Episcopal) who brought not only Christianity but also education and social services to the slaves. The black Christians were at the forefront of the abolitionist movement, alongside the evangelical whites. There were also secular and humanistic reformers who were just as profoundly opposed to slavery on moral grounds.

But the battering rams in the very early days came from evangelicals like Wesley and Whitefield, Wilberforce and others, like Charles Spurgeon (1834–92), an English Particular Baptist preacher. His sermons were burned in America because of their vehemence. He called slavery 'the foulest blot' which 'may have to be washed out in blood . . . a crime of crimes, a soul-destroying sin, and an iniquity which cries aloud for vengeance'. Spurgeon had been converted to Christianity by reading part of the King James Bible when, aged fifteen, he took refuge in a Primitive Methodist church in a snowstorm. The text of that day read: 'Look unto me, and be ye saved, all the ends of the earth, for I am God and there is no one else.' He was to write: 'Bible hearers, when they hear indeed, come to be Bible lovers.' In his lifetime it is estimated he preached to about 10 million people and his sermons were translated into many languages.

Then there is George Bourne whose many books, but most influentially *A Condensed Anti-Slavery Bible Argument* (1845) dissected the biblical pro-slavery arguments. His chapter headings included 'Pro-Slavery Perversions of the Old Testament' and 'Pro-Slavery Perversions of the New Testament'. He was also inflamed at the treatment of women slaves and published *Slavery Illustrated in its Effects upon Women*.

But these were voices crying in the wilderness as far as the epicentre of the problem was concerned. The slave-owning southerners saw no reason to yield their ground and though there were some inroads, these books and sermons and pamphlets had more influence in the North. However, the issue of slavery and behind that the ownership of the truth of the Bible became a serious factor in the growing rift between North and South which would lead to the Civil War.

Meanwhile the slaves were building up their own position through the unexpected but inspiring medium of songs. The early white Methodist preachers gave some encouragement and Methodism was one of the main sources of the early songs. Methodism was renowned for its rousing hymns and notorious in Anglican England for the participation and enthusiasm of its congregations. The Africans took to that, but soon they preferred to find their own way.

We read of secret 'bush' meetings, hidden in the swamps and woods, which could attract thousands of slaves to listen to passionate itinerant preachers. And to sing. As these songs emerged, they became the voice of the slaves, spirituals. From these beginnings, by an alchemy of liberation, talent and the profound seduction of the music and the words, they became three centuries later, through soul and jazz and rock 'n' roll, the voice of America, America's priceless gift to the culture of the world.

The Bible was their Great Book and their unique source. A favourite song was 'Go Down Moses' – also known as 'Let My People Go'. This was rooted in Exodus viii, 26: 'And the Lord spake unto Moses: Go unto Pharaoh and say unto him, Thus saith the Lord, Let my people go, that they may serve me.'

That was translated into the spiritual:

> When Israel was in Egypt's land: let my people go.
> Oppress'd so hard they could not stand: let my people go.
> Go down Moses
> Way down in Egypt land,
> Tell old Pharaoh
> Let my people go.

The effect today even on white Anglo-Saxon Englishmen can be to release that surge of emotion which somehow detonates both hope and joy the way that only music and lyrics can do when they send a depth charge into feelings.

Many of the songs talked of home: heading home to 'Sweet Canaan, the Promised Land' or 'Bound for Canaan Land'.

> Wher're you bound?
> Bound for Canaan land.
> O, you must not lie
> You must not steal
> You must not take God's name in vain.
> I'm bound for Canaan's land.

It is to be marvelled at that people who had known very little but inhumanity were singing songs not only of home but also of a morality so far above that of their slave holders. To combat the brutality they endured they turned to the Ten Commandments. In other songs, it was the words of Jesus which inspired them.

There were political songs, referring to the 'Underground Railway' – the route taken by those slaves who made a break for freedom and struck north, moving from 'station' to 'station' as helpers, at great risk to themselves, harboured them for a while before seeing them on to the next stage of that epic journey. There's 'The Gospel Train' and 'Wade in the Water', referring to the dangerous Ohio River, the boundary seen as the final passage to the North and to freedom. 'Swing Low Sweet Chariot', refers to a specific place where fugitive slaves were welcomed.

The fashion for spirituals has waxed and waned but they are always there, the foundation music. This music was grafted on to the biblically inspired lyrics from the King James Version. Together they made a rallying cry and a soundtrack for those who fought their way out of slavery. The Black Renaissance in the twentieth century saw the spirituals bloom again.

Paul Robeson gave hugely popular public performances as did Mahalia Jackson. Choirs and choruses took the gospel songs on tours across the United States. In the Civil Rights Movement in the 1950s and 1960s they reappeared at full volume to play their part with 'We Shall Overcome' and 'Joshua Fought the Battle of Jericho' where the words were changed to 'Marching Round Selma'. You could argue that when Elvis Presley changed popular music through his version of rock 'n' roll one reason for the transforming power of it was that Presley, the southern choral boy, had grown up on the gospel music and spirituals which are still vibrant in hundreds of choirs today.

It was a form that occurred only in the United States and empowered enslaved millions who, generation after generation, regrouped and regained their poise.

Through their character, history and intelligence, the slaves who were seen as 'objects' had found in Protestant evangelical religion based on its Bible a way to rebuild tribal and family identities which had been cynically smashed, fragmented and, wherever possible, aborted. But to make the big leap, to be freed, to be emancipated, that would take a civil war.

CHAPTER NINETEEN
SLAVERY AND THE
CIVIL WAR IN AMERICA (2)

A braham Lincoln, who had declared that 'Government cannot endure permanently half slave, half free', was elected President of the United States on 6 November 1860. In December they became disunited when South Carolina seceded from the Union. Within two months, Mississippi, Florida, Alabama, Georgia, Louisiana and Texas had followed suit. In February 1861, the Confederate States of America was formed with Jefferson Davis as President. On 12 April 1861 the Confederates under General Pierre Beauregard opened fire on Fort Sumter in Charleston, South Carolina. The American Civil War had begun.

It led to more than 1 million casualties. About 620,000 soldiers died, two-thirds of them from disease. The southern states which became the battleground were devastated. Their churches were desecrated. Slavery was legally abolished. After the war the circumstances under which former slaves lived were often worse than before. Racism was to take a century to uproot. But slavery was history.

There were many factors which led to the Civil War: economic, political, social. The imbalances of forces were clear from the outset. The Union would have twenty-one states, a population of over 20 million and the growing industrial strength of North

America on its side. The Confederacy, agrarian, with eleven states, had less than half that – 9 million, which included 4 million slaves. Firepower, technology and numbers grew in importance as the war dragged through four years. It was and remains a source of pride to southerners that they put up such a fight for so long. That pride became key to their regrouping in their wasted lands after their inevitable surrender when the odds were simply too great. The residual conviction remained among many that their long continuing view about slavery had been defeated by bullets but not by the Bible and their cause had been just.

The issue of slavery was central to the war. And the Bible was central to the issue of slavery. It bound together all the other causes. It was part of the American striving for liberty and equality which could be tracked back to the first English settlers at the beginning of the seventeenth century. It was also allied to America's notion of its historical 'exceptionalism': again in direct descent from the Presbyterians who had crossed from England and increasingly the rest of Britain in the seventeenth century and whose core members considered themselves to be the Chosen People. For all the humanitarian impulses, the essential debate over slavery and the war between the states was over how the Bible was to be interpreted.

In their introduction to *Religion and the American Civil War*, the editors write: 'Religion . . . was found everywhere the war was found – in the armies and the hospitals; on the farms and plantations and in the households; in the minds and souls of men and women, white and black . . . God was truly alive and very much at the centre of this nation's defining moment.'

It was asserted that 'the United States was the world's most Christian Nation in 1861 and became even more so by the end of the war . . . Organised religion provided the spine of an otherwise "invertebrate America".'

Politicians on both sides invoked God and used the King James Version to justify their actions. There were prayer meetings in the soldiers' camps and in their homes. Millions of Bibles and Prayer Books were printed and distributed. The language of the King James Bible was the language that the politicians and soldiers and writers and civilians on both sides had in common.

While by no means a re-run of the British Civil Wars more than two centuries earlier, it had strong similarities and little wonder: many of those involved on the battlefields of England and Scotland and Ireland were the direct ancestors of those taking to war in the southern states. Their adhesion to biblical authority had been unchanged by 3,000 miles of sea, a War of Independence and 200 years of exposure to a continent so unlike the West European islands they had abandoned.

The Great Awakenings in the eighteenth century swelled Church membership which surged again in the lead-up to the Civil War. Bible classes, Sunday schools, religious newspapers, popular fiction: wherever eyes strayed to print or the ears listened to teaching or preaching, the Bible would be the heart of the matter. This was bolstered by the American 'exceptionalism'. This was the conviction that they lived in what their Puritan founders had called the 'city on a hill', that they were a 'redeemer nation', that they were appointed by God and by their very devotion anointed to carry out a 'manifest destiny'.

When the Puritan John Cotton had set sail from England with other early Puritans, he had preached on a sentence from Samuel: 'Moreover I will appoint a place for my people Israel and I will plant them, that they may dwell in a place of their own and move no more.' More than two and a half centuries later, when the Civil War was about to begin, Francis Vitton spoke in Trinity Church, New York: 'The people of the United States, under the Federal Constitution, are ONE NATION, organic, corporate, divinely established, subject to government and bound in conscience to obedience. Disloyalty to the constitution is therefore impiety towards God.'

The war, which could be defended politically as a defence of the elected government against the unconstitutional breakaway rebels in the South, was also a war of the Bible. The constitution was built on the Bible, the Bible was in the sinews of the constitution. It was not a theocratic state: it was more complex and unusual than that. America had taken the Word of God to safety in New England and since then, despite an increasing number of religious people of other religious persuasions and of no religious persuasions, that original King James Version had been the stubborn root and a fertilising cause of the astonishing growing of America.

To many Americans, the Bible was historically accurate. It was the Word of God and though it had to be interpreted, its fundamental authority and supremacy should not be questioned. It is not easy to enter into the minds of previous historical periods even one as near as mid-nineteenth-century America. But without that act of empathy and imagination, the study of history is pointless.

To dismiss the Bible today without much of an inward glance is one thing: to dismiss the tenaciously and profoundly thought-through beliefs and opinions of those every bit as intelligent as we are but alive some time ago and in a different context is, as I have mentioned, to miss the developments and changings in the laboratory and the library of the human mind. Abraham Lincoln read and lived by the Bible. So did labourers and slaves. One riveting aspect of the American Civil War is that the opposing sides, as Lincoln pointed out, 'read the same bible'. And according to Mark A. Noll, they read it 'in the same way'.

That is, they read it, Noll writes, as 'God's revealed word to humanity'. He goes on: 'it was the duty of Christians to heed carefully every aspect of that revelation. If the Bible tolerated, or actually sanctioned, slavery, then it was incumbent on believers to hear and obey.'

Noll's essay on 'The Bible and Slavery' illustrates the awesome problems that led to. The crisis was in the interpretation: the variance in the interpretations provoked the crisis. Preachers and their congregations in the South (though some in the North, too; lines were broadly drawn but not wholly exclusive) concluded that the Bible sanctioned slavery in passages such as Genesis xiv, 14, Leviticus xxv, 44 and Corinthians vii, 21. Therefore true Christians should accept this. The Bible was the supreme and the Divine Authority.

These passages had been strongly challenged by the abolitionists who also argued that the presence of slavery in the Bible was not a justification for its existence in the United States. This was reinforced by those who claimed a distinction between the letter of the Bible and the spirit of the Bible. Hair-splitting as this might now seem, this was at the core of the rationale for the war. Underlying everything was the deferential attitude that believed that any attack on the Bible was unacceptable to God. Noll summarises it as 'a forced dichotomy – either orthodoxy and slavery, or heresy and anti-slavery'. This was the theological battle line on the eve of the war.

The unprecedented numbers of literate people in America at that time, often those whose learning was reinforced by regular, lengthy and demanding sermons, meant that the minds of millions were engaged, daily and with serious purpose, on these questions. The battle was an extension of their arguments. The King James Version provided the intellectual and emotional structure for the politics of the Civil War. It was widely believed that 'every direction contained in its pages was applicable at all times to all men.' The God-given common-sense reading by Americans of the Holy Scriptures had led to that conclusion and also to the rapid burgeoning of a civilisation staked out in a hostile continent.

Noll points out the intensive similarities in the background of the preachers: 'In 1863 a convention of southern ministers appealed to their fellow Christians in the world . . . 94 of the 96 signatures came from Baptist, Methodist, Episcopal, Presbyterian and Disciples churches, all branches of English-speaking reformed Protestantism. A study of northern sermons during the war [showed that] well over 90 per cent came from the same ecclesiastical family.' It was not always Cain versus Abel but Abel versus Abel or Cain versus Cain.

It would be overly simplistic to conclude that the Bible alone 'caused' the Civil War. The Bible was the gate through which the thoughts and passions of the majority were marshalled. Had the Bible not been there . . . ? Well, that is a question without an answer, or a question with too many answers. Had the Bible not been there America as it was in 1861 would not have been there: slavery as it was in 1865 would not have been abolished. It was a time and a place of faith and however much we mock it or feel indifferent to it nowadays, it altered for the better what was already a vital and dynamic new force in the world.

The Bible was America's national book. It spoke directly to the individual reader and he or she could take up the sentences to try for themselves. It could and did provoke deep thought and study. And it led to moral crusades of which that concerning slavery was the most mighty to date.

When the black preachers spoke of the Bible, they too championed its literalism as sincerely as their white contemporaries. Their own readings were different in some aspects – a greater emphasis on prophecy, on dreams, on magic, on liberation – but the absolute belief was no less. And they found political and social ammunition there. For example, Psalm 68 verse 31 was often quoted: 'Princes shall come out of Egypt, and Ethiopia shall soon stretch out her hands unto God.' And equally popular, from Acts,

Thomas Paine, a radical and a democrat but not a Christian, still found in the Bible a template and a language for revolution.

William Wilberforce (left) and Mary Wollstonecraft (right) were both profound Christians and it was their belief, nourished through intense study of the King James Bible, which drove them on.

Five generations of a slave family, South Carolina, 1862. The slave trade between Africa and America and the treatment of the slaves tested the King James Version to its limit, but finally it was key to the liberation of the slaves.

A black preacher delivering his sermon. The battle for the abolition of slavery was fought with Bibles on the plantations in small churches built by the slaves themselves.

The Fisk Jubilee Singers, former slaves, gave public performances of gospel songs and spirituals to audiences of 10,000 and more.

The United States Christian Commission went, unarmed, onto Civil War battle fields and brought supplies, distributed Bibles and worked in hospitals.

A young Confederate soldier with a Bible in his pocket. There were many stories of Bibles in breast pockets stopping bullets during the American Civil War.

A YMCA poster of World War I shows a soldier reading the Bible.

Mother—I promised to read it *every day*

The Bible Class Discussion Group helps you keep the promise. It keeps you true to home ideals.

Fits you to face the folks and the tasks back home.

YMCA

Ask the "Y" man.   Sign up today!

BIBLE STUDY WEEK JAN. 5th to 12th

A page from the New England Primer c.1690 was used by colonial children. It contained the alphabet, hymns, prayers and stories inspired by the Bible.

Postcard of a young baseball player used to encourage Sunday school attendance.

William Carey went to India in 1794 as a Baptist
minister and stayed there for forty-one years. His greatest
achievement was to translate the scriptures into Bengali.

An American missionary with Bible women at the Foochow Mission in China, 1902.

Mary Magdalene washing the feet of Christ. The curse of Eve has been upon her until recently.

Judith (right) with the head of Holofernes. The most unexpected woman in the Bible, she used virtue, courage and leadership as an effective combination to achieve greatness through service to her people.

Abraham banishes Hagar and Ishmael. The trials of Hagar have grown in the consciousness of Christians in the last few centuries, partly because of their resonance in the African-American Christian communities.

Octavia Hill was a major force throughout the charity and welfare organisations of the nineteenth century, inspired by the King James Bible.

William Booth, founder of the Salvation Army wrote of the extraordinary phenomenon of the 'Slum Sister', seen here rescuing an abused child in 1912.

Keir Hardie said 'The impetus that drove me first of all into the Labour movement and the inspiration which has carried me on in it, has been derived more from the teaching of Jesus of Nazareth than all the other sources combined'.

Barack Obama takes the oath at his inauguration ceremony in 2009. Michelle Obama holds the same Bible used by Abraham Lincoln in 1871.

A US soldier in Iraq, 2008, wears a scarf printed with verses from Psalm 91.

God 'made of one blood all nations of men for to dwell on all the face of the earth'.

But slavery proved no less intransigent than race. 'In the United States,' the scholar David Davis wrote '. . . the problem of slavery . . . had become fatally intertwined with the problem of race.' The economic system in the South depended on slavery: slavery was perceived to be a racial issue. To be black was to be marked out from birth as a slave. Race was as deep a biblical-political problem as slavery. There was the curse of Noah; there were the children of Canaan. There was the mark of Cain. There was rich profit from free labour on the labour-intensive plantations.

And through long habit and need and a sort of implacable wish-fulfilment, it was, after so many years, ingrained in the attitudes of many whites, in the South, that the blacks were just plain inferior. They looked around, they saw chained largely illiterate bondsmen and women and children and over centuries it had mainlined into their perception that they were a lesser breed: 'common sense' was all you needed to see that. A chasmic contradiction appeared: slavery could be admitted to be wrong and unjust: but blacks could not be trusted to be part of a civilised society. In this regard, prejudice spoke louder than the Word of God.

After the war, Presbyterians in the South proposed to ordain African Americans as clergymen. This was strongly opposed by speeches in the Synod of Virginia in 1867. 'The righteous rational . . . of pious minds,' one advocate said, 'would deny ordination of black preachers in a white church.' There was an attempt to justify the 'convention that among the peoples of the earth, only Africans were set aside for chattel bondage'. There is no biblical authority for that view.

*   *   *

But the Bible has often been used by the cruel, the vicious, the unscrupulous, the vengeful, the power-besotted. For many it was and remains a sacred text. For others it was no more than a useful instrument to be employed as the occasion demanded. Although, of course, there were those for whom it was both these. We know of dictators who swore by the Bible. We also know of many other dictators who came from a different religion or none and were just as dictatorial. What dictators have in common is never a book: it is lust, opportunity, violence, infinite cruelty, charisma and organisational genius.

The King James Version for some people was no more than an excuse, a supplier of acceptable cover stories, a convenient lie, a dummy to keep the people quiet, a useful diverter of energy which enabled those without faith to go about their business of persecution and oppression more comfortably. The slave-masters included all of these.

What transpired after the Civil War was not unlike a phenomenon that some practitioners in psychoanalysis observe: that the removal of a neurosis may leave exposed a psychosis. Slavery was abolished: racism remained dug in. The next century would be devoted to the successful assault on this visceral bigotry.

In the long journey of the history of slavery, it is a relief to celebrate what had been achieved by the end of the Civil War. To note how integral the Bible was, how positive a part it played, in an achievement which would have seemed impossible even four years before it happened. The arguments between North and South, based on or, sceptics might claim, simply using biblical texts, had become virulent. Slave owners compared themselves to God in their benevolence to the slaves. To anti-slavery voices, slavery was to treat people as commodities, an affront to the very meaning of a Christian view of life. Whether it was because of a sincere embrace of the Christian faith or the use of the Christian faith as a means to an end, both sides saw the Bible as their ally and their salvation.

This can best be illustrated by reports on the widespread and often passionate interest that the soldiers took in Bible studies, especially in the camps on the battlefields. One report reads: 'Wilber Fisk, from Vermont, serving with the Army of the Potomac in March 1864, described meetings every night of two hundred men at a time, which was all the tent could hold, and that many had to leave because no seats were available.'

A military press grew up which regularly published several papers and thousands of tracts. 'Wholesome reading purifies and elevates the man,' said the *Record*. Journalists were everywhere in the battle of words. John Leyland wrote of the Bible: 'it inspires him with better thoughts and impulses, it encourages him to that which is good, it restrains him from evil.' The longer the war went on, the more Christian military publications came out. These included, in the South alone, *The Soldier's Friend* (Baptist, Atlanta), *Army and Navy Messenger* (evangelical, Virginia), *The Soldier's Visitor* (Presbyterian, Virginia), *Army and Navy Herald* (Methodist, Georgia). These publications were united in glorifying the heroic and Christian Confederate soldier. Conversions – 140,000 estimated in the Confederate army after three years of war – were celebrated, as was the big increase in 'praying men' in the field. The Reverend Stiles summed it up: 'the simplest way to convert a nation is to convert its army.'

There was the *Soldiers' Pocket Bible* published in 1862 (again an echo from the Civil Wars in the British Isles). This was a selection of prayers and then 'Scripture Selections' from the King James Bible. These were chosen for their inspirational qualities. The soldiers would fight on their beliefs. 'We have might against this great company that cometh against us,' from the Book of

Chronicles, 'neither know we what to do: but our eyes are upon Thee.' More encouragement from Isaiah: 'no weapon that is found against thee shall prosper.' And Deuteronomy: 'Be strong and of good courage, fear not, nor be afraid of them: for the Lord thy God, he it is that doth go with thee: he will not fail thee nor forsake thee.'

The Young Men's Christian Association and the United States Christian Commission, unarmed, went on to the battlefields and brought supplies, distributed Bibles, offered aid, worked in hospitals. There were 4,859 volunteers, Walt Whitman and Louisa M. Alcott among them. Louisa May Alcott later based her novel *Little Women* on her Civil War experience and also produced *Hospital Sketches*, a lightly fictionalised publication of her letters home. Alcott was the first Civil War nurse to publish an account of her time in service and her work contains many references to the spiritual experience of those at war. From *Hospital Sketches*:

On a Sunday afternoon, such of the nurses, officers, attendants, and patients as could avail themselves of it, were gathered in the Ball Room for an hour's service. To me it seemed that if ever strong, wise and loving words were needed, it was then; if ever mortal man had living texts before his eyes to illustrate and illuminate his thought, it was there; and if ever hearts were prompted to devoutest self-abnegation, it was in the work which brought us to anything but a Chapel of Ease.

With regard to Whitman, the following extract comes from *Treasures of the Library of Congress*: 'Walt Whitman made dozens of small notebooks from paper and ribbon to carry with him as he visited wounded Civil War soldiers in Washington area hospitals between 1863 and 1865. In them he comments on the food provided at the Armory Hospital. Other notebooks describe the horrors of war. As a volunteer delegate under the Christian Commission, he consoled the sick and dying and often wrote letters to their families.'

Abraham Lincoln wrote to the Christian Commission congratulating it on the work it did: 'Your Christian and benevolent undertaking for the benefit of the soldiers is too obviously praiseworthy to admit any difference of opinion. I sincerely hope that your plan may be as successful in execution as it is just and generous in conception.'

Abraham Lincoln, President of what would be the victorious North, had a strong commitment to constitutional democracy. The relationship between the King James Version and democracy is close and Lincoln is a good example of one aspect of it. Lincoln thought that democracy was the system 'through which God's plan for the nation could be worked out'. The Bible had given access to God's word to all men (as Lincoln would have phrased it: women's suffrage was just creeping into the argument but still way out of contact with power). The Bible had no explicit instructions for America but through debate in a democracy that purpose would, the President thought, be arrived at. The secession of the South was not just a rebellion in Lincoln's eyes. It threatened the very process through which Americans would come to play out their divine destiny.

Ronald C. White Jr. who has written extensively on Lincoln states that 'Lincoln's religion, in fact, laid a foundation for his political thinking . . . and the culmination of his religion was his attempt to discern the meaning of the Civil War.' His own struggle with faith seems to be resolved in the short but Bible-pegged Second Inaugural Address. Within that brief speech, he mentions God fourteen times, refers to prayer three times and quotes passages from the Bible four times. It was here that he said: 'both read the same Bible and pray to the same God and each invokes

His aid against the other . . . it may seem strange that any men should dare to ask a just God's assistance in wringing their bread from the sweat of the other man's face. But let us judge not that we be not judged.' Later he says: 'the judgements of the Lord are true and righteous altogether.' Lincoln also said: 'with malice toward none; with charity for all . . . let us strive on to finish the work we are in . . . to do all which may achieve and cherish a just and a lasting peace among ourselves and with all nations.'

In this, Lincoln, very conscious that he was President for the second time but presiding over a country at war with itself, sought a path which might offer a chance of reconciliation. The terms 'moral evil' and 'original sin' had entered the debate. Hatred of the one for the other's position was ratcheted higher every day by reports of new losses. Lincoln wanted an end, an end which came quite soon after that Second Inaugural Address when the bled and battered South, fought to a standstill, surrendered in April 1865.

In January 1865, the US Congress approved the Thirteenth Amendment to the United States Constitution to abolish slavery. In April 1865, Lincoln was assassinated. The Thirteenth Amendment was passed by Congress and fully ratified on 6 December 1865 and slavery was abolished. The Bible, the victors – the abolitionists – claimed, had *proved* that God was on their side.

More than 4 million slaves were freed. The majority came out of shackles into a freedom for which they were wholly unprepared and to which many of them were abandoned. But they had come through! As the stories of the Israelites and the lessons in the New Testament had promised, they had found freedom. They could throw off those chains.

Although there was a constitutional end to the practice of slavery, equality was another matter. That would take another century and even in present-day America with a black President, there are still pockets of hard prejudice. Segregation replaced slavery but the triumph of abolition must not be denied. It was a magnificent achievement: it was world-changing. And the King James Version had played the key role.

There were some who claimed that the lack of support for freed slaves after the Civil War, and the continued disparagement of the 'Negro' left black people worse off. Segregation, they argued, was slavery by another name. The braver ones did not think that. They got on with the new, often disturbed life and, largely through the Churches and a belief in the Word of God and in the mercy and love of God, began the slow build of a civilisation within America which has gradually broken into the mainstream. This was never more dramatically demonstrated than with Martin Luther King with his King James Version-led marches in the 1960s which finally sealed the victory won in 1865.

The number of Christians in the former slave sector grew. In the 1790s, there were 12,000 black Methodists and 13,000 black Baptists. In 1860 this number had gone up to about 400,000. By 1900 there were 2.7 million black Church members out of a black population of 8.3 million. The 2.7 million figure does not include the unaffiliated members. The Words of God in the Churches became the education and the ever-strengthening political muscle in the long, bitter but tenacious struggle for full equality.

Bi-racial Churches all but disappeared. The white Methodist intervention had been a stepping stone. The black preachers now took up their own Methodism, as did other Churches. They took it into the new struggle to construct from the post-slavery debris entirely new communities. This was a very tough and complex task following centuries of chains and objectification and disbarment from any but the most rudimentary social organisation. Even family had been destroyed. Fellowship was found in the Churches after the war just as much as worship; singing, praying, planning, organising and caring for each other began in the Methodist and Baptist Churches.

The century of black progress that followed abolition and secured it, is a compelling time in human history. Whatever religion you might or might not have, you cannot fail to be impressed and moved by the way in which the African-Americans shook off the nullification of their humanity which had lasted for centuries. Their dynamic came through faith, founded in the King James Version. It was by the Bible that they fought their way to freedom and community. In the process they gave the world a new cultural sound and song. This happened through the black denominations, in black Churches in which the Bible was the Sacred Law. The Churches were the major instrument in bringing together, shaping, educating and leading the scattered and abandoned millions who had been told they were no longer slaves but no longer necessary.

The white South had failed. By some alchemy of the human spirit, many of them tried to turn defeat into a moral victory. But they were a society which had been stripped of its meaning and its long-inherited structure. Their destroyed lands and towns and churches, their bankruptcies and the loss, as they saw it, of a large and cheap labour force, threw them back on their own resources. Some went into a century of denial and brutality. Others re-thought and rebuilt.

It was in this regard that women, who had been called upon to do so much of men's work in the war, began to sew the riven society together. Samuel S. Hill, author of *Religion and the Results of the Civil War*, wrote:

During the Civil War, Southern women were called upon to perform many tasks normally fulfilled by men, including meeting the needs of soldiers through soldiers' aid societies, managing plantations, mills and stores in the absence of men, and in many instances 'refugeeing' whole families – finding food and clothing for them when there was little to be found.

After the War, white Southern women rebuilt or aided husbands in building plantations, and often taught school or took in sewing to generate badly needed income. Many women had to support themselves or their families alone. Of the million men who served in the Confederate Army, at least one-fourth died in battle or of disease and many more were incapacitated and unable to support their families.

Women's clubs and Temperance Unions sprang up and by the end of the nineteenth century women were becoming, though not considered of equal 'value', nevertheless a conspicuous presence in the Churches, especially in the Methodist Churches, both black and white.

In the North, the women, according to Hill, were

laying it on the line on behalf of prohibition, suffrage and myriad social Gospel causes. Black women mainly in the South but also in the northern emigration destinations had some of the same agenda, but they worked exclusively through the congregations in their churches – caring for the poor, starting up schools, combating racism, expanding civil rights such as voting and in the area of employment . . . The positive outcome of the Civil War in America was the creation of far more widespread liberties and the opportunities which come from that.

The seismic upheaval of the American Civil War caused waves which swept in high tides across the United States for decades. The abolition of slavery was the one great result but it was as much a beginning as an end. And when the new struggle against racism began it was the churchmen and women, Bible in hand, who led it. Humanists, secularists, atheists, agnostics and the religiously indifferent also joined in the marches, but the cause was fuelled and led by the descendants of those who had suffered most and the leaders of those determined to see the positive consequences of abolition fully realised: and they were Church people.

Martin Luther King came out of the Civil War, speaking what he believed to be Bible truths. His life and his death concluded that historic movement which took African slaves out of bondage, across the river of Jordan, to be set free in what proudly called itself 'the land of the free'. Just under a century and a half after the last guns of war were fired in the southern United States, the world saw an Afro-American, a Christian, in that city on the hill, sworn in on the King James Version as President of the United States of America.

CHAPTER TWENTY
THE BIBLE AND EDUCATION

I t would be fair to claim that for its first three centuries, the King James Bible was, in general, the prime educating force in the English-speaking world. Its impact was stronger in the first two centuries. In the nineteenth century, although there was growing competition from popular fiction and literature, it was still the dominant book. This was the case in the United States before, during and after the Civil War. From about 1850–1900 America was enthralled by the Bible.

People learned to read in order to read the Bible and they learned to read by being taught through the Bible itself. In a substantial minority of cases, Bible reading led on to other religious books: the American Civil War has been called the most religiously literate war in history, as the British Civil War was before it.

Even for those whose apprehension of faith was weak or non-existent, the Bible could be very useful. The flowing poetic prose of the King James Version ran into American speeches, journalism and literature with an enriching effect plainly evident in letters, pamphlets and books from the early seventeenth century and it continues to this day. It was a fine and stately tongue which helped dignify and unify the new States in their conversation just as the Bible unified them in their faith. This, with America's gift for new phrasings, new words and the welcome its English gave to immigrant terms has given it a dazzlingly layered language.

Most of all people were educated in the Christian religion and its history from Creation, through the Jewish Chronicles and prophecies and Psalms – which the Christians absorbed as 'theirs' because they were God's Word – to the New Testament. To the fundamental believers the Bible held an explanation for everything: from the creation of the world to the new Israelites, who became the new 'Saints', first in Britain and then in America, first white and then black.

The widespread concentration on daily learning rituals and practices which were introduced to increase the possibility of good moral Christian behaviour on this earth and eternal salvation in God's heaven, is hard for many of those in secular societies to fathom. But the records show it existed and in force. The King James Bible over centuries educated people who were proud of the privilege of being able to read the Holy Scriptures in their own language. It educated them primarily in faith. It was the call to arms: into the arms of the omnipotent Almighty and to arms in His cause. It was the Word of the Lord. But it also became the means of the unlocking of literary curiosity and ambition.

It was also thought the oracle which spoke mysteries, a guide to behaviour and morality, and the lawgiver full of grave warnings if the commandments of God were broken. For some it held prophecy of the future. It was the centrifugal force in and of all life and it demanded worship and obedience. Millions of people of all backgrounds over those three centuries willingly offered that worship and obedience as millions still do today.

But the Bible had other educative functions. It was a bounty of great stories. There were sacrifices, wars, prostitution, seduction, escapes, love affairs, judgements, conversions, family feuds, murders, disgraceful deeds, fabulous miracles and the astounding good-bad-vengeful-merciful-cruel-wise character of the Old Testament God. There were heroes and villains. There were Adam and Eve, David and Jonathan, Jesus Christ and Judas, Jacob, Nimrod, Samson and Delilah, John and Salome. There was the unblemished mother and the celibate son of God, there were the fishermen who became the fishers of men alongside pharaohs and Roman governors. Mystical writings could be found there and erotic poetry in the Song of Solomon.

There were proverbs to be recited and debated. The purity of perfect love and a perfect society could be cherished. The dark and wild furies of the Apocalypse could be relished by the Doomsday preachers. There was the host that encircled God – the angels and archangels, the seraphim and cherubim and all the company of heaven. And there was the finest jewel of all – the soul – endlessly discussed, full of promise and grace, the gift. Then there was Satan, who reared up at every opportunity to tempt and destroy, to entice and steal that soul away. Satan stalked the Bible and was the darkness of the world which so many of the faithful feared because they had experienced it in the fragile, mostly degraded condition of their daily existence. The book provided a mirror and a window: their own lives were reflected and enlarged.

There are those who claim it held back the shaping of the modern world. Others – including myself in the case of the King James Version – believe that it helped shape it often for the better and was integral in that process. There are those who see its moral qualities, those who can only see it as a breeder of more wickedness than goodness, more error than insight. Few can deny, though, that from 1611 in the English-speaking world, it was the primary education.

*   *   *

Such formal education as there was in America in the seventeenth and eighteenth centuries and in many cases well into the nineteenth, was provided by the Churches. Inevitably it was Bible-led. Rather surprisingly, it was free. This became the norm in America which was the first nation to provide free schooling.

The original settlers in New England demanded that everyone know the Bible. Reading was compulsory. In Massachusetts reluctant parents would have their children apprenticed so that they could 'read and understand the principles of religion and the capital laws of the country'. Connecticut passed a similar law in 1650. By 1700, Richard Middleton a historian of Colonial America tells us, about 70 per cent of men and 45 per cent of women could read and write and the numbers were growing steadily. Middleton points out: 'the New England Primer, used by children, contained the alphabet and a list of syllables and biblical or allied material – hymns, prayers, stories and accounts of Protestant Martyrs.'

New England was well organised. Although education followed a similar pattern elsewhere, it was more patchy. At the centre of the educational system was the Church, usually a nonconformist sect.

It was only in the eighteenth century that other bodies began to move in to education in America with the realisation that commerce, law and administration needed educated men (only men) who would drive the secular engines of this rapidly expanding new continent. There was also the Englightenment project which was welcomed by a number of New World scholars, politicans and intellectuals who saw that national scientific and industrial progress was not anathema to moral progress.

Initially it was the Church schools that had the means, the motivation and the staff. As schools grew in number, teaching became a profession: Harvard was founded in 1636 to provide a trained ministry; it was also determined to offer instruction in 'good literature, arts and sciences'. Teachers as well as preachers (often the same man) came out of Harvard and in 1693 the College of William and Mary was founded and Yale followed in 1701. Even so, many well-heeled Americans still sent their sons to Edinburgh University and to London for their training in law.

Slowly the colleges grew in number and slowly they moved away from the strictly theological curriculum. Benjamin Franklin, a Fellow of the Royal Society in London and the leading figure in the Enlightenment in America, helped to found the Academy of Philadelphia in 1751. This was the first secular institution to impose no religious test for admission. Despite Franklin's measured adulation of the English Methodist charismatic preacher George Whitefield, he saw the future of the country in science and not in religion and he set the example for the North. The Philadelphia Academy emphasised what was useful – arithmetic and accounts, for example, and a course to attend to the 'improvement of agriculture and mechanics'.

When, in 1754, New York obtained its first college, the Anglicans and the Presbyterians competed and failed in their attempts to make of it a partisan religious institution. When it opened, it was non-denominational and its curriculum was centred on 'languages and liberal arts and sciences'. The secularisation of American education had taken a grip.

Yet despite this, the Bible culture held on in many of the educational establishments, especially, as described in the previous chapter, in the southern states where the Church retained its hold for much longer.

This is not to say that the Churches were eased out of education. But the government did not have a constitutional stake in any religious denomination. There were numerous sects and they brought their religion into the schools and even more successfully into the Sunday schools. But there was no state-directed religion;

no authorised religion although the Authorised Version provided a common ground between the denominations.

They ordered things rather differently in the British Isles, where Anglicanism was the denomination that bound the crown to the constitution and the monarch was the Head of the Church of England as well as being the King or Queen and thereby constitutionally head of the country.

In the seventeenth century, apart from the very small numbers in the Presbyterian congregation who took literacy seriously from the outset, education for the vast majority of children in Britain barely existed. The wealthier boys were educated privately and some of them were groomed for Oxford and Cambridge – the only two universities in England, or for Edinburgh and St Andrews in Scotland. There was from the beginning the familiar English anxiety, as Derek Gillard author of *Education in England* points out, 'that . . . education would only lead to the working poor being discontented with their lot.' The fear of the upper classes of the potential disruption which would surely follow any education or liberation of the masses was unrelenting.

When education on a larger scale got under way it was managed through charity movements. The largest of these was a Protestant organisation which came out of the Society for the Promotion of Christian Knowledge (SPCK), founded in 1698, a domestic missionary project which built up a network of primary schools in England and Wales. There were similarly based enterprises in Scotland and in Ireland. At the end of the eighteenth century, Robert Raikes set up Sunday schools in Gloucestershire. These Sunday schools were the educational salvation of hundreds of thousands of poor children and only ten years later they were giving elementary education to three-quarters of a million children.

Derek Gillard point out that the SPCK formed the National Society for the Education of the Poor throughout England and

Wales. Thereby the Protestant Church got a hold on elementary and often secondary education which they have not lost. The Church was in the schools and the schools were in the Church. The King James Bible was used for assemblies and prayers every school day and Religious Instruction was in the syllabus. The local vicar considered it his right and duty to visit the local school whenever he wanted to and he would be on the board of governors. The Bible would be as prominent in the school halls as it was in the churches themselves and its authority would be reinforced by reference to people taking their oath on the Bible. These people would include kings and queens as well as witnesses in the well-reported trials in court.

In its own only seemingly bumbling way, the Anglican Church in England and Wales and then – in its different forms – in Scotland and Ireland, was taking up the credo of the Jesuits, who declared that once they had the child until the age of seven, they had the man. From 1811, the King James Bible was fundamental to the curriculum and the numerous Church of England schools were pervaded by its presence. This was often superficial, non-propagandist, even at times no more than a token presence. The reality was far less rigorous than the constitution suggested. Even this was to ease off yet further in the twentieth century. Until then the British Isles could still be described as a Christian country. Despite the mass of the indifferent and the increasing criticism from atheists and the claims of other religions, 'C of E' ruled, often by default. The exception was Northern Ireland, where its clash with the Roman Catholic schools led to intense indoctrination.

In the new industrial cities, the poor were herded to school partly out of charity but partly to give them the elementary education necessary to cope with the Industrial Revolution. 'Coping' could be interpreted as being trained to bear the boredom of the industrial process. This was to be induced by children being subjected to trained silences in uniform groups for hours on end and being delivered a dose of teaching, generally by rote. Obedience was the supreme virtue. The teaching was accompanied by threats of reprisals, earthly and heavenly, should any deviations be attempted. These were often taken with a large pinch of salt and did little to endear religion to many industrial workers. But it was a start.

School attendances rose in the early nineteenth century, a movement which owed much to religious support. In 1816, 875,000 of the country's 1.5 million children 'attended a school of some kind for some period'. By 1855, this was 1.45 million out of 1.75 million. The average length of attendance was one year. Nevertheless, the majority of the population shunted their way forward: writing and arithmetic eventually became a regular part of the school curriculum and later there was an inclusion of other subjects, geography and history.

A new system was introduced late in the nineteenth century, called 'the steam engine of the moral world'. This involved the transfer of the new factory system into the schoolroom. Teachers would walk up and down the aisles between hundreds of small shared desks, not unlike factory foremen or, to be hyperbolic, plantation bosses in the slave fields, and supervise repetitive exercises. In this way, one man could 'teach' hundreds of children the same lessons at the same time and the authority of what was being taught was not in doubt. The stalking master was the Old Testament God in that classroom.

Sunday schools continued to thrive – for adults as well as for children, but only for Bible studies. Writing and arithmetic were considered 'dangerous . . . and even harmful'. In 1807, one Justice of the Peace said, of the poor receiving an education: 'as to writing and arithmetic, it may be apprehended that such a degree of knowledge would produce in them a disrelish for the laborious occupations of life.' The original idea, which had turned into a hard 'philosophy' that the poor must be kept in their place, was still, in many quarters, as active as it had been in the time of Tyndale, when similar arguments had been used to oppose the translation of the Bible into English.

For all the changes in the Reformation, the Civil Wars and the Enlightenment, the masses in the British Isles were treated as if they were at one and the same time, helpless and inferior yet potentially revolutionary. They had to be curbed even though they were already crushed. Yet the King James Bible could be an escape. If the poor had to be given one book only, then the King James Version, in their own language, was as nourishing and as potentially liberating as any.

The Church of England was far from being the villain in all this. For who else cared? Charities were in their infancy: national government was absent and local government was often downright opposed to the expense of education. So the nonconformist Churches looked after their own as they had done for years and there were Dame schools, small private enterprises, and independent establishments which became, in the mid-century, public (i.e. privately paid for) schools. A few public schools such as Eton already existed as did a number of grammar schools. At these schools the study of the classics was more intensive than the study of religion but the religious basis of life was 'taken for granted' with all the long habit and lack of enthusiasm that phrase describes.

The focus of the internal missionary campaign was among the poor and here the Church of England was the main mover. If you thought education to be desirable for children, then the Established Church's dedication was admirable. Many were opposed to it, especially the industrialists and mass manufacturers who employed tens of thousands of very young children.

Religion was the 'First R' alongside 'Reading, Writing and 'Rithmetic'. When the government did begin to give grants to schools they went through religious channels. Piecemeal, unsatisfactory, often well-intended, often negligent, the education of the majority of children achieved a national platform only in 1870 with the Elementary Education Act. This established compulsory education for all children aged five to eleven and was driven on to the statute books by men of religious conviction and biblical learning.

But the state did not drive out the Churches. The Anglican Church took full advantage of the government's offer of funds for new buildings and within fifteen years the number of Church of England schools, at a crippling cost to itself, rose from 6,382 to 11,864. (In the same period, Catholic schools rose from 750 to 892.) Attendance at Protestant Church schools doubled to 2 million.

At the beginning of the twentieth century, the Church schools secured government funding for the secular curriculum but held on to their privileged position in the matter of religious education. In the twentieth century, driven by the National Society set up in 1811, the national religion was still fundamental to the national education, although there were other faith schools, most importantly the Roman Catholic.

The Church schools were served by some admirable men and women whose religious conviction was central to the way they tackled their society. One such was Joshua Watson, who retired from business in 1814, having done well as a wine merchant out of the Napoleonic Wars. He dedicated the rest of his long life – until 1855 – to the provision of a Christian education for the many. He was referred to as 'the best layman in England' and he devoted all his working time and a large part of his great fortune to the National Society, which upheld the religious component in education. His aim was to plant Protestant Christianity in the minds of the impoverished young who would, he believed, benefit both spiritually and materially from a religious education.

He was determined to put a Church school in every parish in the land. At that time, the first half of the nineteenth century, when the Established Church was yet again publicly arraigned for its corruption and its effete nature, this was a bold ambition. He saw it through. Many a village in the remotest parts of the kingdom was to benefit from the small and sturdy little schools which gave the most disadvantaged an educational start in life and hopefully brought to the Church its future congregations. Joshua Watson was at the heart of this achievement. His services to the Church, it was said, were so manifold and so ubiquitous that William Wordsworth suggested that to the petition in the Litany should be added the clause 'To all Bishops, Priests and Deacons' the words 'and also Joshua Watson'.

In a lecture given in 1961 to celebrate the National Society's 150th anniversary, Canon Charles Smyth of Corpus Christi College, Cambridge, used the occasion to revive the reputation of Joshua Watson. He gave him much of the credit for what was a successful educational mission of the Anglican Church inside its own country. Towards the end of his lecture he said:

> Regarded in the light of our modern educational system, with all the resources of the community behind it, this [what Joshua Watson had achieved] may seem very inadequate and unenlightened. But, regarded against the background of the widespread ignorance and brutality of the England of the Napoleonic Wars, it can be recognised as a heroic missionary enterprise, financed by private charity, and designed to illuminate the surrounding darkness and to rescue the children of the poor, particularly in the new industrial and manufacturing towns, from heathenism and barbarity.

The Protestant religion, in the English-speaking world, through its Bible, at the very least opened the doors of education to millions who had been shut out from learning until this book of faith brought them their enlightenment.

CHAPTER TWENTY-ONE
ON A MISSION AROUND THE WORLD

The Protestant mission around the world – it was to include America, Oceania, Africa, India, China, Australia, New Zealand, Canada and more than a hundred other destinations – began, in earnest, some centuries after the Roman Catholic mission. But when it got under way, it had lasting effects. The central instrument was the King James Bible. Those who had not heard *must* hear, for without it, the Protestants believed, their earthly lives would be condemned to sin and an eternal peace would be denied them. And, most vitally, they had the truth in the Word. Did not the one God in their Bible of truth command all Christians according to Mark, when 'He said unto them, Go ye into all the world, and preach the Gospel to every creature'?

It could be argued that the British Protestant mission abroad began when the Pilgrim Fathers reached the east coast of America. There were missions to neighbouring Indian tribes. They were tentative and under-resourced, but that was to be expected from an alien community fighting a neck and neck battle for survival. Nevertheless the indigenous neighbouring population was approached by those who saw part of their Christian duty to spread the Word of the Lord. The King James Bible was translated into Indian languages. The 'prayer towns' were established and it was in these, outside their own settlements, that the dedicated Puritans hoped, as it proved rather over-optimistically, that their seeds might find fertile ground.

But at the end of the eighteenth century – coincidentally at the time of what was thought by some to be the victory of the Enlightenment – there was a London outburst of missionary work. The Reverend Thomas Coke was appointed by the Wesleyan Conference in 1790 as general supervisor of what would be a global reach of Methodist World Missions. As if moved by the spirit of emulation, the Baptists set up their Missionary Society in 1792, the Congregationalists came into the ring in 1795, Anglican evangelicals in 1799, the British and Foreign Bible Society in 1804 and an American Board of Communities for Foreign Mission in 1810.

As Diarmaid MacCulloch points out, 'this activity had a complementary relationship with that feature of British Protestantism unique in Europe, its large sector of churches separate from the established churches.' It had, also, in common, the King James Bible which over almost two centuries had securely established itself as the national book, and for the religious the key to life and the answer to death.

Perhaps the French Revolution and the consequent increase in apocalyptic fears were two of the factors which triggered this apparently sudden movement in London. Perhaps Romanticism encouraged the religiously minded to see in the 'natural' condition of much of the planet a ready earth to farm. Or could it have been a 'London Awakening'? Whatever the combination of causes, by 1830 around 60 per cent of British Protestants were involved in some variety of evangelical religious practice. There was also that visceral recurring fear that the end of the world was nigh: between 1800 and 1840 over a hundred books were published scouring the evidence for the end of the world.

In many cases, colonial and later imperial rule followed the missionaries: and in many cases, devastation of local cultures was the result. It is difficult to tell the missionary story with enthusiastic one-sidedness. While it is impossible to doubt the integrity of the majority of individual missionaries and possible to give their guiding organisations full credit for what they saw as a need for the world to be 'improved', 'saved', and 'brought to Christ', some of the human and cultural results, often the debris, are still with us. And 'enthusiastic one-sidedness' cannot escape blame.

Whether, given the way the nineteenth and twentieth centuries became harnessed to the unbridled horsepower of the industrial and then the technological and then the ideological revolutions, the 'native' peoples would have stood a better chance without Christianity, who can tell? We cannot trust the thesis that all the 'natives' lived in a state of innocence until the arrival of the horrors of the Europeans and the Americans. There is too much evidence in pre-colonial life of mayhem, murder, savagery and oppression. The attempt to zone the world geographically into the *good* and the *bad* does not seem to work: the bad is always present, the good has always had to be struggled for and 'civilisations' come out of that struggle.

Nevertheless there was much to mourn on the part of those who met the zealous brunt of the Protestant missionaries: as there was much to mourn among the missionaries themselves whose lives were cut down, whose teachings were ignored and whose influence was often minimal. Despair and loss were often shared.

Oceania was a priority for the London Missionary Society. It had become England's province of the tropical imagination after the bold voyages of Captain Cook and the botanical harvesting of Joseph Banks. Tahiti would be the goal and a ship carrying about thirty practical English missionaries set out with an expectation not unakin to those of the Pilgrim Fathers. It was an all but total disaster. Some went native in what proved to be a treacherous Eden; others were murdered; at least one missionary went insane – he had tried to teach Tahitians Hebrew, but the connection is not established – until only one missionary remained. Yet his story, of which more later, can be seen as inspirational and in the longer view of the Christian mission can be claimed to be successful.

Other Pacific Islands were boarded with, at first, little success, though there again, the sheer obstinate belief in themselves and their mission which was displayed by a handful of Christian Englishmen bore Christian fruit in longer terms. It was a strange, mad enterprise, looking back, this assault on deep, alien, illiterate, untechnological oceanic cultures by these raw platoons of theologically primed, industrially educated, European-based men. Even stranger when we realise that to these peoples with their own gods, their own ways, they brought what must have seemed such a weird story.

The story was of a monotheistic, invisible, all-powerful, all-merciful God and His Son Jesus Christ whom He had watched crucified on the Cross to save the world from sins which most oceanic people did not see as sins at all. Yet Christ became the figure who was eventually to bridge the divide between these wide-apart cultures.

The Maoris took more readily to Christianity and by 1845 we are told that at least half the Maori population was worshipping in churches – outnumbering European churchgoers. They followed Isaiah's lead in the Old Testament. And they discovered to their relief that nothing in the King James Version forbade tattooing. But when the colonists grew in number, following Roman Catholic colonists in Central and South Africa, and Protestant colonists in North America, they wanted more land, in this case Maori land, without Maori interference or participation. It was easier to murder them and rob them of their territories than to convert them, and this is what happened.

The Churches stood in the way of this ethnic cleansing but the Churches were pushed aside. Lust for land swept aside the Bible however much those who slaughtered might give it homage and, in a bewildering way, respect. And they had read in the Old Testament that God's chosen people in the Old Testament had not flinched from slaughtering whole peoples whom they saw as their enemies. God had not discouraged them. The missionary project exposed the Bible to some sceptics as merely a pawn, just another power-political player on the board. There was one Bible for war and another for peace, it seemed; one for the strong, another for the weak; one for contemplation, another for action; one for murder, another for compassion.

In Australia it was even worse. In all but the rarest cases, the missionaries gave up on Australia's native population and joined sides with the colonial imperialists. Those who tried to 'save' them were swept aside by the conscious and unconscious decision that the Aboriginals were doomed and deserved nothing. There was little attempt to preserve their languages or their culture.

For almost a century and a half innumerable children were ripped away from their natural parents and forced through a mission education which fitted them for little more than deracinated depression and varieties of near slavery. Even here, though, it would be unjust to blame the Church solely. The mission school education was sincerely and correctly thought to be an improvement on the education in the new state that the children could expect elsewhere. They had been abandoned to the marginal remains of their shrinking homelands. The priorities and the firepower of the white British Protestant immigrants chose to ignore the Sermon on the Mount.

Good work was done with those who had been exiled to

Australia for 'crimes', many of which nowadays we would regard as pardonable or trivial. Courageous men of the Churches went into those dangerous early antipodean settlements much as their colleagues braved the dark satanic mill towns of England, and an alternative to the desperation of exiled imprisonment was offered and sometimes taken up.

In time white-dominated New Zealand and white-dominated Australia laid fair claim to be part of a Christian – an Anglican-nonconformist Roman Catholic – global fraternity, and the Pacific Islands were and are also alongside. In that time much of the indigenous culture has been erased.

The African experience was different in crucial ways and, in my view, hardly surprisingly, it mirrors the African-American experience which came out of slavery. In short, the Africans took Christianity and moulded it to fit their own religions just as the African-Americans took nonconformist Christianity and made it theirs.

In Africa, the Christian missionaries met other strong faiths – Islam, Hinduism and Buddhism, and the greatest of these was Islam. It seemed, according to MacCulloch, that 'in the early 19th century, the most plausible picture of the future was that black Africa would have become overwhelmingly Muslim, and Muslim growth there remained spectacular throughout the century.' However, the Christian mission in that same century made even more spectacular progress. The British missionaries took breath-taking risks in their pursuit of converts.

There were key features in Christianity which meshed with many of the African belief patterns. These patterns were not the messages which were being preached by those who brought their Bible learning into Africa, but they were deep in Christianity and they became the binding that fed the rapid growth of an African evangelical Christianity. Today in some African countries, it is as vibrant and confident as any in the world.

The King James Bible is a book of signs and wonders, miracles and coded messages revealing to the spiritually aware and to the initiate that this is how God shows his face. Africans were used to looking for such signs and interpreting such wonders and messages. The Bible spoke of spirits – commonly present in African religions – and explained in mysterious terms but in terms demanding to be believed, how the world came about. It described in detail the descent of the family of man. The genealogies were a perfect fit with African familial traditions.

Polygamy was a stumbling point for the Christian missionaries but not for the Africans who knew their Old Testament and admired the marital customs of the great patriarchs. Certain enlightened missionaries admitted that the Africans' argument from the Bible was sound. John William Colenso, a Cornishman who became the first Bishop of Natal, argued that the Zulus made a good biblical case for polygamy. He wrote about this in 1862 in a pamphlet addressed to the Archbishop of Canterbury. He was condemned as a troublemaker.

It was a subject which did not go away. In 1917, sixty-five Yoruba ministers were expelled from the Nigerian Methodist Church for polygamy. They went off and founded their own Church: the United African Methodists. Later there was a growing feminist voice which criticised and condemned polygamy. In countries where women were often the most dedicated and gifted Christians, theirs became an increasingly influential argument.

Meanwhile the Churches went about their wider agenda by funding schools – in South Africa the Xhosa word for 'Christians' was 'schools'. And the Bible itself was not only the location of the Word of God, it became a sacred object which to touch was to be calmed or healed.

India, by contrast, was a failure for the Protestant missions. There were those, most prominently Bishop Samuel Horsley, who was a supporter of the Society for the Propagation of the Gospels, who did not think it was part of God's plan that Britain should seek to change the religion of another country. In the Caribbean he had supported the mission because he had seen no religion.

The East India Company, so powerful that its own army was bigger than the British Army, agreed with Bishop Horsley. They were most reluctantly forced to support the missionary movement in 1813 after a campaign led by William Wilberforce. Proselytisers saw this massive subcontinent as an unparalleled opportunity to bring millions of souls to God. But Hinduism and Islam were deeply entrenched and Taoism and Buddhism had a strong hold: these deep faiths were not to be overturned easily. It proved that they were not to be overturned at all, despite some small gains for the Protestant mission. And the East India Company's insistence on favouring Christianity instead of maintaining a traditional neutrality was one cause of the Great Indian Rebellion of 1857, the most serious mutiny against any European colonial power in the whole of the nineteenth century. The company was to rue the day it abandoned its successful policy of leaving indigenous religions alone.

After that rebellion, Queen Victoria ended the ascendancy of the East India Company and ordered the new government to 'abstain from any interference with the religious belief or worship of any of our subjects'. The lesson had been hard learned. The zeal of Wilberforce and others had unexpected consequences of an undeniably negative nature.

The belief that there was one God only who reigned to rule all the world and that this God had to be made known to the world that had lived in darkness without His light, was gone. The royal decree of King James in 1611 had declared the Bible to be the Word of the sole God and he had declared himself to rule by Divine Right. That was extinguished. Christianity from now on was but one religion among many and Protestantism was but one branch of Christianity.

This did not stop the missions. It did not for many years strip individuals of their conviction that the Word of the Christian God had to be spread abroad and the way of the path of Jesus Christ was the only road to sinlessness and salvation. It did, though, mark a turning point. In India, Christianity, admittedly with few representatives but nevertheless with the might of 250 years of the Protestant Advance behind it, had come up against Hinduism and Islam in their implacable might: and retreated.

In China there was a momentous episode of Christian fanaticism which sparked a war called 'the most destructive civil war in world history' – worse in casualties and damage than the American Civil War and almost as devastating as the First World War. This was led by Hong Xiuquan, who had been encouraged to read Christian books by an American missionary. Hong, who had suffered several nervous breakdowns, received many visions from 'God'. The mix of his new philosophy and the breadth of his appeal included a wish to return to the Ming Dynasty, a promise to end corruption and a vow to bring about social equality. He brought about massacres.

The missions of the Protestants, which followed earlier missions of the Jesuits in China, made converts and held on to them after the collapse of the Hong Xiaquan phenomenon. But as in Japan and Korea, the twentieth-century tornados of ideological change swept away all but a valiant few.

The most stunning success for the Protestant mission was in the United States of America. In 1815, active Church membership was around a quarter of the population, which then stood at 8.5 million. A century later it was about 50 per cent of a population which had reached 100 million. MacCulloch writes: 'that growth reflected the dynamism, freedom, high literacy rates and opportunity available in this society, and the Christian religion seemed to owe its success to a competitive and innovative spirit as much as did American commerce and industry.' More subdivisions in the Protestant Church seemed to spring up by the year. The idea of a mission became part of a wider American vocabulary. The overall mission was to do God's work in America, though knowing what would bring Godly benefits was not always certain. The evangelicals, for example, fuelled the temperance movement or mission which led America to prohibition which led to widespread organised crime. This, perhaps, is a classic example of the road to hell being paved with good intentions.

The Mormons – the Latter Day Saints – were another mission and despite the ridicule and persecution, the Mormons persisted and persist. Their polygamous ways trouble the authorities. These same authorities also find another group, the Jehovah's Witnesses, troublesome. They refuse to bear arms or acknowledge the state. They are on an endless world mission. The Jehovah's Witnesses still knock politely on doors throughout the English-speaking world.

The determination of these Bible societies was to spread the Word of God and one sure method, they believed, was by printing and distributing as many Bibles as possible. Bible societies began in the late seventeenth and eighteenth centuries in Britain and America. The most ambitious of the British societies was the British and Foreign Bible Society (BFBS), established in London in 1804. This benefited from the energy, wealth and connections of Wilberforce and by 1811 there were offices in Cairo and the beginnings of a network across Europe. In the middle of the nineteenth century the society undertook to provide translations of the King James Bible in all the languages of the British Empire. A hundred years later, the BFBS had over 7,500 auxiliaries. In 1901, the law that the Bible could only be printed in the King James

Version was lifted but it was the King James Version which was still dominant well into the twentieth century. New English versions have been criticised as adulterations, shadows, even betrayals of the original.

The American Bible Society was formed in 1816 and at their first meeting in New York, the representatives of thirty-five Bible societies agreed to work for the distribution of 'the Holy Scripture without note or comment'. In the twentieth century, more than 125 new Bible societies emerged – in Australia, but also in Cambodia, Hong Kong, Austria and Chile. By 1904, the American Bible Society had supplied nearly 181 million copies of the Scriptures and spent about £14 million on translations and their distribution. During the Second World War, the society circulated an estimated 45 million copies of Scripture. No book in history has matched the general distribution achieved by the King James Bible. The command to the Apostles to broadcast the Gospels was accomplished around the globe. In 1946, the United Bible Societies were founded, an alliance of 135 national Bible societies working in more than 200 countries. The King James Version now spoke to the world in many tongues, including an English which would have been foreign to King James.

These missionaries, mostly from the nonconformist Churches, preponderantly Methodists and Baptists, provide heroic stories in the history of faith. Henry Nott, for example, a bricklayer, joined the mission ship *Duff* which, as I have mentioned, sailed to Tahiti in 1797. It left the thirty missionaries on the island and went back to England for new supplies which were not to arrive for five years. During that time several of Nott's fellow missionaries deserted, died, were murdered or went insane.

Nott was the only survivor and spent the five years' wait learning the Tahitian language. He would eventually translate the

King James Bible into Tahitian. He attempted to befriend the fearsome King Pomare II but in those five years while waiting for the *Duff* to return from England he made not a single convert. He returned to England only twice in forty-seven years. This island and others like it were far from the sun-kissed innocence romantically relayed from the inaccurately reported experiences of Fletcher Christian (so desperately romantic in fact that it lured him into murder and mutiny). One group of Tahitians killed their children as soon as they were born: King Pomare's chief wife belonged to that sect. There were constant wars after which the houses of the defeated were burned, prisoners butchered, their bodies pounded to pulp with large stones, then dried out, holed in the middle and worn like a poncho. Children were sacrificed to idols: Nott estimated that in his thirty-year reign, Pomare sacrificed 2,000 victims to his idols.

Henry Nott's line of defence and attack was to quote from the Bible, especially and, he records, repeatedly from the Gospel according to St John, chapter 3 verse 16: 'For God so loved the world, that he gave his only begotten Son, that whosoever believeth in him should not perish, but have everlasting life.' It had been the favourite line of Martin Luther, who is said to have repeated it three times in his death throes.

Nott's house was destroyed; his possessions stolen; his printing type melted down for bullets. By 1810, alone and beggared, Nott described himself as 'troubled . . . persecuted . . . cast down . . . but not in despair'. He held to his faith that one day Christ would triumph in those islands.

It is not so easy to dismiss such resolution and such faith. Perhaps it was all a delusion. Perhaps Nott and the many other missionaries like him were in a trance of fanaticism, mesmerised by a promise which devoured their reason. Or perhaps through their religion they dug more deeply into their inner resources than most do and found there a source of conviction which carried its own knowledge. Perhaps they believed because they knew something hidden from most of us.

After eighteen years, Nott's persistence was rewarded: or he might say his call to faith was answered. Pomare had a chapel built; 31 natives agreed to renounce idolatry and the number sped up to 800. King Pomare won a great battle and after his victory he destroyed all the heathen idols and altars he could find. Schools were established and a huge church was built at Papara – 712 feet long, 54 feet wide, containing three pulpits, 260 feet apart, so that three sermons could be preached simultaneously. In 1819, King Pomare was baptised, watched by more than 5,000 of his subjects. Henry Nott, the bricklayer from Bromsgrove, had, as he would see it by the grace of God, helped Tahiti to see the true light and become an active Christian community and put aside its murderous heathen ways.

William Carey, a cobbler, went to India as a Baptist missionary at the age of thirty-three and stayed there for forty-one years. He never returned to England. He was part of what was admitted to be an unsuccessful mission but it was not for want of trying on his part. He had schools built, and travelled thousands of miles across the subcontinent preaching the Word. By the time of his death in 1834, Carey had helped to set up more than thirty different missionary stations in different parts of India. His greatest achievement was to translate the Scriptures into Bengali, which set off a spate of translations into fifteen other languages – Sanskrit, Hindustani, Person, Maratha, Guajarati, Oriya . . . The small but tenacious congregations of Christians in India today still honour him.

There is Alexander Mackay, a Scot, an engineer missionary who arrived in Zanzibar in 1876. It took him two years to achieve his first goal and get into Uganda. He spent fourteen years there without once returning to Scotland. Mackay built 230 miles of road, and translated Matthew's Gospel. He died of a virulent tropical disease having seen his bishop murdered, his pupils burned and his converts and friends strangled or clubbed to death. 'Prepare ye the way of the Lord' was the injunction that inspired him and so he did.

Uganda's Christian community had grown out of the example of Mackay who, it was reported, when surrounded by mayhem and threats of death, 'met it with calm blue eyes that never winked'. Another missionary wrote of him: 'it is worth going a long journey to see one man of this kind, working day after day without a syllable of complaint or a moan and to hear him lead his little flock in singing and prayer to show forth God's kindness in the morning and his faithfulness every night.' Perhaps his example eventually led to the consecration of John Sentamu as Archbishop of York in 2005.

There were many like him: Samuel Marsden in Australia; Mary Slessor, a Scot, in Africa; another Scot, James Chalmers, in the Cook Islands for ten years and New Guinea for twenty-four, until he was murdered by cannibal tribesmen; and yet another Scot, James Gilmour, who went to Mongolia and died there at the age of forty-seven after twenty-one years of service. J. Hudson Taylor, an English missionary to China, founded the China Inland Mission, which at his death included 205 mission stations, 800 missionaries and 125,000 Chinese Christians.

In 1885, there were the 'Cambridge Seven' – seven young graduates from Cambridge. They had a wide influence in inspiring student volunteer movements and their remarkable successes in China were published in *The Evangelisation of the World*, which was distributed to every YMCA and YWCA throughout Britain and the United States.

The records of these people, mostly working alone in initially alien and hostile cultures with languages hard for Europeans to grasp, must inspire respect at the very least, even from the most case-hardened agnostics and atheists. Unless they are thought to be utterly misguided, their undoubted energies misdirected, their intrusions into foreign cultures undesirable. In which case what they did is to be written off and even damned.

Yet the emphasis on education can be seen as a benefit. It is relevant to quote from a speech by King M'Tesa of Uganda:

> The Arabs and the white men behave exactly as they are taught in their books, do they not? The Arabs come here for ivory and slaves; as we all know they do not always speak the truth and they buy slaves, putting them in chains, beating them and taking them far away to sell. But when white men are offered slaves they say 'shall we make our brothers slaves? No. We are all sons of God.' When the explorers Speke and Grant came here, they behaved well. Indeed I have not heard a white man tell a lie yet. I say that the white men are greatly superior to the Arabs and I think, therefore, that their book must be a better book than Mohammed's.

There must have been some authoritarian, brutal missionaries. Accounts of various missions are scarce. There will always be the divide between those who see the missionaries as prejudiced and interventionist, out to destroy an existing culture, and those who see them as bringers of light, who prepared the way for their inevitable takeover by the rampaging West.

What happened, in my view, is that the idea of empire and especially the British Empire, because it was the biggest and the most recent, got such a bad name that its reputation stained that of the missions. All empires have always behaved badly which does not mean that everything within them is bad. Moreover in the UK Christianity waned rapidly in the second half of the twentieth century, after the British Empire was finally dissolved, and there grew in strength a sense of disillusionment, almost of being cheated, which contaminated everything to do with Christianity. And the voice of the non-believers grew louder in the land and became more acceptable and energising for the media. The novelty of their zest recalls the early evangelicals.

None of this, I think, should take away from the efforts of valiant and often good people to bring to quarters of the world they considered in peril the opportunities to embrace a religion, in the New Testament, of high morality and kindness. That it failed on many occasions is not especially surprising, given its entanglement with the lusts of empire-building and the complications of civilisations which they encountered and of which they knew very little at the outset. That it succeeded could be regarded as a loss or a gain depending on your point of departure. That it, the Word of God in the King James Bible, sent out across the world cohorts of outstandingly brave and virtuous people and that some good came of it can hardly be denied.

But to Christians, these missions were all admirable and their results a testament to the glory of God. That there have been setbacks is disappointing but they should not be a cause of despair. The missions go on. The Bible they believe dwells in eternal life. The world still has to be saved and by repeated efforts Christians believe that it will be saved. Such is the prayer and the faith of the dedicated today who find inspiration in these early attempts to spread the Word.

CHAPTER TWENTY-TWO
THE BIBLE AND SEX

When men began to look for ways to control society, language, firepower and sex followed fear as the best available methods. The Bible is packed with examples of both fear and sex. God exemplified the authority to crush and terrify: the characters in the Bible provide a gallery of sexual activities which could be examined for many a different version of heaven or hell.

There was polygamy among the most respected patriarchs; there was incest and the prostitution of daughters by their fathers. There were mass rapes. There were banning orders on a range of sexual activities which were successfully broken, often to positive and much applauded effect. Adultery was practised and denied. Seduction was an art which could either further or thwart the will of divine destiny. The erotic was celebrated in sexually abandoned verse so lightly disguised that a fig leaf would have seemed like an overcoat. There was the repudiation of all eroticism. There was the introduction of sin to sex and guilt to sin. Then, for the brave, a sensual and dark engagement with the brew of guilt, sin and sex, more dangerous eroticism spurred on by such dramatic constraints. The Bible has provoked a multitude of variations, often to spite it, sometimes in the strict obedience to it.

There were heroines of sexual liberation and hordes of women condemned to sexual servitude. Sexual meekness was a bond and a virtue but it also became an object to desire in itself, heightened further by protestations of chastity. There is prostitution and celibacy, orgies and the love between men which is accepted and sex between men that is abominated. There is onanistic sex for which the Lord slaughters you. There is a fuse of mystical sex with the divine Creator of all things visible and invisible. There are detailed lists of prohibitions which imply much licentiousness and rampage. There is sexual assault and tenderness, cruelty, the wreckage of jealousy and the severe duty to breed, protect and build up family. We read of Eve begetting the human race in original sin according to St Augustine; Mary conceived of Christ in immaculation to redeem and to save the human race, according to the Gospels; and Salome the slut.

Interpretations of what these and other women represent fill volumes, from phallocentric essays to the relatively recent scholarly counter-attacks by feminist authors. There is in the Bible almost all that sex can offer: and the King James Version's ubiquitous availability over the four centuries has broadcast it far and wide.

The classicist author, Edith Hamilton, has written that the Bible is the only book in the world up to the twentieth century which looks at women as human beings no better and no worse than men. The Old Testament writers, she argues, described them just as impartially as they did men, free from prejudice and even from condescension.

Eve is born out of the body of Adam to be the mother of the human race. Yet when she yields to the beguiling serpent and eats the apple she condemned that race, according to the early commentators. In some ways the story of the history of the Bible is how it is able to fit the story to the changing face of authority. The Middle

Ages especially targeted Eve for this original sin because it suited their rule, and Milton took it up in *Paradise Lost*.

Eve was punished for this sin, as forever after was woman. Hers was to be a life of sorrow and pain in childbirth and child loss and unquestioning obedience under the heel of her husband. Men who wanted to keep women in domestic slavery invoked the spoiling of the Garden of Eden at every turn: women, when they were allowed their full public voice, pointed out that Eve was created out of a man: all men and women since were created out of women. But Eve became the exemplar of satanic sexual temptation's greatest triumph: 'and the serpent beguiled her, and she did eat.' From then on, until deep into the modern age, woman was cast as the temptress, the untrusted, the seducer, the sexually rapacious, ungovernable, to be kept chained. An extreme of this was in 'Malleus Maleficarum' (The Hammer of Witches), in which two German Dominicans, in 1486, took the central notion, as they saw it, of the sin of women, to launch three centuries of persecution of 'witches'.

Eve became the temptress long before the Bible was translated into the King James Version. All the women discussed in this chapter have histories which precede 1611. But the printing and the unprecedented distribution of the Bible to the ambitious, increasingly populous and avidly literate English-speaking world brought Eve and other biblical women to a wider, a more interrogative, a more intrigued public than ever before.

Biblical women were irresistible to writers. High culture stepped up to the plate from John Milton's *Samson Agonistes* to Oscar Wilde's and Cavafy's *Salome*. Popular culture weighed in through films – from *All About Eve* to the *Last Temptation*, which portrayed Mary Magdalene as Eve's direct prostituted heiress. There were popular songs, from 'Jezebel' to 'Delilah'. And in the layering of many novels, plays and poems we find direct and glancing references to Mary the Mother of God, to Ruth, to Jezebel in Lesley Hazleton's trilogy *Jezebel: The Untold Story of the Bible's Harlot Queen*, and the many accounts that include Mary Magdalene. Sex and the treatment of women were widely discussed after the King James Version made its way.

One claim, which came after 1611, was that Adam and Eve hold out the model for monogamy. One woman is created for one man. Eve is wrested from Adam's rib which emphasises that they were once one. As they will be again. 'Wherefore a man shall leave father and mother, and shall cleave to his wife: and they shall be two in one flesh.' And in 1 Corinthians xi, 11–12, Paul says: 'For as the woman is of the man, even so is the man also by the woman.'

The consensus today is that Eve has been sinfully misused. Pamela Norris in her book *Eve: A Biography* argues that the story of Eve has been used consistently 'to manipulate and control women'. Eve has also become a repository of male fears and fantasies. The story of Eve, to modern feminists, is the source of patriarchal misogyny in Christianity. The accusation in Genesis was that she had been tempted to eat of the Tree of the Knowledge of Good and Evil despite being forbidden to do so by God. That act was the root of all wickedness and for that alone women must be kept subject to men. It was very convenient for men.

Then there is Hagar. The story of Hagar has grown in the consciousness of Christians over the last three centuries partly because of its resonance in the African-American Christian communities.

Sarah, wife of Abraham who was to be the fountainhead of not one but three monotheistic religions – Judaism, Christianity, Islam – could not conceive. She offered her slave Hagar to Abraham who takes her, and a child is born, Ishmael. Sarah in her envy torments Hagar but she stays to be with the child. Some years later, Sarah conceives and Isaac is born. Sarah then forces Abraham to drive out Hagar and Ishmael with minimal provisions, destined for death by hunger. But Hagar's prayer to God saves them and they continue to live – though they stay outside society in the wilderness.

Hagar was victimised by the great commentators from St Augustine – who wrote that she symbolised the sinful condition of humanity – to Thomas Aquinas and John Wycliffe, who wrote that the children of Sarah were to be redeemed but the children of Hagar were 'cursed by nature and mere exiles', and were not to be redeemed.

This transparent and (by non-patriarchal standards) grotesque injustice has since been recognised. In America, several black feminist biblical historians have seen Hagar as someone with whom it is easy and important for former slaves to identify. She is seen as a slave forced into a pregnancy for the convenience of Abraham and the determination of Sarah that he should fulfil his dynastic destiny. Then she is expelled for no fault of her own, out of jealousy and the possessiveness of the non-slave wife when she has no need for her. She is, like the African-American slaves, a thing, an object, to be used at will and rejected when the use is over and thrown out without a thought for her future life or that of her child.

The theologian Dolores S. Williams writes:

Hagar has 'spoken' to generation after generation of black women because her story has been validated as true by suffering black people. She and Ishmael together, as family, like many black American families in which a lone woman/mother struggles to hold the family together in spite of the poverty to which ruling class economics consign it. Hagar, like many black women, goes into the wide world to make a living for herself and her child with only God by her side.

Hagar is a perfect example, I think, of how the contradictory and clashing nature of the Bible can re-address the world across the centuries. The Hagar 'story' was changed utterly by a reading radically at odds, scarcely even resembling, the original and acclaimed progress of Abraham and his seed. The one does not eradicate the other but it stands in powerful opposition to it.

Sarah is the establishment, the ruling caste, Hagar the slave, the abused outsider but also the survivor. These women bring other dimensions to the portrayal of women in the Bible. Though driven by procreation, it is not simply the gender and sex of Eve which shadows and colours other strong biblical women. As with Sarah and Hagar the context is vital. Sarah the unbearably barren and then unbearably jealous wife, only to become a competing mother is still with us now. Hagar's casting off is common.

Salome and Jezebel are more to be thought of as the expected daughters of the old Eve. Each of them has been revisited by modern feminists with rich rewards. We see how the characters become a caricature which fitted the dominant male culture of the time: more intriguingly, we are afforded subtler and plausible interpretations of the lives and actions of these women. Jezebel for example is traditionally a lustful unlicensed worshipper of the goddess of love who lured upstanding Israelites from their own God to Baal through her deployment of temple prostitutes. An evil power behind the throne, Jezebel is thrown, literally, to the dogs by fanatics. A modern reading sees her as an assertive woman baited and foully murdered by representatives of a male-dominated religion.

Judith gives us another strand: the use of sexuality to achieve greatness through service to her people. When Nebuchadnezzar's Persian army lays siege to Bethulia, the inhabitants think that God has abandoned them. Judith, a wealthy and beautiful widow, leaves the town at night, seeks out the leader of the army,

Holofernes (perhaps by posing as a prostitute?). She makes him drunk, hacks off his head, returns to the town and displays the severed head on the ramparts. The Persians panic: the Israelites charge out and slaughter them.

Judith is a heroine.

She was an example of the warrior queen, a woman as brave, cunning and successful in war as a man. She must have seduced Holofernes even if only through conversation and promises; she must have used those wicked feminine arts so feared and despised by the men who had cast women into the outer darkness and stigma of sinful sex. Yet her story rises above that. Judith is the most unexpected woman in the Bible: virtue and courage and leadership as an effective troika.

Mary Magdalene provokes inexhaustible reappraisals. Her presence in the life of Jesus Christ is unique. If we track her story, we begin in the Gospel according to St Luke. He reports that Jesus 'went throughout every city and village, preaching and shewing the glad tidings of the Kingdom of God: and the twelve were with him. And certain women, which had been healed of evil spirits and infirmities. Mary called Magdalene, out of whom went seven devils, and Joanna the wife of Chuza, Herod's steward, and Susanna, and many others, which ministered unto him of their substance.' Mary seems to be a woman of substance. As was to happen repeatedly over the next 2,000 years, women of a certain education and wealth were important early supporters of the Apostles and their heirs and successors.

There are four accounts of Mary Magdalene being present at the crucifixion – Matthew, Mark, Luke and John all refer to her. Luke and Matthew report that she was there when the body of Jesus was sealed in the tomb of Joseph of Arimathea; she could confirm that he was dead and she prepared the spices needed for the proper burial. Most significantly of all, according again to all four Apostles, it was Mary Magdalene who was the first person to see the risen Jesus, the first witness to the greatest of all miracles. This was the Christian proof of the God-in-Christ, the Resurrection with its promise of life everlasting. It was shown first before all others to Mary Magdalene. It was Mary Magdalene who told Peter and the other Apostles 'He is Risen' – this again recorded in all four Gospels.

She had an outstandingly privileged and unique role in what for Christians is the stem narrative of their faith. Yet the curse of Eve has been on her until quite recently. She has been represented by male commentators and film makers, lasciviously and certainly voyeuristically, as a prostitute, albeit an ultimately repentant prostitute. Much more damning that she should have been a prostitute. It fits in with centuries of stereotyping. It also encompasses the wishful thinking of some men whose constructs of sin and sex have seen and still see prostitution as an exciting and irresponsible access to carnal pleasure.

Scholars have looked in the Apocryphal texts and found a different story. They often contain evidence which seems as reliable as that which was waved through into the New Testament. In the Apocrypha, Mary Magdalene is portrayed as 'The Apostle to the Apostles' – which makes sense of her several key appearances in the Christ story. In some texts she is described as a visionary and a teacher of the early movement, and one who was loved by Jesus more than all other disciples.

We could be forgiven for seeing a conspiracy theory here: perhaps the excision of the Apocryphal books was not prissiness but yet another attempt in the institutional Church's ignominious history of reshaping the Word of God to suit the earthly politics of the men who led and ran the institution. These cuts arouse legitimate suspicions that a woman of such significance in the life and work of Christ disturbed the early Church's ordering of things too much to be tolerated. In several Gnostic Gospels, for instance, Mary is seen as a special disciple of Jesus who has a deeper understanding of His work and is asked to interpret it to the other disciples.

Even with just the evidence we have in Matthew, Mark, Luke and John, her 'specialness' is unquestionable. Her closeness to Christ undeniable. Her maternal support for him is a stated fact. Not a big leap to speculation that she was more educated than the fishers of men who formed the core of the twelve? More used to the discussion of ideas? Not unlikely. Nor is it at all unlikely that had the centrality of Mary Magdalene been acknowledged and celebrated from the beginning of the written Gospels then perhaps the history of Christianity and certainly the history of women in Christianity would have been radically different.

Was Mary Magdalene rubbed out to preserve a monopolistic male mafia? It is within the bounds of possibility and the psychology of those who decided to organise a work that became such an attractive and substantial force in the empire. Organisers are often at a distance from the activists, the doers. The Church of wealth, the Church that crowned emperors and excommunicated kings had to be a matching Church militant in those masculine societies. A woman as favoured by Christ as Mary, perhaps a woman of independent mind and means, was not helpful.

Some have gone further, unsupported by enough evidence, and claimed that Mary Magdalene was the wife of Christ and bore his children. If it could be proved, that would change the Christian world for ever: and perhaps for the better?

The Song of Solomon begins:

> The Song of Songs which is Solomon's. Let him kiss me with the kisses of his mouth: for thy love is better than wine. Because of the savour of thy good ointments thy name is as ointment poured forth. Therefore

do the virgins love thee. Draw me, we will run after thee. The King hath brought me into his chambers: we will be glad and rejoice in thee: we will remember thy love more than wine: the upright love thee. I am black, but comely, O ye daughters of Jerusalem, as the tents of Kedar, as the curtains of Solomon . . . Behold, thou art fair, my love . . . Thou hast doves' eyes . . . Behold, thou art fair, my beloved, yes, pleasant: also our bed is green: the beams of our house are cedar and our rafters of fir . . . He brought me to the banqueting house and his banner over me was love . . . His left hand is under my head, and his right hand doth embrace me . . . thy two breasts are like two young roes that are twins, which feed among the lilies . . . my beloved put his hand by the hole of the door and my bowels were moved for him. I rose to open to my beloved and my hands dropped with myrrh, and my fingers with sweet smelling myrrh, upon the handles of the lock. I opened to my beloved but my beloved had withdrawn himself and was gone; my soul failed when he spake: I sought him, but I could not find him; I called him, but he gave me no answer . . . I charge you, O daughters of Jerusalem, if ye find my beloved, that ye tell him that I am sick of love . . . there are three score queens, and four score concubines and virgins without number . . . Return, return, O Shulamite, return, return, that we may look upon thee . . . I am my beloved's, and his desire is toward me. Come, my beloved, let us go forth into the field: let us lodge in the villages . . . set me as a seal upon thine heart, as a seal upon thine arm; for love is strong as death, jealousy is cruel as the grave . . . many waters cannot quench love, neither can the floods drown it . . . Make haste, my beloved, and be thou like to a roe or to a young hart upon the mountains of spices.

The eroticism and the sensuality are explicit. To some its inclusion in the Bible is a puzzle. To others it is evidence that the Bible encompasses all of human life and does so here in a poem to sexual passion.

*   *   *

Eroticism and seduction are credited with being the principal weapons of bold women in the Bible. One of the boldest women was Delilah, who seduced Samson, the strongest man. The Philistines recruited her to unman Samson and destroy this destroyer of their nation. She seduced him and discovered his secret, cut off his hair thereby nulling his strength and condemning him to slavery. Despite some efforts, it has not been easy to elevate her reputation. Samson can be and has been ridiculed by feminist writers as a rather mindless butchering bully boy. Even so, Delilah used sex for information to destroy the man she professed to love. But is that any worse than any other spy or indeed any other tactic by a spy? It is a territory that has not been entered with much confidence. Delilah remains the harlot with the heart of stone and confirms the poisoned gift of Eve.

To say that female seduction is not uncommon in the Bible is to say not much more than that female seduction is not uncommon in life: in almost all times among all classes in all tribes and states and nations. Sometimes it can be defended as a virtuous strategy as when Ruth goes to the bed of Boaz and seduces him so that they might marry. And Esther seduced the King of Persia in order to protect the Jews and hang those in the Persian Empire who sought to destroy them. She is much commended for that. In the First Book of Moses, Genesis, we read of Tamar using sex to get justice for a broken promise of marriage. She poses as a prostitute when her promised husband is passing through the town. She seduces him, takes his ring and staff as surely and when she is pregnant, informs him and returns the ring and staff. The Bible does not suggest she was immoral and her new husband declares that 'she was more righteous than I.'

For all the sexual pleasure evident in the excerpts from the Song of Solomon, for all the allure of the seductive women of the Old Testament and the openness of love in the New, official Christianity, once it got going, thought it better to build up its congregations by putting a stop to tempting celebrations of sex. It was decreed that sexual satisfaction was not an option outside procreation. Genesis decreed: 'God said unto them, "Be fruitful and multiply, replenish the earth." ' But did that mean be fruitful *only* to replenish the earth? Onan, son of Judah, 'spilled [his seed] on the ground', therefore Genesis once more, 'the thing which he did displeased the Lord: wherefore he slew him also.' It became rather complicated.

The control demanded in the First Book of Moses on the sexual practices of millions of human beings for millennia afterwards is one of the more amazing of the spells which the Bible has cast over its followers. Of course many people ignored it, but there was hell to pay for that. It could be argued that the directions of Genesis were given to a partly nomadic, limited population whose survival depended on the perpetuation of the herd. Infant mortality would rack up the odds against this and therefore common sense ordered: 'Breed and keep breeding.' The intention was to weld in the notion to the believer that nothing but sex for procreation would be permitted.

In the English-speaking world, until the Tyndale and then the King James Bibles made the Scriptures widely and commonly available for individual scrutiny, the interpretation of God's Word was monopolised by the priests. Whatever its virtues – and there were some – the Church tended, like all monopolistic organisations which gain vast sway, to become corrupt and obsessed with its own best interests and hang everything else. To be able to decide on the sexual practices of all humankind was an unmissable opportunity of which the Church took full advantage to the consequent frustration, guilt and misery of millions of its faithful.

Another consequence of the act of Onan – apart from the persisting rumour let loose among adolescent boys that it made you blind – was to stress the sacredness of the seed. The Roman Catholic Church used this for its savage campaign to prohibit birth control with, yet again, consequences which included the frustration, guilt and misery of its faithful. The faithful were frequently bullied, tormented and rebuked. Nor did the Protestant Church lag far behind in seeing part of its duty until recently to instil into its congregation an acceptance of the sacredness of God-given life which began in the womb and must not be aborted by mere humankind.

To put the padlock on non-marital sex they brought in sin. Eve again was a useful example. But, to reinforce her evil legacy, just three chapters on from her historic yielding to the wiles of 'the serpent . . . more subtle than any beast of the field', when by some unexplained process the sons of Adam and Eve had all gone forth and multiplied, 'on the face of the earth', the message of the inadequacy of the human race was hammered in. 'And God saw that the wickedness of man was great in the earth and that every imagination of the thoughts of his heart was only evil constantly. And it repented the Lord that he had made man on the earth, and it grieved him at his heart. And the Lord said, I will destroy man whom I have created, from the face of the earth . . . But Noah found grace in the eyes of the Lord.'

And with Noah God's evolution began again. This was believed by faithful congregations for centuries and those who manipulated these matters made sure that the underlying notion of God's limited patience with the wickedness of man was linked with the root of that wickedness: sex. So began the battle between instinct and authority, between joy and repression, between liberty and control. It was a battle kept active as often as not by potentates who disobeyed all the rules they enforced on their congregations. It was a battle riddled with bold characters who risked hell and damnation for sex and pagan pleasures. But a battle which, until quite recently in the history of the influence of the Bible, succeeded in shepherding the long-suffering, the fearful and the obedient into paths, they were promised, of earthly righteousness and heavenly glory.

The outcomes were obfuscated but the message was very clear. The message was 'thou shalt *not* . . .'. The outcomes, in the stories – thought for so long to be historically accurate – were confusing. David, for instance, who had slain Goliath and written the Psalms and loved Jonathan and had many wives, committed adultery with Bathsheba.

> And it came to pass in an eveningtide, that David arose from his bed, and walked up on the roof of the King's house; and from the roof he saw a woman washing herself; and the woman was very beautiful to look upon. And David sent and enquired after the woman. And one said is this not Bathsheba, the daughter of Eliam, the wife of Uriah the Hittite? And David sent messengers and took her; and she came in unto him and he lay with her (for she was purified from her uncleanliness) and she returned unto her house. And the woman conceived and sent and told David, and said, 'I am with child'.

David then arranged for her husband Uriah the Hittite to be killed in battle. After Bathsheba's time of mourning for her husband, she became a wife of David. 'The thing that David had done displeased the Lord' and their son was 'struck' by the Lord and was 'very sick'. Despite David's prayers and fasting the son died. David then 'comforted Bathsheba his wife, and went into her, and lay with her, and she bare a son and he called his name Solomon . . . and the Lord loved him.'

Where does that leave us? The adultery leads to a form of murder, God takes his revenge but then appears to relent since the marriage to the adulteress brings him Solomon, whom he loved. Yet the first act of adultery was punished by the death of the child.

Most remarkable of all, I think, is in the book of the Apostle John, when the scribes and the pharisees brought a woman to Jesus while he was in the temple teaching the people.

They say unto him, 'Master, this woman was taken in adultery, in the very act. Now Moses in the law commanded us that such shall be stoned: but what sayest thou?' This they said, tempting him, that they might have to accuse him. But Jesus stooped down, and with his finger wrote on the ground, as if he heard them not. So when they continued asking him, he lifted up himself, and said unto them, 'He that is without sin among you, let him first cast a stone at her.' And again he stooped down, and wrote on the ground. And they which heard it, being convicted by their own conscience, went out one by one, beginning at the eldest, even unto the last: and Jesus was left alone, and the woman standing in the midst. When Jesus had lifted up himself and saw none but the woman he said unto her, 'Woman, where are those thine accusers? Hath no man condemned thee?' She said, 'No man, Lord.' And Jesus said unto her, 'Neither do I condemn thee: go, and sin no more.'

Forgiveness. And that would appear to have been if not the end, then the decisive opinion on the matter of adultery. Yet Christ would speak again. And both Exodus and Deuteronomy declare, 'Thou shalt not commit adultery' with the force of a law which would trigger punishment. And it is that line rather than the story of Jesus and the 'woman taken in adultery' that became the rod to beat the congregations into line. Yet Hosea had a wife who committed adultery constantly, Jeremiah claimed the whole of Israel was committing adultery and did Lot commit adultery when he slept with and had children with his two daughters?

No matter that there were contradictions in the evidence, the most fervent users of the King James Bible – the evangelicals and the varieties of Presbyterians – clasped the Books of Exodus and Deuteronomy to their bosoms and enforced unrelieved monogamy: nothing more; or less. There were abundant useful biblical references.

'Marriage is honourable in all' says the Letter to the Hebrews in the New Testament, 'and the bed undefiled: but whoremongers and adulterers God will judge.'

Proverbs talks about keeping

thy father's commandment and forsake not the law of thy mother . . . for the commandment is a lamp; and the law is light; and reproofs of instruction are the way of life; to keep thee from the evil woman, from the flattery of the tongue of a strange woman. Lust not after her beauty in thine heart; neither let her take thee with her eyelids. For by means of a whoreish woman a man is brought to a piece of bread and the adulteress will hunt for the precious life . . . whoso committeth adultery with a woman lacketh understanding: he that doeth it destroyeth his own soul. A wound and dishonour shall he get: and his reproach shall not be wiped away.

And Christ himself adds to the confusion. Having forgiven the woman taken in adultery and saved her from death by stoning, he takes wing in Matthew after the Sermon on the Mount to join forces with the Old Testament he has declared he came to overthrow. 'Ye have heard that it was said by them of old time, Thou shalt not commit adultery: but I say unto you, That whosoever looketh on a woman to lust after her hath committed adultery with her already in his heart.'

Immediately following is a passage of God-of-Vengeance intensity

– and an intensity turned on itself – that is barely credible in the mouth of the man who has just preached the Beatitudes. He says: 'And if thy right eye offend thee, pluck it out, and cast it from thee: for it is profitable for thee that one of thy members should perish and not that thy whole body should be cast into hell. And if thy right hand offend thee, cut it off and cast it from thee: for it is profitable for thee that one of thy members should perish and not that thy whole body should be cast into hell.' And the sermon goes on, without pause, to: 'It hath been said, Whosoever shall put away his wife, let him give her a writing of divorcement. But I say unto you, That whosoever shall put away his wife, saving for the cause of fornication, causeth her to commit adultery: and whosoever shall marry her that is divorced committeth adultery.'

Is he equating the casting out of an eye, the cutting off of a hand with the self-punishment resulting from adultery? Or is it all a metaphor? Where has the forgiveness gone?

There was always enough to keep a punitive sexual restraint near the top of the Christian agenda. Paul told the Thessalonians that God wanted them to be completely free from any sexual immorality. And Leviticus in chapter 18 lays out twenty-three laws of acceptable sexual behaviour.

These include never having intercourse with anyone of your own blood, nor with your stepmother or stepsister or granddaughter or aunt or daughter-in-law or a woman and her daughter together, or your neighbour's wife, or with a man as a woman, or with an animal.

Much of this is understandable for the protection of the health of a small tribe. Some seem excessive; others, with regard to homosexuality for instance, are offensive. But the weight of it in Leviticus and Proverbs, and the insistence on strict monogamy in Paul to the Corinthians all confirm the reason taken from that one act of Eve: sexual women had to be reined in.

There is more about the perils of forbidden sex than the casualities of unjust, including genocidal, wars. It has been seized on so often and so forcefully to shape and order society in a form not always guaranteed to suit the best interests of the majority. Nor has it been kind to minorities.

Women who have sought abortion, for instance, have for centuries been driven to often criminally inadequate abortionists. They have faced persecution and ostracism. The Bible gives licence for the hounding of these women through its call on the sacred nature of the womb. In Job: 'Did not he that made me in the womb make him? And did not one fashion us in the womb?' Isaiah: 'Thus saith the Lord that made thee, and formed thee from the womb.' Jeremiah: 'Before I formed thee in the belly I knew thee; and before thou camest forth out of the womb I sanctified thee, and I ordained thee a prophet unto the nations.' Psalms: 'By thee have I been holden up from the womb: thou are he that took me out of my mother's bowels; my praise shall be continually of thee.'

There are those who agree with passion and sincerity that life begins once conception is under way and that to abort is to kill a living being. This has Church authority on its side; it has other supporters who see human life as sacred from the seed to the death. It takes no account of rape, accidents whose outcomes carry a variety of dangers and the claim or right of a woman to determine as far as possible the fate of her own body. It has been a bitter struggle and in some countries it still is. But increasingly the blanket negative of the Bible is being ignored. It is a similar story with contraception where again the Church's authority is now largely obsolete. Neither abortion nor contraception carry stigma any more except in a few remaining repressive boltholes. Fornication can still bring public opprobrium even in liberated societies.

'Flee fornication' urges St Paul to the Corinthians. By which I take it he includes all extra-marital, including pre-marital, sex. To the Galatians he includes it in a comprehensive listing: 'Now the works of the flesh are manifest which are these: adultery, fornication, uncleanness, lasciviousness, idolatry, witchcraft, hatred, variance, emulations, wrath, strife, seditions, heresies, envyings, murders, drunkenness, revellings, and such like: of the which I tell you before, as I have also told you in time past, that they which do such things shall not inherit the kingdom of God.'

Then there is homosexuality. Once again Paul is adamant: to the Romans he writes: 'And likewise also the men, leaving the natural use of the woman, burned in their lust one toward another; men with men working that which is unseemly.'

Leviticus was blunt: 'Thou shalt not lie with mankind as with womankind: it is abomination.' This is in such contrast to attitudes in the classical world which Christianity challenged and then replaced that it is possible to see it as part of a conscious 'difference', a rebuttal of the superiority of classical claims on the world. It is also worth noting that several commentators see and find homosexuality in the Old Testament – David and Jonathan – and in the New – the closeness of the disciples. The Spartan and the Apostolic elites have been thought to have much in common.

There are gay militants today who tear out of the Bible the page on which that verse of Leviticus is printed. Perhaps it might be better to put a note in the margin instead. 'David and Jonathan' is one simple suggestion. Yet in some Christian countries – Nigeria is a leading example – Leviticus is held to be right and with St Paul speak for Church law. The Anglican communion is riven between the traditionalist Nigerian faction and a liberated faction determined to have homosexuals as priests and bishops. English Anglicans are uneasily trying to find a middle ground, not least by continuing their own long tradition of unobtrusively accepting homosexuality in their own priesthood.

There is the growing view that the Church should keep out of private life. The boundaryless world of a hegemonic religion which believed it could direct and micro-manage not only life before birth but life after death and all that happened between these two, is, in the secular world, long gone and not missed. It is good riddance. In this regard, as with its edicts on women and homosexuality, the Bible dogmatists and literalists have suffered in direct proportion to people and nations becoming more tolerant. History is on the side of those attempting the choppy waters of increasing individual liberty and an increasing willingness to take responsibility for one's own destiny. The modern secular world has reached back to the classical world and the waters have closed over certain unsustainable prejudices in the Bible.

One of the positive aspects of the last century in Bible studies in the English-speaking world (and elsewhere, though for obvious reasons I am limiting myself to the English-speaking world) is the entrance of the feminist critique. This has not only identified the abuse and marginalisation of women in the Church and in the Old and New Testaments, it has refreshed their stories in the act of reinterpretation.

Some stories are hard to redeem – the rape of Tamar, Jepthah sacrificing his daughter, Lot offering his daughters to the men of Sodom, and the many cases in which women are the property, the enslaved, of men.

At times it can seem that one of the closet aims of the Bible is to calumniate women. Some of the key verses which feminist commentators use to show the Bible in what understandably they see as its true colours include this from Paul's Epistle to Timothy in the New Testament: 'Let the woman learn in silence with all subjection. But I suffer not a woman to teach, nor to usurp authority over the man, but to be in silence.' And Paul to Corinthians: 'Let your women keep silence in the churches: for it is not permitted unto them to speak; but they are commanded to be under obedience, as also saith the law. And if they will learn any thing, let them ask their husbands at home: for it is a shame for women to speak in the church.'

Not surprisingly, it was the Quakers, in the seventeenth century, who found an authoritative voice to challenge all this. Margaret Fell, a northerner, known as the 'Mother of Quakerism', would have none of it. In her book *Women's Speaking Justified*, she found key biblical arguments to support the place of women in Church leadership. As in the British Civil Wars, the King James Bible found itself as ammunition for both sides of the debate.

Curiously, given the apparent obsession in the Old Testament with woman as the source of evil, the wicked seducer, the harlot and the temptress, it is in the Old Testament that certain verses appear which are the pillars for a new non-misogynistic world. Margaret Fell goes to Genesis: 'And I will put enmity between thee and the woman, and between thy seed and her seed; it shall bruise thy head and thou shalt bruise his heel.' There is an undeniable equality here.

Margaret Fell also points out that in Isaiah, Jeremiah, Psalms and Revelation, the Church is known as a woman. Therefore to speak against women is to speak against the Church. Christ's teaching mission is also invoked. Mary Magdalene has already been referred to, but Margaret Fell points out that in the Gospel according to St John, Jesus preaches equally to women and to men. He preaches to the Samaritan woman at the well and to Martha, both of whom testified to their belief in Christ as the Messiah at a time when few others accepted Him.

She rebuts Paul's admonitions by imagining that he was speaking of irreverent women and ungodly women only. Margaret Fell appears to have set in motion what has eventually become a thriving and intellectually satisfying re-examination of the place of women in the Bible and therefore in Western history. It is not difficult to leap from Margaret Fell's seventeenth-century Quakerism to the formidable and numerous feminist scholars of today.

Among them are David Baker who studied the Pentateuchal stories and pointed to the mother-centred voices that challenge the patriarchy which is so much in the foreground. Then there is Musa Shoman-Dube who starts with the adage that when the white man met the African, the white man owned the Bible, and the African the land. Soon it was reversed. This not only brings in the colonialist heritage but, tellingly, includes the story of the Canaanite woman's daughter. In another book which she edits, Musa Shoman-Dube introduces the subject of women in African oral storytelling. In establishing a new balance, it can help to depress the prominence of men.

Barbara J. Essex's book *Bad Boys of the Bible: Exploring Men of Questionable Virtue* subjects to scrutiny the heroic and moral status given to Adam, Cain, Abraham, Lot, Jacob, Jepthah and Samson. Several books examine the women who saved the life of the child Moses abandoned in the bulrushes. Jane Schalberg in *The Illegitimacy of Jesus* suggests that is just what it was – a normal but illegitimate birth. This, if true, would establish an 'illegitimacy tradition' and could open up 'fuller human and deeper theological potential'.

James I, whose name is so closely associated with the 1611 Bible, was a biblical scholar, widely erudite, but also, as King James VI of Scotland, a notoriously zealous persecutor and executor of witches. The great majority of these were women and every one, we can safely assume, was innocent. Every one of these women was victimised in large part because of a masculine, controlling, darkly sexually charged obsession with the alleged evil brought into the world by Eve. Four hundred years after the King James's publication it is a new generation of the daughters of Eve who are rolling back 2,000 years of perverse and destructive prejudice.

It is a vigorous, positive analysis which has reformed traditional ideas by discovering deeper and other possibilities latent in the very stories that once denigrated and all but denied half the human race. The women of modern scholarship have liberated the women in the Bible and led them out of Egypt. Material in the Bible has proved the defence of what was most offensive about it. Those whom it tried to silence have used it to speak out and claim their equal rights.

For centuries, men used the Bible to reduce the great majority of women to little more than objects, vassals, marginal creatures. In the last century, women have used that same Bible to reinforce the liberated, complex, rich history and future of women. When God is referred to nowadays, it is very often as *She*.

CHAPTER TWENTY-THREE
THE BIBLE AND WOMEN

As early as the seventeenth century, women began to outnumber men in the congregations in the Protestant, especially the nonconformist, churches. Sometimes the attendance was two-thirds women, one-third men. In the more radical groups, like early Quakerism, women were given roles denied them by all other Churches. It became a currency of congregational conversation that, as Richard Allestree, an English clergyman, and Cotton Mather, a minister in Massachusetts, said, women were more spiritual than men. Men, they thought, inverting Eve, were slaves to passion. 'Devotion is a tender plant,' said Allestree, 'that requires a supple, gentle soil; and therefore the feminine softness and plyableness is very apt and proper for it . . . I know there are many Ladies whose Examples are reproaches to the other Sex, that help fill our congregations, when Gentlemen desert them.'

Mary Wollstonecraft was to abominate that stereotyping of women, but in one way it was a useful beginning. Without the stereotyping as pliable, docile, devoted, there might have been a lesser chance of women beginning their long journey, still unfinished, to equality in the Church. Those remarks of the Anglican Richard Allestree were radical in that they challenged and contradicted the great Church Father St Augustine – enemy of

Eve – who had condemned the uncontrolled passion of women, their sinful wilfulness.

Women came to see the Church as a place in which they could fight their cause. Politics were barred; universities were barred; the law barred them from its offices. But the Church had chinks in its armour and the rapiers of clever and brave women pierced it. It provided a path both to join and to challenge the Established Order.

Mary Astell, for instance, whom Diarmaid MacCulloch describes as 'a celibate High Church Anglican Tory with a lively interest in contemporary philosophy', attacked John Locke, whose philosophy of freedom excluded half the human race; and in the 1690s, set out her own version of Christian feminism. 'That the custom of the world,' she wrote, 'has put Women, generally, in a state of Subjection, is not denied; but the Right can no more be proved from the Fact, than the Predominancy of Vice can justify it . . . one would . . . almost think that the wise disposer of all things, foreseeing how unjustly Women are denied opportunities of improvement from *without*, has therefore by way of compensation endowed them with greater propensions to Vertue, and a natural goodness of temper *within*.'

A century later, another gentlewoman, from Devon, Joanna Southcott, a Methodist, gave vent to visions and prophecies that led to a large-scale apocalyptic movement which retained female leadership, despite challenges from men who wanted to be at the forefront of this uprising. Joanna Southcott's box of prophecies which caused so much alarm and excitement is still to be opened – but only in the presence of twenty-four Anglican bishops.

There were others. Two Scottish sisters for example, Isabella and Mary Campbell, said to be of rare holiness, spoke in unknown tongues and inspired what became a charismatic and widespread Pentecostal movement. In 1853, a Congregational Church in New York ordained Antoinette Brown as a minister; the first woman outside the Quakers to hold such an office in modern Christianity. Women volunteered for missionary work, the Great Awakening released into activity thousands of women who made the Church their transport through society and the King James Version their guide. These and many others were the forerunners who pointed the way to the 'Bible Women' who did so much to alleviate the scarcely credible destitution of the poverty-stricken.

The English word 'charity' comes from the Bible, a translation of the Latin word 'caritas' which could also mean 'care' or 'love'. Charity combines both and in St Paul's letter to the Corinthians it is given its crown. 'And now abideth faith, hope, charity, these three; but the greatest of these is charity.' The King James Version is the only English Bible version to translate 'caritas' as 'charity' rather than as 'love'.

Charity had been seen by the Christian Church as part of its purpose from the time of Christ. It had been considered a Christian virtue. Its administration was largely left to the Church. The consequences of the publication of the King James Bible included a growing belief on the part of individuals that the pursuit of charity was an obligation and a responsibility for the individual: the individual who had been released into full participation with their Creator and their Redeemer.

In Victorian Britain and in roughly the same period of history in America, there was a spectacular surge in the creation of charitable organisations which took on the desperate condition of the outcast impoverished, often diseased and malnourished masses cramped into the slums of the new industrial cities. These organisations were Bible-led and that Bible was the King James Version.

There was something simple, basic and good about their mission, which was to help the weak. But there was also the colouring of the times: the weak had to prove that they were deserving.

The role of government was very limited. The government's argument was that doling out large sums of relief to the poor would only encourage poverty, especially among the undeserving poor. There was an accepted level of destitution. The general view was that poverty was the result of personal failure – laziness, idleness, greed, or sin. In that respect – the moral sphere – it was thought the Bible could make a crucial contribution. This view was challenged by individuals like Henry Mayhew, who argued that this was not a moral problem but a social problem. The poor were not poor because they were immoral. If they were immoral it was because they were poor. They were poor because they could find no work and accumulate no money.

The Co-operative Movement and the Friendly Societies, connected through membership with the nonconformist branches of the Protestant Church, took a slightly different view. They encouraged self-help and reached out to those unable to rise to that challenge. They did not bring in what could in practice be a rigid and unhelpful distinction between the undeserving poor who brought neglect upon themselves and the deserving poor, to be rewarded and worthy of salvation.

Then there were individuals: Octavia Hill (1838–1912). She worked as a child with her sister in a toy workshop. By the age of fourteen she was running it. Her workshop, which from the description was appalling, was thought to be better than most of the sweatshops which were making Britain the 'workshop of the world'. The toy workshop was subsidised by Christian Socialists. This group was to have a strong part in the British charity movement and it gave to Octavia Hill a desire for social reform which melded with her strong Christian principles.

Octavia Hill's impact is proof that an individual, however skilfully she might seem to be riding on the tide of an economic and social turn of history, can make a substantial difference. She was convinced that young, unmarried Christian women of the middle class should go into the world of extreme poverty and serve God and the poor. They acted as rent collectors and supervisors. Ellen Ranyard, founder of the 'Bible Women', deliberately hired women from the working classes. She thought they would be more able to make easy contact with the women they went to help and to whom they sold Bibles.

Octavia Hill led by example and was a major force throughout the charity and welfare organisations of the nineteenth century. She campaigned successfully for social housing and for the availability of open spaces for the poor, a campaign which was key in the establishment of the National Trust. She was a founder member of the Charity Organisation Society (now the charity Family Action) which formed the basis of modern social work.

The latter society emphasised Bible study and encouraged attendance at Sunday school and Church. The Bible was the enabler in all of this. A strong prevailing idea was that those in poverty were so placed because of their ungodliness. Bible study and the practice of the Christian faith were to be made crucial to rehabilitation. Many of the poor, we are told, grudged the enforced Christianity as the price they had to pay. Those ignored for so long by Christianity or atavistically wary of its claims on them were often reluctant to accept the faith even though they benefited from the works. But they were made well aware that the Bible was part of the cure.

Just as vigorous as Octavia Hill was her contemporary, William Booth (1829–1912), who founded the Salvation Army. He came from the school that believed that poverty, vice and crime were indisputably linked to sin. His army took up the King James

Version as it marched into the slums and war zones, banners flying, drums beating, tambourines cascading with shimmering sounds. Booth wrote *In Darkest England and the Way Out*: he knew his ground on the first part of that title: the second he found in the Bible.

In the book, he sets out the cityscape, in which he worked:

To the dwellers in decent houses, who occupy cushioned pews in fashionable churches, there is something strange and quaint in the language they hear read from the Bible. Language which habitually refers to the Devil as an actual personality, and to the struggle against sin and uncleanness as if it were a hand to hand death wrestle with the legions of Hell. To our little sisters who dwell in an atmosphere heavy with curses, among people sodden with drink, in quarters where sin and uncleanness are universal, all those Biblical sayings are as real as the quotations of yesterday's price of Consols are to the City man. They dwell in the midst of Hell, and in their daily warfare with a hundred devils it seems incredible to them that anyone can doubt the existence of either one or the other.

Booth describes these Christian women, the Bible Women, who were so outstanding on the battlefields of nineteenth-century charity. Booth in this instance writes of the remarkable phenomenon of the 'Slum Sister'.

The slum sister is what her name implies, the Sister of the Slum. They go forth in Apostolic fashion, two-and-two living in a couple of the same kind of dens or rooms as are occupied by the people themselves, differing only in the cleanliness and order, and the few articles of furniture which they contain. Here they live all the year round, visiting the sick, looking after the children, showing the women how to keep themselves and their homes decent, often discharging the sick mother's duties themselves; cultivating peace, advocating temperance, counselling in temporalities, and ceaselessly preaching the religion of Jesus Christ to the outcasts of society.

Those of religion will recognise such people. In the current secularism of British society it is worth drawing attention to the practical dedication of those who came not so long ago before us and brought comfort and relief to many 'outcasts' and acknowledge that this was inspired by what were believed to be the Words of God and Jesus Christ. I am sure it can be proved that non-religious women behaved just as well, applied themselves just as devotedly. That does not detract from those whose vocation was inspired by the King James Bible. These British Bible Women who, they might have said, were 'about their Father's business', are now foreigners here in what was once their land. We know them not. But they helped make it the better land it became and William Booth, flags flying, tambourines shaking, knew what he was praising.

Booth wrote that his experience of the work of the Slum Sisters gave him a 'greater respect for true religion'. These are two from many examples. There is a strong connection, in my view, between the work done here and that which Christ sent out the Apostles to do.

'Mrs. W—of Haggerston slum. Heavy drinker, wrecked home, husband a drunkard, place dirty and filthy, terribly poor. Saved now over two years. Home A.1, plenty of employment at cane-chair bottoming; husband now saved also.'

'Mrs. R—Drury Lane slum. Husband and wife, drunkards; husband very lazy, only worked when starved into it. We found them both out of work, home furnitureless, in debt. She got saved and our lasses prayed for him to get work. He did so, and went to it. He fell out again a few weeks after, and beat his wife. She sought employment at charring and office cleaning. Got it.'

Catherine Booth, wife of William, was as energetic and effective as he was. She was a devout Christian, daughter of a coachbuilder in Derbyshire, and by the age of twelve she had read the Bible eight times. Despite William's opposition to her feminism, she went her own way and in 1860, in Gateshead Bethesda Chapel, she began to preach. A strange compulsion seized her, she reported, and an inner voice taunted her: 'She will look like a fool and have nothing to say.' Catherine decided that this was the devil's voice and replied: 'That is just the point. I have never yet been willing to be a fool for Christ. Now I will be one.' Her sermon so impressed William that he changed his mind about women preaching and she went on to develop a reputation as a powerful speaker, especially in the Dockland parishes of the East End of London.

The Salvation Army was not welcomed by the establishment. Lord Shaftesbury called William Booth 'the Anti-Christ'. But they went marching on and in 1882, a survey in London found that on one weeknight, there were about 1,700 worshipping with them compared to 1,100 in ordinary churches. The 'Sally Army' reached out and fed and comforted those whom the Anglican Church could not or would not embrace.

Catherine Booth went on to be the leading figure in transforming the condition of the 'sweat-shops', then mostly employing women. Her chief activity was with the match factories where the vile overcrowding and the pittance wages (9d a day) were made even worse by the use of yellow phosphorous which caused the widespread illness known as 'phossy jaw' (necrosis of the bone). The whole side of the face turned green and then black, discharged pus and led to early death. Catherine helped the workers to get the use of yellow phosphorus banned.

There is a sense in which intelligent, brave women who were excluded from all the commanding heights of the state, found, through their faith nurtured by the King James Version, that the unexpected consequence was access to the power to change society. There are so many examples.

Josephine Butler, for example, came from a very well-connected family. Her father was the cousin of Earl Grey, the Prime Minister, who led the Whig government from 1830 to 1834 and introduced the Great Reform Act. She was, claimed Prince Leopold, 'the most beautiful woman in the world'.

She was an Anglican and saw the King James Version as her text when she immersed herself in charity work. She wrote and campaigned for improved educational and employment opportunities for single women. Most notably of all she campaigned with others to end what was known as the 'white slave traffic' – child prostitution then rampant in London. She was spat on and vilified but eventually Parliament passed an Act that raised the age of consent from thirteen to sixteen. This and her work in securing the repeal of the Contagious Diseases Act, which applied only to women and gave the police the right to arrest any woman they considered might be a prostitute, proved that these women of the Bible could and did engage in politics and on a very controversial issue. Religion was not only a commitment and a faith, it had become, especially for women in the nineteenth century, a gateway to bring about essential social change.

America was also accelerating and expanding its Christian charity with characteristic buccaneering effectiveness. The Charity Organisation Society founded in England in 1869 soon crossed to America, where it became more 'scientific', but still used 'friendly visitors', mostly women. It established the first professional training school for social work – the New York School of Philanthropy.

The Social Gospel Movement was the cavalry of the Protestant

Christian intellectuals and it rode into battle against inequality, alcohol, crime, racism, slums, child labour and poor schools. There was within the movement a strand of conviction that the Second Coming would not arrive until society had cleansed itself through its own efforts with the help of the Bible. Self-help before salvation. There were crusades against the twelve-hour day; there was the establishment of the YMCA to help young people from the country adjust to the city without falling for its temptations; and there were the settlement houses, such as Jane Addams's Hull House.

Jane Addams was born in 1860. Her Presbyterian father ran the local Bible class. She herself, as she grew older, did not follow his example: she was not personally religious. However she said that she had no doubt that the Bible and her father's teaching had led her to the charitable social work which was to consume her life. She would use religious language and imagery to get her message to Christian communities. On the site devoted to Christian charity workers we read:

> Although she was baptised in the Presbyterian Church, Addams remained aloof from organised religion. Yet she saw her work in Hull House and in social reform as consonant with the great humanitarian spirit that animated the early Christian movement, and that now sought to embody itself 'not in a sect but in society itself'. While it tended to promote 'personal virtue', the time had come, she believed, to promote the exercise of 'social virtue' in the service of humanity.

In her impact she can be compared with Octavia Hill but her social politics seem closer to those of Henry Mayhew. She saw the distress in the most indigent and underprivileged areas of society and addressed it not as a vice or a crime but as a social problem.

Hence her unique and lasting contribution, the US settlement movement, which began at Hull House in Chicago, Illinois, in 1889. She became just the second woman to be awarded the Nobel Peace Prize.

In Karen Whitney Tice's book *Tales of Wayward Girls and Immoral Women* she outlines the steady professionalisation of social work in America. In it she describes the effect the 'Bible Women' (her phrase) had on their visits to slum homes. In 1911, for example, one woman spoke of her efforts in martial terms. 'Our ammunition of war consisted of a broom, a scrubbing brush, a pail and a Bible.' Whitney Tice surveys the relevant books and lists recommended to social workers – fiction and non-fiction – all of them citing the Bible. She also stresses the importance of the physical presence of the Bible in the work of the Bible Women.

She writes: 'What brought middle class observers and reformers into the daily lives of the poor was the practice of home-visiting . . . religiously motivated explorations that searched for those in the throes of odious circumstances gave rise to home visits, which took men and women out of church confines and into slum homes.' Home visitor narratives of 'last ditch repentance (on a deathbed of rags)' and stock characters such as the 'fallen woman, starving seamstress, and ragged match girl' appeared in the annual reports of tract societies as well as in published fictional sketches at the end of the nineteenth century. Not for the first time, a claim was made for the particular suitability of these visiting women, their 'unique moral virtues sustained by the sheltered domestic sphere they occupied'. It became known as 'benevolent femininity'. This notion, according to Karen Whitney Tice, 'carried the expectation that women's influence should, like the "dew of heaven", act in divine ways'.

In 1861 in London, Henry Mayhew published a survey of *London Labour and the London Poor*. This was widely researched and considered then and since as a groundbreaking revelation. As mentioned earlier, his analysis of the condition of the poor considered that its cause lay in their inability to earn enough to live on and the desperate remedies they sought to try to escape the pain of that distress.

Yet he too was immensely impressed by the Bible Women, often very young 'Christian ladies', who went out into the slums with their Bibles to sell and to instruct and aid the 'moral plight' of the poorest in London. The scope for patronage and even hypocrisy is not hard to spot. The sense of an exciting brief encounter with the devil might have been part of it. The phrase 'slumming it' soon signified a self-serving attempt to drop down a class or two for the frisson. Provided you could escape 'up' again whenever you wanted to. Nevertheless, good work was done and Mayhew, no religious fellow traveller, was not only persuaded but enthusiastic.

The appointment of these female colporteurs has been attended with the most beneficial and encouraging results, for not only has the sale of Bibles been facilitated among classes almost inaccessible to such influences, but opportunities have been afforded of help to some of the most wretched and morally debased of our population . . . the lowest strata are thus reached by an agency which takes the Bible as the starting point of its labours, and makes it the basis of all the social and religious improvements which are subsequently attempted . . . at the present time there are 152 of these agents [women] employed . . . During the past year the Bible women in London disposed of many thousand copies of the Scriptures among classes which, to a very great extent, were beyond the reach of ordinary means used to effect this work; and their circulation was attained not by the easy method of gift but by sale . . . the very poorest being willing to pay by small weekly instalments.

When literally millions of Bibles were being printed every year and its distribution reaching numbers never before imagined, it could be seen as odd that the Bibles were sold and not given to the 'very poorest'. But the notion of buying the Bible and therefore owning it personally was an acknowledgement of dignity. This part of the visit was not charity only. You had to become part of that larger commercial society which denied you entry to so many of its rewards. You had your own, owned property in that market. It is not far from the transaction in psychoanalysis where payment, it appears, is an expression of your commitment.

In any event, many of the poor paid up. The London City Mission alone, in 1861, employed 381 Bible Women who made 1,815,332 visits, 237,599 to the sick and dying; 2,721,173 religious tracts were given away, there were 584,166 readings of Scripture in visitations; 681 fallen females were rescued or reclaimed and 10,058 children were sent to school. It is unlikely that any of that would have happened without the Bible Women. In 1893–4, William Howe, who produced surveys of charitable bodies, showed that the income of the London charities reached £2.25 million in 1874–5 and rose to £3.15 million in 1893–4. This was about one-third of the figure spent by the Poor Law authorities at the time and there have been claims that charity – overwhelmingly Christian – exceeded state expenditure on the poor.

The theory that poverty is the result of a lack of will and virtue, that indolence and sluttishness and drunkenness and crime render you undeserving of help until you take the path of reform through religion is now, in most of the English-speaking world, spoken of, if at all, with a shake of the head or with contempt for those misguided Victorian days. All antisocial behaviour is thought to be capable of repair through computed social adjustments. It may be a kinder way. It may be a better way. But it does not detract from the determination and the faith of those Bible Women who, with broom, scrubbing brush and pail and the King James Bible, went into the sewers of society on a mission to save souls by way of mending and redirecting ruined lives.

CHAPTER TWENTY-FOUR
CHRISTIAN SOCIALISM AND
THE SOCIAL GOSPEL

When Keir Hardie entered Parliament in 1892, he was the first independent workers' representative to secure election. He was a Scot who had been a trades union organiser and before then, a coal miner. While it would be inappropriate to suggest any direct comparison between the working classes of the industrial UK in its most labour-intensive time and slavery, there were affinities.

To Keir Hardie, born in 1856, the memory of children as young as six working in the coal mines would have been still current in the talk and oral history of his community. He would have known of women, even pregnant women, working in the pits, dragging trucks of coal along the rails to the shaft, chained to those trucks. He would have known of pitiful safety measures, pit disasters, early deaths through pneumoconiosis, pittance wages, the relentless exploitation of man by man.

As a trades unionist he was part of a movement – reflected in the United States and in other countries also involved in the industrialised 'advance' – which was determined to better the lot of the oppressed, the undervalued, what Marx and Engels called the proletariat. It became an ideological debate, a power struggle between the workforce and the owners, the masters and the masses, and an increasingly urgent political issue.

But for Keir Hardie there was a different and a deeper perspective. 'The impetus which drove me first of all into the Labour movement and the inspiration which has carried me on in it,' he said, 'has been derived more from the teaching of Jesus of Nazareth than all the other sources combined.' This continued in the British Labour Party for over a century, a line which includes George Lansbury in the 1930s and Stafford Cripps in the Labour reforming government of 1945. In 1996, in the Labour Party Shadow Cabinet, 50 per cent were in the Christian Socialist movement.

It seems a good fit. The New Testament and the Social Gospel movement in North America, and the Labour movement in Britain, joined together Christ's teachings – especially the Beatitudes – with the growing determination that there was an equality in mankind which had to be recognised and brought into the light.

This was not new in the nineteenth century nor unique to it. The Church at its best through its monasteries had fed and housed the poor for centuries when other institutions did little more than ignore, hound or imprison them. Ideology had appeared in England in the fourteenth century with the radical preacher John Ball, an admirer of John Wycliffe, who was a leading actor in the 1381 so-called (miscalled) Peasants' Revolt which came within a whisker of overwhelming established hierarchies in England. 'When Adam delved and Eve span,' he said in one of his sermons, 'who was *then* the gentleman?'

But it was the King James Bible which unlocked a sense of justice which had been repressed for so long. Most notably in the Civil War there were the Diggers and the Levellers who preached a form of communism, and the Methodists who supported the Tolpuddle Martyrs. These are just a few examples from a radical tradition still undervisited and undervalued in our histories of ourselves. What these groups had was their Bible in English, a

Bible in print and therefore available in unprecedented quantities, a Bible that enabled many people to talk on the basis of a shared book. For the first time, each of them could be equal.

Christian Socialism in Britain gathered this together in the middle of the nineteenth century and saw the politics of socialism and the philosophy of the New Testament as interrelated. Christ had spoken against the established religious authorities of the time: the egalitarian anti-establishment movement of nineteenth-century socialists aimed to do exactly the same. 'Whoever uncouples the religious and the social life has not understood Jesus,' wrote Walter Rauschenbusch (1861–1918), a Baptist minister and theologian and a central figure in the American Social Gospel movement which grew from the same roots as Christian Socialism in the UK. He went on: 'whoever sets any bounds for the reconstructive power of the religious life over the social relations and institutions of men, to that extent denies the faith of the Master.'

He spoke for a group of educated people, mostly men, given the educational context of the day, who found in the King James Bible their justification and their agenda for what became an assault on centuries of under-addressed deprivation. In Britain those men were mostly clergymen, writers and activists. The Christian Socialist movement (which bred others such as the International League of Religious Socialists, in twenty-one countries) could be said to have begun in Anglicanism and not, rather surprisingly, in one of the nonconformist groups which had instigated so much change.

F.D. Maurice, an Anglican clergyman (who had a deep influence on the young Octavia Hill), declared in 1848 that socialism was an outcome of Christianity and it was he who coined the phrase 'Christian Socialism'. He worked closely with another clergyman, Charles Kingsley, author of *The Water-Babies*, a fairy tale of Christian Socialism which swept up a massive readership and spread the movement's message across the land. One benign and lasting consequence was to set up numerous co-operative societies which were to play an integral part in the betterment of working-class life. In its quiet way, it was revolutionary. Its founders were clear that this revolution was based on the Scriptures as well as on economically and politically driven ideals.

The idea was not as widely embraced in America but nor was it a negligible contributor to the social advances in American society. In 1889, in Boston, W.D.P. Bliss set up the Society of Christian Socialists, which emphasised the brotherhood of man and criticised the contemporary social order. In her book *The Bible in America: Versions That Have Played Their Part in the Making of the Republic*, Marion Simms writes: 'one difficulty with both socialism and communism is that they expect entirely too much from purely economic changes. Man does not live by bread alone. The socialistic and communistic experiments that had a religious foundation always lasted longer than those which did not. Those who do battle for a just social system make a mistake when they push religion aside.' Humanist materialists and atheists would disagree. Nevertheless it is impossible to deny the amount of good work done by those who drew their inspiration from the Bible, then and still now.

The Christian Socialist movement in the UK was and continues to be active: faith and works. Christians are encouraged to take up politics, to campaign against prejudice and abuse of power, as well as to seek the Kingdom of God. It looks not only to the New Testament but to prophets – Micah and Amos – who spoke of injustice. F.D. Maurice, the founder, set the pace.

Though Maurice became an Anglican in his late twenties, his roots were inside that nonconformist world which has given so much to radical thought and action since 1611. His father was a

Unitarian minister who worked with Joseph Priestley in Hackney in London in a church which became an unofficial nonconformist university. He went to Anti-Slavery Society meetings and he was a regular attender of the Bible Society. When he became the Anglican chaplain at Lincoln's Inn Fields in London, he entered the legal establishment and found an influential platform.

It was his book *The Kingdom of Christ*, published in 1838, that made his mark. Politics and religion were inseparable, he asserted, and the Church should be active in redressing social injustices. He was against individualism which he associated with selfishness.

In 1853, following the formation of the Christian Socialists, his development of these ideas led King's College to deprive him of his post as Professor of Theology. So he set up a scheme for a Working Men's College and became its first principal. Later he went to Cambridge University as Professor of Moral Philosophy but still continued to run the Working Men's College in London. It was a life lived out according to his beliefs and with him as with the many like him, the motivation came from the Bible. Would he have done all that without the Bible? Likely not. Did others who were not religious at all or not as religious as Maurice accomplish what he and his colleagues accomplished? Some did. But these Christian Socialists were the role models and the leaders in the field.

A more prominent member of the group was Charles Kingsley, previously mentioned. He is still best remembered for his children's book *The Water-Babies: A Fairy Tale for a Land Baby* (1863) about a boy chimney sweep miraculously washed clean and swept into eternal happiness. It carried a sentimental but strong and emotionally persuasive message, converting its target audience for generations. I still remember reading it when I was about seven or eight. With the memory still comes a warmth of optimism. Charles Kingsley (1819–75) was the son of a clergyman. He himself became a clergyman and, like his brother, a novelist. He was appointed Regius Professor of Modern History at Cambridge, as distinguished an academic post as any in England, and yet he renounced it to go to Chester, where he took up the comparatively humble role of a canon of the cathedral. Maurice's book *The Kingdom of Christ* had influenced him greatly and he wanted to serve both his religion and society. Politics was the sway to bind them together, he thought, and the Christian Socialist movement provided his political base.

Kingsley made his contribution through his writing. His novels carried the sentiment; his articles, in *Politics for the People* and the *Christian Socialist*, carried the argument which, broadly, aimed to demonstrate that democracy and egalitarianism came from the Bible and therefore to work for the social improvement of the weaker in society was to do the work of God. He, like Maurice, became involved in Working Men's Associations and set up a famous Night School in Little Ormond Yard.

His reading of the Bible had begun early in his life and remained intense throughout his life. In his early novel *Hypatia*, for example, a book of 491 pages, it takes fifty pages to list the biblical references. In the first ten pages there are quotations from Psalms, Matthew, Luke, Ezekiel, Ephesians and Proverbs. He read from the Psalms every morning and evening. He wrote of the Bible as 'the true poor man's book, the true voice of God against tyrants, idlers and humbugs . . . the Bible demands for the poor as much, and more, than they demand for themselves; it expresses the deepest yearnings of the poor man's heart . . . it is the poor man's comfort and the rich man's warning.'

Men such as Kingsley and Maurice were not in the mainstream of the nineteenth-century religious establishment which was more like that which the novelist Anthony Trollope wrote of in its hierarchical, snobbish, satirised, Anglican, landowning, socially acceptable venal character. There were exceptions and there is a heroic roll call of Anglican preachers at work in the new slums of the newly industrialised cities. But the Christian Socialist movement sprang directly out of convictions aroused through study of the King James Version and a close knowledge of the poverty in the country which led to a compulsion to act for the betterment of those most in need.

Keir Hardie spoke for many political figures, in the USA and around the English-speaking world as well as in the UK. These people saw in the Bible the means and the encouragement to take on the growing varieties of social injustice in a proliferating industrial society. They also brought vision.

Octavia Hill has been referred to earlier but her work through contact with the Christian Socialists shows how far-sighted and effective they were in identifying and helping these increasingly populous agglomerations of the poor to steer towards a better world for the living as well as to aim for a better world after death. Octavia Hill was conservative in many ways – accepting that there was a male 'sphere' which was not to be broached; speaking in public, for instance. Yet her actions went to the core of public need.

John Ruskin, the art critic, loaned her money in 1864 to begin what proved to be one of her most successful and influential Christian enterprises. With Ruskin's money she bought slum properties in Little Hill in Marylebone Place in London. She renamed it Paradise Place. She rebuilt and rented these properties at very low rents to poor tenants. This scheme then took off both in the UK and abroad. The Ecclesiastical Commissioners approached her to manage similar properties in Southwark and in Lambeth and Wandsworth. This was not cosmetic. They became huge undertakings – involving demolition, new roads, recreation grounds, community facilities. And for many poor people they were indeed thought of as a metropolitan paradise.

Octavia Hill saw her mission to include the moral as well as the material improvement of the poor. Therefore she decreed that tenants who did not pay their rent on time were to be evicted. She was determined to instil a sense of responsibility and would not tolerate laziness. There were the 'deserving' and the 'undeserving' poor: any forgiveness had to be earned. What was even more striking was that Octavia Hill saw the importance of the larger environment and, like Wordsworth, she saw it in moral terms; she believed that a true appreciation of nature could teach and improve you. First, though, in her new 'Paradise' nature had to be available. For this she insisted on parks and gardens within easy reach of the new settlements and if possible part of them.

Her career took her into key developments in what eventually became desired social policy ambitions in many countries in the second half of the twentieth century. Though denied, through her gender, a place on the Royal Commission on Housing, she was appointed to the Royal Commission on the Poor Law in 1905, the first female commissioner to be allowed on to that body. She was methodical, she used trained volunteers, she laid the foundations of modern housing management with her 'Fellow Workers'. She not only cleared slums and rebuilt new properties, she set the example and standard for doing so. Her methods were taken up in other countries, including Holland, Ireland and the USA. There is still a flourishing Octavia Hill Association in Philadelphia. Her example led many women to take up professional roles in social work. 'By the last quarter of the 19th century,' writes Jane Lewis, 'the large numbers of unpaid visitors were middle class women, bent on leaving their homes in order to instruct working class women how to manage theirs.'

Not all of these women were Christian Socialists, but they were in the vanguard. Octavia Hill's personal example, her achievements and the obvious need for her efforts undoubtedly led the way. Similarly her Kyrle Society formed to 'Bring Beauty Home to the People', for which she enlisted William Morris, is considered the forerunner of the Civic Trust. She looked to improve the quality of life for the poor across the spectrum. Hospitals and schools were to be decorated, open spaces purchased and made into gardens for the people, trees and flowers planted in the congestions of cheap urban brick. Everywhere, to create Paradise Place on earth was to be one of the two great objectives of her mission: the other was to save immortal souls. And on she went: she helped found the Women's University Settlement movement and in 1895 she helped form the National Trust. She had already proposed what she called a 'green belt' to link together and protect the open spaces around London.

These are just a few of the people who took what they had found in the Bible into a wider society. They acted in a tradition. They were modern-day Apostles whose 'miracles' tended to be organisational rather than divine. It is difficult to quantify the effect the Christian Socialists had: it spanned work in the slums, the writing of pamphlets and novels, social management, urban and city planning, cultural upgrading and conservation. It came from the companionate egalitarianism which can be found in the Bible.

The movement was not as strong in America but Walter Rauschenbusch promoted the notion of what he called the Social Gospel. He had an original way of looking at the death of Christ. This, he wrote, was because of 'six sins, all of a public nature'. The idea of 'social sins' was key to his mission to improve the social conditions. These six social sins were: 'religious bigotry, the combination of graft and political power, the corruption of justice, the mob spirit (by the 'social group gone mad'), and mob action, militarism and class contempt . . . every student of history will recognise that these sum up constitutional forces in the Kingdom of God.'

332

Socialism to Rauschenbusch was not an ideology but the best practical answer to the problems of the day: and Christianity, he believed, both informed that socialism and steered it. 'His writings,' wrote Martin Luther King, 'left an indelible impact on my thinking.'

Christian Socialism is underpinned by a vision of the Kingdom of God. It takes into account human self-interest and attempts to guide it to socially useful ends and it directs people into politics to bring about change. The new word 'socialism' which entered the language in the early 1830s (oddly enough at the same time as the word 'science') was soldered on to the egalitarian strand in Christianity. There were other movements, such as that pioneered by Robert Owen in his New Lanark cotton mills: a commitment to social engineering outside the established Churches but emanating from Owen's Christianity.

Alongside this, throughout the century, was an atheistic social movement which was going in much the same direction. It is arguable that Marx was influenced by the Judaeo-Christian tradition but he was more influenced by Feuerbach in his rejection of the Christian consciousness. From 1844 onwards, Marx advocated the abolition of religion – 'the opium of the people'. He saw it as an impediment to progress. Marx's vision of the inevitable triumph of the proletariat was as prophetic as any of the prophets of the Old Testament but his God was the working out of economic determinism. He thought there was no need for God. There was no need for Christianity. Charity, the individual enterprise of helping the poor, all the work to be done by Octavia Hill and so many others was trivial compared to the destiny of the proletariat promised by the engines of the Marxist system.

Yet Christian Socialism has left a legacy which is substantial. It could be argued that the godless statist socialism of Marx and Engels and their apostles led to far more violence, misery and damage than the altogether pacific Christian Socialists could ever have dreamed of. The Christian Socialists, by combining what they saw as the sacred with the social, built on firmer and better ground. Marxism is dead save for its historical-philosophical interest to universities. It is conceivable that the time of Octavia Hill and Keir Hardie might be revived.

CHAPTER TWENTY-FIVE
THE BIBLE AND DEMOCRACY

Democracy, as it took root and developed in Britain and then in America in the seventeenth century, owed an essential debt to the Reformation and to the King James Bible. This could be its greatest achievement.

Together with the growth of early modern experimental science and the new encounters with civilisations beyond the long confined boundaries of the post-Roman European stagnancy this marked a great culture shift. It was the Bible in English, both what it said and the way in which it licensed its listeners and readers to attempt new thoughts that proved to be the vital catalyst. The Bible was the keystone in the bridge to democracy. In *Wide as the Waters*, the biblical scholar Benson Bobrick wrote: 'without a vernacular bible, the English Bible in particular, through its impact on the reformation of English politics, there could not have been a democracy as we know it, or even what today we call the "free world".' I have touched on democracy several times in the course of this book – this is to draw it together and finally emphasise the biggest of the unexpected consequences and impact of that publication in 1611.

The Bible was *the* book for most people for centuries. As has been mentioned, because of its size, and variety, its rich

335

contradictions, its exhilarating prophecies, its exalted promises and its vivid 'characters' with heroic, fragile or damned lives, it could be embraced on many levels.

It provided a universal basis for arguments on morality, on war, and above all, and most importantly, on the question of authority. Where did authority come from? Whose territorial world was it? This English translation let loose a deluge of knowledge unlike anything that had happened before in human history. And as the waters irrigated what had been the deliberately uncultivated minds of millions, new shoots appeared: and the most remarkable of these, over time, was to be democracy.

The powers in the land spotted this from the beginning. Henry VIII, once such a proud lieutenant of the Pope, joined a Protestant movement he loathed and feared in order to father a legitimate heir. His dynastic imperative took precedence over his faith and the faith of the overwhelming majority of his subjects. One unforgivable unforeseen consequence included his vandalism and looting of some of the finest monasteries in Europe. The other and far more seismic unexpected consequence – the replacement of the Latin with the English Bible in churches throughout his kingdom – proved to be the rock on which his God-given idea of kingship was to be wrecked.

He himself saw that when, a few years after he had authorised the reading of the Bible in English, he lamented to Parliament, in 1545, that the Bible was 'disputed, rhymed, sung and jangled in every alehouse and tavern'. It was the access by the lower classes that grated. They were the growling beasts of the realm kept down by well-exercised oppressions: now their baying could be heard and the old and golden age and God-given hierarchical order of things would start to fall apart.

There was a Protestant pride in the liberation afforded by the Bible in the common language. As early as in the sixteenth century

Bishop John Jewel wrote: 'we allure the people to read and hear God's Word . . . We lean unto knowledge, they [Catholics] unto ignorance . . . unless thou know thou canst not judge: unless thou hear both sides thou canst not know.' That new phrase 'hear both sides' could be an early encapsulation of the democratic process.

The 'uneducated' proved swift to learn. Thwarted and rendered frustrate by the bits of Latin that were whispered at the high altar, they now had meat. Christopher Hill notes: 'the Biblical sophistication of the lower class Marian martyrs [Protestants burned at the stake by the Catholic Queen Mary and her government in the middle of the sixteenth century] is one of the most remarkable things about them. They took on bishops and scholars, out-argued and out-texted them. The memory of this did not die easily.' The Catholics warned against this rampage of the peasants. In 1554, John Standish expressed Roman Catholic fears when he wrote that uncontrolled Bible reading 'would set man against wife, master against servant and vice versa. Women have taken upon them the office of teaching: servants have become stubborn, forward and disobedient to their masters and mistresses.' A decade later, Anthony Gilby complained that soldiers and serving men can talk so much Scripture that they 'are no longer respectful to their betters'.

This was the first great fissure in the medieval Church-state's grip on power. And it came from the translated Bible which not only gave an intellectual landscape common to all, but provided ammunition for arguments. These arguments pierced the pomps and ceremonies and above all the claims to sole and unique authority of the establishment, at first in the Church but quite soon to follow in the state as well.

It is significant that the defenders of the status quo feared the overthrow of previous hierarchies in the everyday workings of life, man-wife, master-servant. It was in at the roots, and this was the evidence of the real danger. The plague of learning had got among the people, had reached to the bottom of the barrel, had got into the foundations and was gnawing away. 'When God gave Adam reason,' wrote Milton, 'he gave him freedom to choose, for reason is but choosing.' Through the translated Bible the great blessing of being able to decide for themselves now reached the people: they used it to choose. And it was in Protestant England that this was put to the test, in the Civil War.

So central was the use of the Bible in the Civil Wars, in pamphlets and meetings and among the numerous preachers, that when Charles II reintroduced monarchy in 1661 he passed an 'Act for the Safety and Preservation of His Majestie's Person and Government against Treasonable and Seditious Practices and Attempts'. This attempted to outlaw what the Restoration government saw as a prime cause of the Civil Wars – the religio-political tracts and sermons which had led to the case being made against the King. It was intended to make the King yet again unassailable. The Act was passed but a generation later, when James II attempted to reintroduce Catholicism he was swept away in the 'Glorious Revolution'. The subsequent 'Bill of Rights' established a landscape of discussion – rooted in the Civil War – which legitimised the trek towards a more democratic state.

The early democratic dialogue was fed by the pull between two ideologies. One was that of the Divine Right of Kings, vigorously claimed by James I and fatally held on to by his son Charles I. Opposed to that was the ideology of John Calvin and other nonconformists where anyone with the blessing of God and under proper authority can oppose tyranny and therefore any government perceived to be unjust can be brought down. The people could be God-supported in challenging an ungodly government and with God on their side and not on the side of the King or tyrant, where was the firm ground of government? It spread into calls for freedom of speech and, in the eighteenth and nineteenth centuries, attempts to give a place in the political world to the common man (and much later woman) on a par with their equal place in the intersecting sphere of religion. For religion in those centuries was the language and the arena of politics.

The strongest flavour of the roots of the democratic flowering comes from a debate in a church, St Mary the Virgin, in Putney, now a rich suburb of London. In 1647 it was a country village just two or three miles up the Thames from Parliament. What were known as the Putney Debates began on 28 October 1647 and lasted until the 11 November.

They were initiated by the Puritans' New Model Army in its cavalry regiments. It was here that the fervent Puritans were at their most radical and determined. They demanded 'one man, one vote'; that Authority be invested in the House of Commons and not with the King. Certain rights they called 'native' and these were to be inalienable: freedom of conscience and equality before the law. Thomas Rainsborough spoke for all of them, 'for really I think that the poorest he that is in England hath a life to live as the greatest he . . . and I do think that the poorest man in England is not at all bound in a strict sense to that government that he hath not had a voice to put himself under.' The Bible in English had given these men equality before God; now they wanted equality before government. The democratic game was afoot.

The Chairman of these Debates was Oliver Cromwell, who would not at that stage agree that the King should be removed. His son-in-law, Henry Ireton, spoke for Cromwell and others on his side and argued that only landholders should have the vote. He said 'no man hath a right to an interest or share in the disposing of the affairs of this kingdom . . . that hath not a permanent fixed interest in this kingdom.'

In 1647 Cromwell and Ireton's view prevailed.

But the fuse had been lit and that simple phrase 'the poorest hee . . . hath a life to live as the greatest hee' became the spark that was to light the fire which eventually razed centuries of tyranny, monarchy, feudalism and oligarchy. From now on the search and the fight for a new space for democracy was on. And behind it was the authority and confidence given by having the Bible in their native tongue.

In America, the first colonists held their first assembly also in a church. As time went on, the colonists claimed more and more religious freedom. The church assembly was the model which guided them towards greater political freedom. Nowadays, in a secular society, it seems easy to diminish the part played by religion in the reorientation of the modern world. But in the journey towards a full democracy there can be little doubt that the experience of a religion which grew out of the wide reading of the King James Version was the defining condition, the initiative for most people and certainly for most activists.

Having discussed and even disputed the Sacred Scriptures, the state held no ideological fears for these activists. In the Declaration of Independence, 1776, seen to mark the formal arrival of democracy in America, the words 'We hold these truths to be self-evident, that all men are created equal, that they are endowed by their Creator with certain inalienable rights' took the roots back to God and the Bible of the founding Puritans.

In the middle of the nineteenth century, the French essayist, Alexis de Tocqueville, was to write: 'the Americans combine the notions of Christianity and of liberty so intimately in their minds, that it is impossible to make them conceive the one without the other; and with them this connection does not spring from that barren traditional faith which seems to vegetate in the soul rather than to live.'

It had been a determined journey to arrive at the condition

described by de Tocqueville. Noah Webster, whose Bible-based educational books had such a widespread influence, wrote that 'our citizens should early understand that a genuine source of correct republican principles is the Bible, particularly the New Testament, and the Christian religion.' That early understanding was clear to the first colonists. Their numbers swelled greatly, with the Great Awakening, which has already been referred to.

In the middle of the eighteenth century, Jonathan Edwards was dismissed from his church in Northampton, Massachusetts, for ending his grandfather's policy of open (i.e. general) communion. Edwards instead favoured and emphasised personal (individual) communion, personal salvation, an individual and not a community decision. Furthermore, individuals could choose between different Churches. The idea of the individual as the hub of society was beginning to replace the still prevailing notion of the Church as the community. Once the individual was given authority, herding and mass control were not so easy to take for granted and the voice of a single person had to be heard.

Edwards was a key player in the Great Awakening of the mid-eighteenth century. Its transforming effect on the religious lives of the hundreds of thousands who came to hear the charismatic preachers was a prologue to its eventual effect on their sense of themselves in the politics of the day. Though the message of the Great Awakening was biblical, it was also egalitarian and emphasised that the grace of God could fall on anyone who sought salvation. Salvation became independence, and independence sought the entitlement to a vote. Now you had a place on earth equal to the place provided by the grace of God in heaven.

Edwards clarified and changed the emphasis of the Christian message. He moved it back to the ways of the original Apostles as many progressives failed to do. It was its own version of the

Renaissance, the rediscovery of the past in order to energise and re-order the present. As has been mentioned, Edwards was fore-shadowed by the Wesley brothers and by George Whitefield, who were also key influences in the devolution of the Church.

Now it took only the conversion of the 'heart' to take the soul into the Kingdom of Heaven. This reinforced almightily the shift to the individual being the determinant of his or her own fate. It reached to the poor and marginalised as never before. Following the literate preachers, hitherto the theological masters of the universe, there grew the army of the poor and the marginalised who now had a status. Democracy was creeping in, a part of salvation.

Thomas Paine was an Englishman, a radical, a democrat but not a Christian. Yet, in the crucial year 1776 he published, in America, a pamphlet, *Common Sense*, which quoted extensively from the Bible. For example, he writes:

> Near three thousand years passed away from the Mosaic account of the creation, till the Jews, under a national delusion, requested a king. Till then their form of government (except in extraordinary circumstances when the Almighty interposed) was a kind of republic administered by a judge and the elders of the tribes . . . and when a man seriously reflects on the idolatrous homage which is paid to the person of kings, he need not wonder that the Almighty, ever jealous of his honour, should disapprove of a form of government which so impiously invaded the prerogative of heaven.

In the Bible the non-religious Tom Paine found a template for revolution. He picked out the positive points of the embryonic nation of America like an archer arrowing into the dead centre circle again and again. If the Jews were under a 'delusion', then the Americans were not alone; indeed they had venerable forebears and examples to follow. The Bible fed his hunger for democracy.

The Almighty was given due omnipotence. Christians were secure with that. The phrase 'a kind of republic administered by a judge and the elders of the tribes' was a canny perception of the state of a country with its eyes beginning to open to the possibility of a republic. This was in step with its 'judges' and its nonconformist assemblies run by 'elders'. 'Idolatrous' was good, the king to be associated with the graven image, would bring onside those who believed 'thou shalt not worship any graven image.'

The phrase about the Almighty 'ever jealous of his honour' spoke both to an often expressed characteristic of the Old Testament Jehovah, god of vengeance and to the ideal of 'honour' which took the curse off any possible offence.

Paine's adoption of passages in the King James Version as a means of communication was successful beyond any expectation: 150,000 pamphlets sold within a few weeks, and *Common Sense* was exported to London and Paris where it caused an equal sensation and set Paine on the road to be the world revolutionary-threat-in-chief.

Abraham Lincoln though possibly a Christian was never a Church member. But he, too, like Paine, used the language and drew on its reserve of history, suffering, struggle and its triumphs. Perhaps he was essentially closer to it than Tom Paine, as when, in his Second Inaugural Address in the middle of the carnage of the Civil War, he refers to both sides in that war as appealing to the same Bible and praying to the same God. He might have added that they were instructed by an almost wholly identical cohort of nonconformist divines. And he appealed to prayer, a central Christian instrument. 'Finally do we hope – fervently do we pray – that this mighty scourge of war might pass away.' That their President was praying alongside them would have mattered greatly to the many Christians embroiled in that conflict. Lincoln's speech was approved in Europe as well as in America. The theologian Philip Schaff wrote at the time: 'I do not believe that any royal, princely or republican state dreamt of recent times can be compared to this inaugural address for genuine Christian wisdom and gentleness.'

George Washington took up the song. 'Of all dispositions and habits which lead to political prosperity, religion and morality are indispensable supports . . . 'tis substantially true that virtue or morality *is a necessary spring of popular government*' (my italics).

In Britain the road to democracy was not marked out by quite such vivid and enthusiastic figures. But movements for social reform were far more often than not lit into life by those whose theory came out of the New Testament. Political developments – notably the trades unions and the birth and growth of the Labour Party – owed more to Methodism than to Marxism.

And underneath it all were the two pillars of wisdom: the first was the Reformation which demanded freedom of thought on what were then the most pressing and awesome issues of the day – the teachings of the Bible. The second was the translation of the Bible into the vernacular, which happened in many countries but in Britain resulted in a book which became the university for those who were barred from them, the education for those who had hitherto been denied it, and the national book giving access for all to the high table of debates on life and death and eternity. The King James Bible is a book which has informed and enriched two English-speaking empires over 400 years and carried many of its messages around the globe. It set off consequences no one could have imagined in 1611, nor, in many cases, would they have approved. It has been well used and abused. It has been a transforming force, often making our world a better place.

In its beginnings was the call to faith. In those beginnings were other hidden calls to people who would listen to them. Its impact has been immeasurable and it is not over yet.

AFTERWORD

I encountered the King James Bible in 1945 when I was six. My uncles had hauled me into the choir of St Mary's, the Anglican church in the north Cumbrian town of Wigton. A town at that time of twelve churches. Wigton's population was about 5,000.

In the service of the Nine Lessons and Carols, the tradition is that the youngest choirboy reads the first lesson. It was a tough call. The words I had to read, from Genesis, were incomprehensible: 'and the serpent beguiled her and she did eat.' The church was packed, floor and gallery, candlelit, parents and relatives somewhere in that mass of congregation, all of whom wore their best, their 'Sunday' clothes. I remember as I tried to peer over the eagle-masted lectern that it was so very strange: this voice was not mine, out there was something both me and not me. But it got done. 'Here endeth the first lesson,' and the page was turned for the next reader.

My mother, a Wigton girl, was christened and confirmed in that church. She was married there and at some time soon will join my father who is buried there.

The church was a strong strand in my childhood. Choir meant regular attendance and the choir practice, church services, Sunday school, the church youth club (the Anglican Young People's Association), debates, outings, games and dances in the Parish

Rooms. The Bible came into the school in morning assemblies, prayers, hymns and lessons called Religious Instruction. I was caught up in it, doused in it, bound in it, and then, in the heady liberation of adolescence, unbound. But there has continued to be a residue, stronger than a 'trace memory', but much less, as I said in the book, than the total Christian demand on a believer.

This book grew out of that early experience. The language of the King James Version flowed into me, its stories and characters fed the imagination and its various promises and threats provided both meat for argument and grist for guilt.

St Mary's is a handsome Georgian church on the site of a huddled medieval church pulled down without any recorded regret. There are several fine stained-glass windows but on the north side there were three large empty windows which, a few years ago, I decided to fill with stained glass as a tribute to my parents and family and as a thanksgiving to the church for what I had got out of it.

This was an unconscious education. The stories and words of the King James Bible and the Book of Common Prayer, the Psalms and hymns, were sung and listened to for many years. They are still lodged in my mind. They were a gift. The music, too, the anthems we sang, the organ voluntaries we heard and the quiet ceremonies of a then benign, easy, undemanding church built up a hidden store of knowledge and sensations, church bells and candles, bowing to the altar, versicles and responses.

I wanted the three new windows to bring the town into the church. Other windows told stories from the Bible. I wanted stories of Wigton, representing the congregations which had been the Church in that town for more than 800 years. To illustrate this I chose not only the school and the church itself, but the factory, the cattle auction, the rivers, the once prosperous now obsolete mills, the streets, terraced houses, the special features of the place and the people. The King James Bible brought them into the church with eyes and ears at last fully opened to the Faith they practised. Over the centuries many had lived and died for it.

Brian Campbell, an artist and long-time friend, made the designs. Alex Haynes, crafted the stained-glass final version.

Occasionally I go to the church when I am in the area. Its numbers have fallen as they have all over the country. I think there's a gallantry about those who still assemble there. You see this most clearly when you go into one of our magnificent cathedrals in the late afternoon to listen to the incomparable music of the Choral Evensong. The choir can outnumber the congregation.

They are few. But they have been few before and they hang on. Perhaps out of habit or nostalgia or perhaps because of an apprehension or hope for some intimation of the mystery of things – things that the recent President of the Royal Society said we shall never know about but sometimes think or feel that we sense.

The whole idea – God, Genesis, Christ, Resurrection – is now to me a moving metaphor, a poetic way of attempting to understand what may be for ever incomprehensible. When I was six it was the truth about all of life.

But in what those remembered words in the Bible hold, there is still for me a sonic echo of something Isaac Newton – a mathematician, and a Christian – said at the end of his life. He described his work as having been like that of a boy merely collecting pebbles on the shore 'whilst the great ocean of truth lay all undiscovered before me'.

ACKNOWLEDGEMENTS

Hannah Whittingham has been invaluable in helping with the research for this book. She is widely gifted and I have been lucky that she found the time to work so energetically on this project.

I am once again in debt to my friends Vivien Green and Julia Matheson whose counsel and practical help have been unstinting. I have been very fortunate to know and work with them over so many years. My wife, Cate Haste, has been unfaltering in her support.

To the authors listed in the bibliography I owe a lot. This Book of Books has been built on books. Books are written to be read and studied: and to be used by later writers of other books. None more than the King James Bible.

I am grateful to my publishers, Hodder & Stoughton, especially its exemplary non-fiction editor Rupert Lancaster and to Sam Richardson who was in at the beginning.

Finally my warmest thanks to my friend Richard Simon, of whose generous reading and knowledge I was a beneficiary here, as I have been for many years.

PICTURE ACKNOWLEDGEMENTS

© Alamy/Pictorial Press: 2 below. © The British Library: vi (C.35.I.11), 1 (C.188.a.17, CXIV), 6 above right (G.11631), and below (C.70.aa.3). © Corbis Images: 5 below, 8 below, 10 below, 12 below, 14 above left/attributed to Giotto, 14 centre right/painting by Cristofano Allori, 14 below/painting by Guercino, 16 above/photo Jim Bourg, 16 below/photo Goran Tomasevic. © Mary Evans Picture Library: 4 centre right, 10 centre right, 13 above, 15 centre left, 15 below right/Marx Memorial Library. © Getty Images: 2 above/Time & Life Pictures, 3 above/portrait by Nathaniel Hone, 3 below/painting by John Collet, 4 above and below, 5 above left and centre right, 6 above left, 7 above left, 7 below left/photo Alfred Eisenstaedt/Time & Life Pictures, 12 above. © The Huntington Library and Art Gallery, San Marino, California: 9 above/portrait by Bass Otis/photo Bridgeman Art Library. Library of Congress Prints and Photographs Division, Washington DC: 7 above right/engraving by Samuel Hollyer, 8 above/photo Arthur Rothstein, 10 above/photo Timothy H. O'Sullivan, 11, 13 below. © National Portrait Gallery, London: 15 above right/portrait by John Singer Sargent/NPG 1746. Private Collection/photo Bridgeman Art Library: 9 below right/portrait by John Keenan. © Rex Features: 7 below right. © Wilberforce House, Hull City Museums and Art Galleries: 9 below left/portrait by John Rising/photo Bridgeman Art Library.

SELECT BIBLIOGRAPHY

Anderson, Christopher, *The Annals of the English Bible*, London: William Pickering, 1845

Bobrick, Benson, *Wide as the Waters: The Story of the English Bible and the Revolution it Inspired*, Simon and Schuster, 2001

Bourne, George, *A Condensed Anti-Slavery Bible Argument*, 1845

Bragg, Melvyn, *The Adventure of English: The Biography of a Language*, Sceptre, 2004

Bragg, Melvyn, *12 Books That Changed the World*, Hodder & Stoughton, 2006

Bruce, Frederick Fyvie, *The King James Version: The First 350 Years*, OUP, 1960

Bruce, Frederick Fyvie, *History of the Bible in English*, Cambridge: Lutterworth Press, 2002

Campbell, Gordon, *Bible: The Story of the King James Version 1611–2011*, OUP, 2010

Crystal, David, *Begat: The King James Bible and the English Language*, OUP, 2010

Daniell, David, *The Bible in English: Its History and Influence*, YUP, 2003

Davies, Julian, *The Caroline Captivity of the Church: Charles I and the Remoulding of Anglicanism 1625–41*, Clarendon Press, 1992

Dawkins, Richard, *The God Delusion*, Bantam, 2006

Fox, John, 'The Influence of the English Bible on Literature', *Princeton Theological Review*, Vol. 9, No. 3, 1911

Harris, Sam, *Letter to a Christian Nation*, Bantam, 2007

Harrison, Eugene Myers, *Blazing the Missionary Trail*, Chicago, Ill.: Scripture Press Book Division, 1949

Hill, Christopher, *The English Bible and the Seventeenth-Century Revolution*, Penguin Books, 1993

Hills, Margaret T. (ed.), *The English Bible in America: A Bibliography of Editions of the Bible and the New Testament Published in America, 1777–1957*, Greenwood, 1991

Jayne, A.G., 'The Bible in English' in Henry Barker, *A Tercentenary Celebration of the Authorized Version of the English Bible*, New York Bible and Common Prayer Book Society, 1911

MacCulloch, Diarmaid, *A History of Christianity: The First Three Thousand Years*, Allen Lane, 2009

Mayhew, Henry, *London Labour and the London Poor*, Penguin Classics, 2006

McAfee, Cleland Boyd, *The Greatest English Classic: A Study of the King James Version of the Bible and its Influence on Life and Literature*, New York: Harper and Brothers, 1912

McGrath, Alister, *In the Beginning: The Story of the King James Bible and How it Changed a Nation, a Language and a Culture*, Hodder & Stoughton, 2002

Middleton, Richard, *Colonial America: A History, 1565–1776*, Blackwell, 2000

Miller, Randall M. (ed.), *Religion and the American Civil War*, OUP, 1998

Nelson, Scott Reynolds and Sheriff, Carol, *A People at War: Civilians and Soldiers in America's Civil War, 1854–1877*, OUP, 2007

Nicolson, Adam, *God's Secretaries: The Making of the King James Bible*, HarperCollins, 2003

Noll, Mark, *The Civil War as a Theological Crisis*, University of North Carolina Press, 2006

Norton, David, *A Textual History of the King James Bible*, CUP, 2005

Rowse, A.L., *William Shakespeare: A Biography*, Barnes & Noble, 1995

Scrivener, Henry Ambrose Frederick, *The Authorized Edition of the English Bible, 1611, its Subsequent Reprints and Modern Representatives*, CUP, 1884

Shaheen, Naseeb, *Biblical References in Shakespeare's Plays*, University of Delaware Press, 1999

Taylor, Alan, *American Colonies: The Settling of North America*, Penguin, 2001

Walsh, W. Pakenham, *Modern Heroes of the Mission Field*, New York: Fleming H. Revell, 1915

Wheeler, J.M., *Satan, Witchcraft and the Bible*, London, 1895

WEBSITES

http://www.tyndale.org/TSJ/3/mansbridge.html

http://www.legislation.gov.uk/ukpga

http://www.educationengland.org.uk/history/chapter01.html

http://www.natsoc.org.uk/society/history/

http://www.gideons.org

http://www.biblesociety.org.uk

http://www.usccgettysburg.org/

http://www.av1611.org/kjv/reagan.html

http://www.ymca.net

INDEX

'KJB' indicated the King James Bible.

Abel 79, 232, 248
abortion 304
Abraham 79, 290–91, 308
Abravanel, Isaac ben 232
Adam 187, 233, 288, 290, 308, 338
Adams, John 67
Addams, Jane 319–20
adultery 287, 300–303, 305
Africa 276–77, 284
African Methodist Episcopal Church
    238
African-Americans 97, 124, 178,
    205, 206, 231
Ahab, King 116
Alcott, Louisa May 252
Alfred the Great 12, 14
All About Eve (film) 289
Allestree, Richard 310
'Am I my brother's keeper?' 127–28
America
    the Bible and literature 164–81

Great Awakenings 92, 94, 96, 97,
    101, 103, 106, 236, 245, 312,
    341
missionaries in 279–81
new world founded 10, 39, 60
slavery and civil war 229–42,
    243–58
American Bible Society 166, 281
American Board of Commissioners
    for Foreign Missions 272
American Civil War 172, 230, 232,
    240, 243–54, 256, 257, 259,
    279, 343
American English 64–66
American Indians 64
    see also Native Americans
American Social Gospel movement
    326
American War of Independence
    (1775–83) 101, 105, 165,
    245
Andrewes, Launcelot, Dean of 38,
    45–46, 178

Anglican Church 9, 90, 100, 218,
    238, 265, 268, 269
    see also Church of England
Anglican Young People's Association
    345
Anglo-Saxon 50, 123
Annesley, Reverend Samuel 152
Anti-Slavery Society 328
Antwerp 29
Antwerp Polyglot (1572) 44
Apocrypha 47, 294
Aquinas, St Thomas 111, 112, 291
Aramaic 18, 147
Aristotle 111, 112
Arnold, Matthew 136, 149
Arundel, Thomas, Archbishop of
    Canterbury 122
Astell, Mary 311
Athelstane, King 12
Auden, W.H. 178
Augustine, St 98, 111, 112, 187,
    231, 288, 310–11
Austen, Jane 158–59, 219
Australia 275–76, 284
Australian Aboriginals 198, 200, 275
Authorised Version *see* King James
    Bible

Babylon 79
Bacon, Francis 24–25, 79, 110, 158,
    185
Baker, David 308
Ball, John 14, 325
Balzac, Honoré de 143
Bancroft, Bishop (later Archbishop)
    48

Banks, Joseph 273
Baptists 238–39, 248, 255, 256,
    272, 281, 283
Barker, Robert 49, 83
Barker, Thomas 49
Bathsheba 137, 168, 300
Bay Psalm Book, The 165
'Be fruitful and multiply' 127, 298
Beatitudes 7, 25–26, 73, 132, 159, 303
Beauregard, General Pierre 243
Beckett, Samuel 207
Bede, Venerable 14
Bega, Theodore 44
Beresford family 219
Bible, the
    use in the Civil War 338
    first version in English (1382)
        13–17, 25, 44
    'interpretations' 69
    Latin translations 44–45
    a pit of fertile contradictions 70
    popularity and influence at its
        height 135
    power of 78
    and sex 287–309
    a well of adaptable wisdom 70
    the word 'bible' 135
Bible Society 222
Bible Women 312, 314, 315, 316,
    320–23
Big Bang 8
Bill of Rights 88, 338
Bishops' Bible (1568) 37, 51, 68
black Churches 255–56
Blake, William 9, 136, 153–55
Bliss, W.D.P. 327

Bloom, Harold 143
Bloom, Paul 206
Blunden, Edmund 172–73
Boaz 297
Bobrick, Benson 335
Boleyn, Anne 29
Book of Common Prayer 346
Booth, Catherine 317
Booth, William 314–17
Bourne, George 239
Bowdler, Dr Thomas 125
Boyd, Sir Robert 114
Boyle, Robert 110, 111, 113
Bradford, William: *Of Plymouth Plantation* 54–56
Brinsley, John: *The Third Part of the True Watch* 59
British and Foreign Bible Society 272, 280
British Empire 225, 280, 285, 286
Brontë, Charlotte 161
Brontë sisters 161
Brophy, Brigid 207
Broughton, Hugh 50–51
Brown, Antoinette 312
Brown, George Gordon 157
Bryson, Bill 56, 57
Buckingham, Duchess of 221
Buddhism 276, 278
Bunyan, John 149–51, 159, 161, 170, 222
Burgess, Cornelius 75
Burke, Edmund 213
Burton, Richard 222
Butler, Josephine 318
Byron, George Gordon, Lord 156–57

Cabbala 189
Cain 79, 232, 248, 249, 308
Calvin, John 83, 338
Calvinism, Calvinists 53, 95, 104
'Cambridge Seven' 284
Cambridge University 45, 90, 217, 264, 328
Campbell, Brian 347
Campbell, Isabella and Mary 311–12
Canaan 167, 231, 232, 241, 249
Canaanites 231–32
Canterbury, Archbishops of
    Simon Sudbury 121
    Thomas Arundel 122
    Thomas Cranmer 29, 142
Carey, William 283
Case, Thomas 77
Castalio, Sebastain 45
Cavafy, Constantine P. 289
Cavaliers 76
Caxton, William 121
Cecil, Robert 48
Celts 64
Chalmers, James 284
charity 312–23, 333
Charity Organisation Society (later Family Action) 314, 318
Charles I, King 57, 59, 69, 71–78, 82, 83, 85, 88, 116, 184, 338
Charles II, King 71, 82–83, 84, 88, 89, 109, 184, 338
Chaucer, Geoffrey 16, 120, 122
    Canterbury Tales 121
Cheke, Sir John 124
child abuse by Roman Catholic priests 197–98

China 279
China Inland Mission 284
Choral Evensong 9, 347
Christian, Fletcher 282
Christian Brethren 22
  see also Lollards
Christian Commission 253
Christian Evidence Society 114
Christian Socialists 313, 325–34
Church Mission Society 222
Church of England 9, 38, 90–91,
  99–100, 219, 265, 267, 268
  see also Anglican Church
Church schools 262, 268
Churchill, Sir Winston 9, 10, 51
Civic Trust 332
Civil Rights Movement 242
Clarkson, Thomas 216
Co-operative Movement 313
Codrington Plantation, Barbados
  238
Coke, Sir Edward 71
Coke, Reverend Thomas 272
Colenso, John William, Bishop of
  Natal 277
Coleridge, Samuel Taylor 136, 137,
  157–58
College of William and Mary,
  Williamsburg 263
Collinges, John 79
Cologne 23, 24
Commonwealth 59, 78
Complutensian Polyglot (1517) 44
Confederate Army 257
Congregationalists 89–90, 272
Constantine, Emperor 14

Contagious Diseases Act 318
contraception 304
Conway, Lady Ann 117
Cook, Albert Stansborough 130
Cook, Captain James 273
Cook Islands 284
Cook, Professor Albert Stanborough
  52
Cooper, Dr Lane 125
Copernicus, Nicolaus 112
Corpus Christi College, Oxford 39
Cotton, John 245
Counter-Reformation 210
Coverdale, Miles 29, 37
Cranmer, Thomas, Archbishop of
  Canterbury 29, 142
Crick, Francis 208
Cripps, Stafford 325
Cromwell, Oliver 59, 60, 78, 82, 85,
  339
Cromwell, Thomas 29
Crystal, David 126–27, 128
Culverwell, Nathaniel 186
Cunningham, Valentine 152, 153

Damasus, Pope 14
Dame schools 267
Daniell, David 28
Darwin, Charles 110, 113, 128, 196
David and Goliath 300
David and Jonathan 305
Davis, David 249
Davis, Jefferson 235, 243
Dawkins, Richard 8, 194–209
Declaration of Independence (1776)
  340

Defoe, Daniel 152, 153, 155
Delilah 297
democracy 335–44
Descartes, René 112, 193
Dickens, Charles 7, 9, 143, 159
Diggers 149–50, 325
Diodati, Giovanni 45
Dirac, Paul 110
Disciples churches 248
Dissenters 98, 212, 213, 214, 217
Dissenting Protestantism 113
Divine Right of Kings 35, 39, 42,
    70, 72, 114, 278, 338
Dobneck, John 24
Doddridge, Philip 221–22
Donne, John 145–47, 179
Douay-Rheims New Testament
    (1582) 37, 124, 165
Dryden, John 151–52
dualism 206–7
Duff (mission ship) 281, 282
Duns Scotus, Blessed John 111

Early Modern English 37
East India Company 223, 278
Ecclesiastical Commissioners 330
Eddington, Arthur 113
Edinburgh University 263, 264
education 259–70
Edward VI, King 184
Edwards, John 117
Edwards, Jonathan 102–3, 105,
    341–42
Edwards, Sarah 105
Egypt 79, 200, 309
Einstein, Albert 113, 196, 207, 209

Elementary Education Act (1870)
    268
Eliot, George 159–60
Eliot, T.S. 9, 45–46, 130, 136,
    178–81
Elizabeth I, Queen 32–33, 34, 37,
    38, 45, 49, 60, 71, 184
Elizabeth II, Queen 1, 9
Engels, Friedrich 324, 333
English Civil War (1642–51) 59, 69,
    75–78, 80–83, 90, 92, 110,
    210, 232, 238, 245, 251, 259,
    267, 338
Enlightenment 182–93, 209, 210,
    211, 215, 233, 263, 267
Episcopal churches 248
Erasmus, Desiderius 22, 23, 26, 27
Essex, Barbara J. 308
Esther 297
eternal life 94
ethnic cleansing 274–75
Eve 187, 233, 288, 289, 290, 292,
    297, 303, 308, 310, 311

Faraday, Michael 110, 113
Farrer, Austin 137
Fast Sermons 74–76
Faulkner, William 169
Fell, Margaret 307–8
Feuerbach, Ludwig 333
Field, John 84
Fifth Monarchists 149
First Cambridge Company 46
First Cause 8, 114, 196
First Oxford Company 47
First Westminster Company 45

First World War 172–73, 279
Fitzgerald, F. Scott 175–76
Flanders, Battle of 173
fornication 304–5
Fox, Charles James 220
Foxe, John: *Book of Martyrs* 29
Franklin, Benjamin 104–5, 110, 263
Frei, Hans 187–88
French Bibles 45
French Revolution 11, 189, 272
Friendly Societies 313
Froude, James Anthony 130
Fuseli, Henry 214

Galileo Galilei 112
Garden of Eden 18, 115, 289
Gardner, Bishop John 89
Geneva Bible (1560) 37, 40, 41–42,
    51, 54, 71, 83, 141, 142, 147,
    230
German Bible 45
Germanic tribes 64
Gettysburg Address 126
Gibbon, Edward 125
Gideon Society 10
Gilby, Anthony 337
Gillard, Derek 264–65
Gilmour, James 284
Ginsberg, Allen 154
Glorious Revolution (1688) 11, 88,
    338
Gloucester, Bishop of 19
Gnostic Gospels 294–95
Godwin, William 214
Golding, William 176–77
Google search engine 206

Goostree gentlemen's club 220
gospel songs 236
Gospels: Alfred the Great has them
    translated 14
Grant, James Augustus 285
Graves, Robert 172–73
Great Awakenings 92, 94, 96, 97,
    101, 103, 106, 236, 245, 312,
    341
Great Bible (1539) 37
Great Indian Rebellion (1857) 278
Greek language 8, 18, 23, 44, 45,
    46, 63, 124, 134, 147
Greenblatt, Stephen 141–42
Grey, Earl 318
Grotius, Hugo 45
Gurney, Ivor 172–73
Guy Fawkes Day 73–74

Hagar 290–92
Hague, William 219
Haldane, J.B.S. 209
Hamburg 23, 29
Hamilton, Edith 288
Hampton Court 36–37, 39, 43, 47,
    71
Hampton Court Conference 39, 47
Handel, George Frideric 9, 192
Hardie, Keir 324, 325, 330, 334
Hardinge, John 47
Hardy, Thomas 142–43, 177–78
Harrington, James 88
Harris, Richard, former Bishop of
    Oxford 206
Harrison, Peter 114–16, 184,
    187–88

Harvard University 60, 262–63
Hawking, Stephen 110
Hawthorne, Nathaniel 164, 168–69
Haynes, Alex 347
Hazleton, Lesley 290
Hebrew language 8, 18, 28–29, 44,
  45, 46, 63, 123, 134, 147
Henrietta Maria, Queen 73, 74
Henry V, King 120, 124
Henry VIII, King 6, 9, 13, 21–22,
  24, 27, 29, 36, 37, 49, 70, 72,
  85, 122, 184, 336
Hill, Christopher 58, 69, 88–89, 337
Hill, Octavia 313–14, 319, 326,
  330–34
Hill, Samuel S. 256–57
Hinduism 276, 278, 279
Hobbes, Thomas 51, 88, 89, 191, 193
Hogarth, William 223
Hogg, James 161
Holland, Thomas 47
Holocaust 173
Holofernes 293
Holy Club 99, 100
Holy Roman Empire 13
Holy Trinity church, Stratford-upon-
  Avon 140–41
homosexuality 303, 305, 306
Hong Xiuquan 279
Hooke, Robert 110, 111, 117
Hooker, Thomas 59, 74
Horsley, Bishop Samuel 277
Hosea 301
House of Commons 10, 75, 224,
  233, 339
Houses of Parliament 73, 224

Howe, William 322
Howland, John 55
Hull, east Yorkshire 216, 217, 221
Hull House, Chicago, Illinois 319,
  320
Hume, David 188
Hunter, J. Paul 174–75

illiteracy 87
incest 287
India 277–79, 283
Indian languages 64–65
Industrial Revolution 189, 224, 234,
  265
International League of Religious
  Socialists 326
Ireton, Henry 339
Isaac 79
Ishmael 290, 291
Islam 191, 276, 278, 279, 290

Jackson, Mahalia 242
Jacob 308
James I, King 184
  a biblical scholar 308
  childhood 34
  crowned in Westminster Abbey 1,
    9, 36
  and Divine Right of Kings 35,
    70, 72, 338
  and the Geneva Bible 83
  inspires the KJB 1, 34, 39–40,
    41, 51, 109
  as James VI of Scotland 33
  journey from Edinburgh to
    London 35–36

persecutor of witches 308
rules for the KJB 48
succeeded by son Charles 57
James II, King 88, 184, 338
Jamestown, Virginia 60
Japan 279
Jasper, David 136
Jefferson, Thomas 165
Jehoichim, King 73
Jehovah's Witnesses 280
Jepthah 306, 308
Jeremiah 301
Jerome, St 14, 18, 19, 45, 51
Jerusalem Chamber, Abbey House,
    Westminster, London 46
Jesuits 265
Jesus Christ
    and Mary Magdalene 293–94
    pamphlet attacks as an 'imposter'
      191
    teaching mission 307
Jewel, Bishop John 337
Jews
    Cabbala 189
    destruction of Jerusalem 190
    expelled from the Iberian
      Peninsula 190
    Thomas Paine on 342
Jezebel 290, 292
John, St 293, 295
Johnson, Joseph 212
Johnson, Dr Samuel 140
Jones, David 172
Joseph of Arimathea 293
Josiah, King 73
Joyce, James 139, 143

Judaism 190, 191, 232, 290
Judith 292–93
Judo, Leo 45

Kant, Immanuel 193
Kelvin, Lord 114
Kepler, Johannes 112
King, Martin Luther 9, 126, 135,
    255, 258, 333
King James Bible
    and American English 66
    Bancroft's fourteen changes 48
    becomes the sole Bible in churches
      51
    and Church of England schools
      90–91
    claimed to be the most pivotal
      book ever written 5–6
    consists of sixty-six different
      'books' 5
    cost of first printing 50
    and democracy 253
    and the English constitution 78,
      84–85
    and execution of Charles I 69
    General Committee of Revision
      48
    general distribution 281
    Hebrew idioms 123
    importance to English-speaking
      peoples 1, 5
    inspired by James I 1, 34, 39–40,
      41, 51
    key role in abolition of slavery
      255
    the King's fourteen rules 48

known as the Authorised Version
or the King James Version
48–49
later versions 50, 83–84, 166
as literature 130–39, 140–63
Miles Smyth's preface 48
misprints 50
over 90 per cent of the words are
Old English 124, 134–35
Oxford Edition 85
power of 78, 172
prepared for publication 42–48
printed in English in 1611 1, 5,
6, 48, 49–50
translations 280
King's College, London 328
Kingsley, Charles 161, 326–27,
328–29
Kingswood 103
Kipling, Rudyard 149
Korea 279
Kyrle Society 332

Labour Party (British) 325, 344
Langland, William 16
Lansbury, George 325
Last Judgement 17
Last Temptation (film) 289
Latin 14–19, 34, 44, 46, 51, 63, 86,
93, 120, 122, 123–24, 134,
147
Latin Vulgate 14, 18, 19, 20, 45
Laud, Archbishop 74, 83, 84
Lawrence, D.H. 137, 170–71
Lecky, W.E.H. 235
Lefèvre d'Etaples, Jacques 45

Leopold, Prince 318
'Let there be light' 127
Levellers 88, 149, 325
Lewis, C.S. 136
Lewis, Jane 331
Leyland, John 251
Lincoln, Abraham 1, 7, 126, 243,
246, 253–54, 343–44
Lincoln Cathedral 36
literacy 93, 95
literature
America and the twentieth
century 164–81
the Bible itself as literature
130–39
English literature in Britain
140–63
Little Sodbury, Cotswolds 22
Lively, Edward 46–47
Locke, John 97, 184, 192, 193, 311
Lockyer, Nicholas 77
Loftus, Elizabeth 198
Lollards 17–18, 22, 24
London City Mission 322
London Missionary Society 273
Lord's Prayer 19, 122, 159
Lot 301, 306, 308
Lowth, Robert 136
Luke, St 293, 295
Luther, Martin 21, 23, 24, 27, 45,
98, 282

McAfee, Cleland Boyd 144, 150–51,
161
Macaulay, Lord 52, 126, 130–31
McCarthy, Cormac 177

McCarthy, Senator 63
McCrea, Dr William 11
MacCulloch, Diarmaid 60, 96, 97,
    98, 190, 192, 232, 234, 272,
    276, 279–80, 311
McGrath, Alister 84, 122, 124, 133
Mackay, Alexander 283–84
Magna Carta 70
Malden, William 122
Mansbridge, Ronald 141
Mansfield, Lord Chief Justice 234
Maoris 274–75
Marian martyrs 337
Mark, St 293, 295
Marsden, Samuel 284
Marshall, Stephen 75
Marston Moor, Battle of (1644) 76
Marx, Karl 324, 333
Marxism 333–34, 344
Mary, Queen 184, 337
Mary, Queen of Scots 34, 42
Mary, Virgin 288, 290
Mary II, Queen 88
Mary Magdalene 289, 290, 293–95
Massachusetts 60, 262
match factories 317
Mather, Cotton 310
Matthew, St 293, 295
Maurice, F.D. 326, 327–28, 329
Maxwell, James Clerk 110, 113
Mayflower 53, 54
Mayhew, Henry 313, 319, 320–21
Melville, Herman 167–69
Mencken, H.L. 8
Methodism, Methodists 89–90, 97,
    98, 101, 106, 126, 218,
    220–21, 236, 238–39, 240,
    255, 256, 257, 263, 281, 325,
    344
Methodist World Missions 272
Mid-Western Bible Belt, United
    States 206
Middle Passage 229
Middleton, Richard 262
Miller, Arthur 62–63
Milner, Isaac 221
Milton, John 11, 88, 138, 147–49,
    151, 181, 289, 338
missions, missionaries 6, 90, 271–86
Mohammed 191, 285
Mongolia 284
More, Hannah 155
More, Sir Thomas 22, 26, 27–28, 85
Mormons (Latter Day Saints) 280
Morris, William 332
Morrison, Toni 7, 178, 181
Moses 18, 79, 81, 115, 117, 135,
    137, 152, 163, 191, 233, 237,
    308
M'Tesa, King, of Uganda 285
Münster, Sebastian 44
My Brother's Keeper 127–28
mystery plays 20

Napoleon Bonaparte 9
Napoleonic Wars (1799–1815) 269
Naseby, Battle of (1645) 76
National Society for the Education of
    the Poor 264–65, 268–69
National Trust 314, 332
Native Americans 96
see also American Indians

Nebuchadnezzar, King 73, 89, 116, 292

Nelson, Admiral Lord Horatio 224

Neoplatonism 189

New England 59, 61, 62, 64, 106, 262

New England Primer 65–66

New Enlightenment 194

New Guinea 284

New Lanark cotton mills 333

New Model Army 76, 88, 339

New Testament
    Douay-Rheims (1582) 37, 124, 165
    Luther translates into German 21
    Theodore Bega's translation 44
    two companies prepare the KJB 47
    Tyndale's translation (1525) 13, 23–28, 31, 37, 44, 84, 122, 222, 298

New York School of Philanthropy 318

New Zealand 274–75, 276

Newton, John 222

Newton, Sir Isaac 8, 9, 16, 110, 112, 113, 114, 116, 117, 189, 199, 347

Nietzsche, Friedrich 170

Nigeria 305

Nigerian Methodist Church 277

Night School, Little Ormond Yard, London 329

Nightingale, Florence 9

Nimrod, King 116

Nine Lessons and Carols, Service of 345

Noah 116, 117, 231–32, 249, 299

Noah's Flood 115–16

Noll, Mark A. 165, 246–48

nonconformists 89–90, 213

Normans 120

Norris, Pamela 290

North, Lord 219

Northampton, Massachusetts 341

Northern Ireland 265

Norton, David 161

Nott, Henry 281–83

Obama, Barack 1, 258

Octavia Hill Association, Philadelphia 331

Old English 8

Old Testament
    Sebastian Münster's Latin translation 44
    three companies prepare the KJB 47
    Tyndale's partial translation 28–29, 31, 37, 45, 46, 298

Olivétan, Pierre Robert 45

Onanism 298–99

original sin 288, 289

Owen, Robert 333

Owen, Wilfred 172–73

Oxford University 12, 90, 98–99, 102, 111, 264

Pagninus, Sanctes 45

Paine, Thomas 213, 214, 342–43

Papara, Tahiti 283

Parliamentary Army 83, 149
Parliamentary Grand Committee 84
Parliamentary Party 83
Patrick, St 231
Paul, St 99, 290, 303, 305, 306–7, 312
Peasants' Revolt (1381) 14, 24, 121–22, 325
Penn, William 64–65
Pennsylvania Gazette 105
Pentateuch 29, 308
Pentecostal movement 311–12
Peter the Apostle, St 95, 294
Philadelphia, Academy of 263
Phillips, Henry 30
'phossy jaw' 317
Pilgrim Fathers 10, 60, 64, 66, 72, 271, 273
Pitt, William, the Younger 220, 222
Plato 186
Plymouth, Devon 53
Plymouth, Massachusetts 53
Plymouth Rock 56
Polkinghorne, John 114
polygamy 277, 287
Pomare II, King 282, 283
Poor Law authorities 322
Pope, Alexander 185
Prayer Book 142
Presbyterian Church 35, 38, 248, 319
Presbyterianism 34, 79
Presley, Elvis 242
Price, Dr Richard 212, 213

Prickett, Stephen 136
Priestley, Joseph 113, 328
printing press 121, 166
Privy Council 33, 38
Proclamation Society for the Reformation of Manners 223
prostitution 287, 288
Protectorate (1653–9) 11
Protestant Church 184, 192, 280, 299, 313
Protestant Reformation 21, 69
Protestantism 38, 60, 115, 129, 156, 211, 214, 248, 272, 279
public schools 267
Pullman, Philip 204
Puritans 38, 39, 43, 47, 58–63
Putney Debates (1647) 339

Quakers 61, 88, 113, 233, 234, 307–8, 310, 312

racism 243, 250, 257–58
Raikes, Robert 264
Rainsborough, Thomas 339
Raleigh, Walter 60
Ranyard, Ellen 314
rape 287, 304, 306
Rauschenbusch, Walter 326, 332–33
Ray, John 113
Reagan, Ronald 1
Rees, Martin 196
Reformation 185, 210, 218, 335, 344
Reina, Casiodoro de 45
Reina-Valera Bible (1569) 45
Renaissance 185, 342

Research Scientists' Christian
  Fellowship 114
Restoration 338
Resurrection 294
Reynolds, John 39, 47
Rhode Island 61
Robeson, Paul 242
Robinson, Mary 155
Roman Catholic Church 14, 15, 16,
  18–21, 27, 94–95, 120, 121,
  183–84, 197, 218, 298, 299
Roman Empire 14, 15
Romantic movement 155, 157, 272
Rome 14
Rosenberg, Isaac 172
Roundheads 76
Rowse, A.L. 142
Royal Commission on Housing
  331
Royal Commission on the Poor Law
  331
Royal Navy 224
Royal Society 109–15, 347
Royalists 83
Ruskin, John 149, 330
Ruth 290, 297

St Andrews University 264
St John's Gospel: Bede translates
  into English 14
St Mary the Virgin church, Putney
  339
St Mary's church, Wigton, Cumbria
  345–47
St Paul's Cathedral, London 26
Saintsbury, Professor 133

Salem witch trials 62–63, 232
Salisbury, Robert Cecil, 1st Earl of
  33
Salome 288, 292
Salvation Army 314–15
Samson 297, 308
Sarah, wife of Abraham 290–91,
  292
Saul, King 73, 116
Saul of Tarsus 215
Schaff, Philip 343–44
Schaffer, Simon 114
Schalberg, Jane 308
Second Cambridge Company 47
Second Coming 319
Second Inaugural Address (Lincoln)
  253, 254, 343–44
Second Oxford Company 47
Second Westminster Company 47
Second World War 173
Sedgewick, William 76
segregation 254–55
Selden, John 44
Sentamu, John, Archbishop of York
  284
Separatists 53–58, 60, 63
Sermon on the Mount 7, 275, 302
Sewall, Judge Samuel 232–33
sex, the Bible and 287–309
Shaftesbury, Lord 317
Shakespeare, William 9, 37, 50, 119,
  120, 125, 129, 135, 139,
  140–45, 147, 151, 209
Sharp, Granville 234
Shaw, George Bernard 149
Shelley, Percy Bysshe 136, 157

Shoman-Dube, Musa 308
Signet Office 120, 121
Simms, Marion 327
Simpson, David 10–11
slavery 6, 96–97, 106, 126, 210,
      215–16, 223–26, 229–44,
      246–49, 250, 254–57, 276
Slessor, Mary 284
Slum Sisters 315–16
Smith, Charlotte 155
Smith, Sydney 223
Smyth, Canon Charles 269
Smyth, Miles 43, 48
Social Gospel 332
Social Gospel Movement 318–19
Society for the Promotion of
      Christian Knowledge 264
Society for the Propagation of the
      Gospel in Foreign Parts (SPG)
      237–38, 278
Society for the Suppression of Vice
      223
Society of Christian Socialists 327
Solomon 301
Somersett, James 234
Somersett's Case (1772) 234
Song of Solomon 295–96, 297
South Africa 277
Southcott, Joanna 311
Spanish Armada 32
Speke, John Hanning 285
Spenser, Edmund 45
Spenser, George 61
Spinoza, Benedict de 190, 191,
      193
spirituals 126, 236, 240–42

Spurgeon, Charles 239
Squanto (Tisquantum) 56–57, 65
Standish, John 337
Stanton, Elizabeth Cady 138
Staunton, Edward 77
Staverdale, Lord 220
Steinbeck, John 173–75
Sterelong, Kim 198
Stiles, Reverend 251
Stowe, Harriet Beecher 164, 231
Sunday schools 264, 266
Swift, Jonathan 153
Synod of Virginia (1867) 249
Syriac 18

Tahiti 273–74, 281–83
Tamar 297, 306
Taoism 278
Taylor, Alan 62
Taylor, J. Hudson 284
Temperance Unions 257
Ten Commandments 19, 128,
      241
Tennyson, Alfred, Lord 162–63
Thirteenth Amendment (1865)
      254
Thirty Years War (1618–48) 59, 70,
      73
Thomas, Edward 172–73
Tice, Karen Whitney 320
Tocqueville, Alexis de 340, 341
Tolpuddle Martyrs 325
Torah 29
Townes, Charles Hard 114
trade unions 344
Treatise of the Three Imposters 191–92

Tree of the Knowledge of Good and Evil 290
Tremellius-Junius Bible (1579) 44
Trevelyan, G.M. 223
Trollope, Anthony 219, 329–30
Tunstall, Cuthbert, Bishop of London 24, 26, 27
Twain, Mark 143
Tyndale, William 11, 12–13, 18, 20, 22–31, 44, 46, 50, 111, 119, 123, 134, 141, 145, 148, 170

Uganda 283–84
United African Methodists 277
United States Christian Commission 252
Updike, John 177
Uriah the Hittite 300

Valera, Cypriano de 45
Van Dyke, Dr 162
Vatican 15
Victoria, Queen 278
Vilvoorde Castle, Belgium 30
Virginia 60, 62
Vitton, Francis 245–46
Voltaire 186

Wallace, General Lew 169
Walsh, Sir John 22
Washington, George 1, 7, 63, 344
Watson, Joshua 268–69
Webster, Noah 166, 341

Wesley, Charles 11, 99, 100, 342
Wesley, John 11, 98–101, 239, 342
Wesleyan Conference (1790) 272
Westminster Abbey, London 1, 9–10, 38
Whichcote, Benjamin 186
White, Ronald C., Jnr. 253–54
Whitefield, George 11, 100, 101–6, 239, 263
Whitman, Walt 177, 252
Wigton, Cumbria 345, 346–47
Wilberforce, William 9, 210–11, 215–26, 229, 231, 233, 234, 278, 280
Wilberforce family 216
Wilde, Oscar 289
William III, King 88
William of Occam 111
William the Conqueror 9
Williams, Dakin 128
Williams, Dolores S. 291
Williams, Roger 61
Williams, Tennessee 128
Winstanley, Gerrard 79, 88
Winthrop, John 60
witch hunts 61–63, 308
Wittenberg, Germany 23
Wollstonecraft, Mary 155, 210–15, 217, 223, 310
Wolsey, Cardinal 22, 24, 36, 39
women
    and charity 312–23
    liberation of 309
    witch hunts 61–63, 308
women's clubs 257

Women's University Settlement
    movement 332
Wordsworth, William 136, 149,
    155–56, 158, 269, 331
Working Men's Associations 329
Working Men's College, London
    328
Wren, Sir Christopher 110, 111
Wycliffe, John 13–18, 22, 25, 44,
    111, 291, 325

Yale University 263
York Mystery Plays 120
Young Men's Christian Association
    (YMCA) 252, 319

Zurich Bible 45